**INTERNATIONAL YEAR
OF FORESTS · 2011**

State of the World's Forests
2011

Food and Agriculture Organization of the United Nations
Rome, 2011

The designations employed and the presentation of material in this information
product do not imply the expression of any opinion whatsoever on the part of the
Food and Agriculture Organization of the United Nations (FAO) concerning the legal
or development status of any country, territory, city or area or of its authorities, or
concerning the delimitation of its frontiers or boundaries. The mention of specific
companies or products of manufacturers, whether or not these have been patented,
does not imply that these have been endorsed or recommended by FAO in
preference to others of a similar nature that are not mentioned.

The views expressed in this information product are those of the author(s) and do
not necessarily reflect the views of FAO.

ISBN 978-92-5-106750-5

Contents

Foreword iv

Acknowledgements vi

Acronyms and abbreviations vii

Executive summary ix

Chapter 1: The state of forest resources – a regional analysis 1

    Africa 3

    Asia and the Pacific 8

    Europe 13

    Latin America and the Caribbean 17

    The Near East 21

    North America 24

Chapter 2: Developing sustainable forest industries 29

    Driving forces affecting forest industries 30

    Strategic choices for the future of the forest industry 43

    Summary and conclusions 56

Chapter 3: The role of forests in climate change adaptation and mitigation 57

    Forests in the Kyoto Protocol 58

    Progress on forest-related climate change negotiations 60

    Forest carbon tenure: implications for sustainable REDD+ projects 63

    Strengthening the role of adaptation in climate change policies 71

    Summary and conclusions 75

Chapter 4: The local value of forests 77

    Traditional knowledge 78

    Community-based forest management and small and medium forest enterprises 81

    Non-cash values of forests 88

    Challenges and emerging issues 92

    Summary and conclusions 98

Annex 99

    Notes on the annex tables 100

    Table1: Basic data on countries and areas 101

    Table 2: Forest area and area change 110

    Table 3: Carbon stock and stock change in living forest biomass 119

    Table 4: Production, trade and consumption of woodfuel, roundwood and sawnwood, 2008 128

    Table 5: Production, trade and consumption of wood-based panels, pulp and paper, 2008 137

    Table 6: Forestry sector's contribution to employment and gross domestic product, 2006 147

References 157

Foreword

The year 2011 has been designated 'The International Year of Forests' by the United Nations General Assembly. This builds on momentum already generated in other international arenas, such as those related to climate change and biodiversity, to bring even greater attention to forests worldwide. Work is progressing rapidly on international forest issues and this edition of *State of the World's Forests* focuses on a number of critical themes designed to stimulate greater analysis during the International Year of Forests.

State of the World's Forests, which is published on a biennial basis, presents up-to-date information on key themes affecting the world's forests. The 2009 issue considered the theme of 'Society, forests and forestry: adapting for the future' by presenting a 'demand-side' perspective on forest trends and topics. The 2011 issue takes a more holistic approach to the multiple ways in which forests support people's livelihoods under the theme 'Changing pathways, changing lives: forests as multiple pathways to sustainable development'. To explore this theme, the report tackles three core subjects – sustainable forest industries, climate change and local livelihoods – and examines their potential to stimulate development at all levels. In addition, we present new regional level analyses drawn from the Global Forest Resources Assessment 2010 (FRA 2010).

The book is divided into four chapters, each dedicated to one of the core subjects mentioned above. Across the chapters, a strong sense emerges of the wealth that forests offer and that can be accessed by utilizing them for industrial purposes; by managing and conserving forests within the context of climate change; and by tapping into local knowledge of the cash and non-cash value of forests. There is no single way in which these pathways are pursued – sometimes their goals and approaches intersect, while at others they occur in isolation. Yet, it is clear that in all cases, forests remain an underappreciated and undervalued resource that could stimulate greater income generation and development.

The first chapter explores some of the key regional trends in the extent of change in forest area, the areas allocated for productive and protective functions, levels of biomass, and employment, among other topics. This provides an indication of the regional approaches to forest resource use and the measures that countries have taken to adapt to changes in biological systems, policies and new management techniques.

Adaptability is also a key theme in our second chapter on developing sustainable forest industries. This examines a traditional development pathway based on industrial utilization of a natural resource. Over many decades this has been the main way in which forests have enabled countries and people to generate income. This chapter reviews the extent to which the forest industry has developed based on a number of key global drivers, and how it can strategically modify its approach to the use of forests. A key message of this chapter is that the forest sector continues to make a real contribution to employment and economic growth for many countries.

Climate change occupies a prominent position in international discussions, and forests have a particular role to play in the global response. In recognition of this, the report presents an update on the negotiations underway in the climate change convention and programmatic aspects related to forests and climate change. In particular, chapter three focuses on developments in reducing emissions from deforestation and forest degradation, and in conserving and enhancing carbon stocks (REDD+). The agreement reached on REDD+ in the Cancún negotiations in December 2010 could lead to transformational changes in conservation and management of tropical forests while safeguarding the livelihoods of indigenous peoples and forest-dependent people. Secure and equitable forest carbon tenure has a major role to play in ensuring the sustainability of these activities. The chapter provides a snapshot of some emerging legal guidance on forest carbon tenure and different approaches to determining ownership of the resource. New localized project activities on climate change need to be accompanied by sound forest carbon tenure arrangements, which take into consideration the needs of local communities and ensure long-term sustainability and equitable benefit-sharing.

The theme of the International Year of Forests makes people a central focus of activities during the Year and our last chapter highlights the importance of forests to local livelihoods, through a discussion of traditional knowledge, community-based forest management, small and medium forest enterprises and the non-cash value of forests. These approaches have historically been an essential part of local development, yet our knowledge of their value is

still relatively poor. Further analysis is needed during the International Year of Forests, to emphasize the connection between people and forests, and the benefits that can accrue when forests are managed by local people in sustainable and innovative ways.

The present edition of *State of the World's Forests* provides an introduction to the above ideas, which will take greater shape during 2011 and beyond. Together we must continue to pursue multiple pathways towards sustainable development using forests at all levels. I invite you to contribute to the discussion on these key themes during the International Year of Forests.

Eduardo Rojas-Briales
Assistant Director-General
FAO Forestry Department

Acknowledgements

The preparation of *State of the World's Forests 2011* was coordinated by Lauren Flejzor, with editorial assistance from Sophie Higman at Green Ink. Special thanks are given to the authors of and data analysts for the chapters, who took time out of their busy schedules to contribute to this important work. They are: Remi D'Annunzio, Monica Garzuglia, Örjan Jonsson, Arvydas Lebedys, Mette Løyche Wilkie and Hivy Ortiz-Chour (Chapter 1); Jukka Tissari and Adrian Whiteman (Chapter 2); Pierre Bernier, Susan Braatz, Francesca Felicani-Robles and Danilo Mollicone (Chapter 3); Michelle Gauthier, Sophie Grouwels, Sam Johnston, Fred Kafeero, Sarah Laird, Rebecca McLain, Rebecca Rutt, Gill Shepherd and Rachel Wynberg (Chapter 4). Additional thanks to others who offered reviews or contributed to other aspects of the report: Jim Carle, Ramon Carrillo, Peter Csoka, Marguerite France-Lanord, Fran Maplesden, R. Michael Martin, Andrea Perlis, Maria Sanz-Sanchez, Tiina Vähänen and members of the World Business Council for Sustainable Development. Acknowledgements are also given to the helpful technical assistance provided by Giselle Brocard, Paola Giondini and Daniela Mercuri. Paul Philpot (Green Ink) helped create a workable design for this special edition of *State of the World's Forests*.

Acronyms and abbreviations

APF	Adaptation Policy Framework (of UNDP)
AWG–KP	Ad hoc Working Group on Further Commitments for Annex I Parties under the Kyoto Protocol (of the UNFCCC)
AWG–LCA	Ad hoc Working Group on Long-term Cooperative Action (of the UNFCCC)
CATIE	Center for Investigation and Teaching of Tropical Agronomy
CBD	Convention on Biological Diversity
CBFM	community-based forest management
CDM	Clean Development Mechanism
CEPF	Confederation of European Forest Owners
CEPI	Confederation of European Paper Industries
CIFOR	Center for International Forestry Research
CITES	Convention on International Trade in Endangered Species of Wild Fauna and Flora
CO_2	carbon dioxide
COP	Conference of the Parties
CSR	Carbon Sequestration Rights
DFID	UK Department for International Development
ETS	Emissions Trading Scheme (of the EU)
EU	European Union
EUA	European Union Allowances (for CO_2 emissions)
FAO	Food and Agriculture Organization (of the United Nations)
FC	Forest Connect
FCPF	Forest Carbon Partnership Facility (of the World Bank)
FRA	Global Forest Resources Assessment
FSC	Forest Stewardship Council
FTE	full-time equivalent
GACF	Global Alliance for Community Forests
GDP	gross domestic product
GFP	Growing Forest Partnership
GHG	greenhouse gas
GPS	global positioning system
Gt	Giga tonnes
HWP	harvested wood product
IAITPTF	International Alliance for Indigenous and Tribal Peoples of Tropical Forests
IFFA	International Family Forest Alliance
IGC	Intergovernmental Committee on Traditional Knowledge, Genetic Resources and Folklore
IIED	International Institute for Environment and Development
IPCC	Intergovernmental Panel on Climate Change
ITTO	International Tropical Timber Organization
IUCN	International Union for Conservation of Nature

IUFRO	International Union of Forest Research Organizations
KP	Kyoto Protocol
LCA	life cycle analysis
LFP	Livelihoods and Forestry Programme (of DFID)
LULUCF	land use, land-use change and forestry
MA&D	Market Analysis and Development toolkit (of FAO)
MDF	medium density fibreboard
MJ	megajoule
MRV	monitoring, reporting and verification
MT	metric tonne
NAPA	National Adaptation Programme of Action
NC	National Communications (on climate change)
NFP Facility	National Forest Programme Facility
NGO	non-governmental organization
NWFP	non-wood forest product
PEFC	Programme for the Endorsement of Forest Certification
PROFOR	Program on Forests (of the World Bank)
REDD	reducing emissions from deforestation and forest degradation
REDD+	REDD plus the role of conservation, sustainable management of forests and enhancement of forest stocks in developing countries
SBI	Subsidiary Body for Implementation (of the UNFCCC)
SBSTA	Subsidiary Body for Scientific and Technological Advice (of the UNFCCC)
SFM	sustainable forest management
SFPA	Smallholder Forest Producers Associations
SMFE	small and medium forest enterprises
SOFO	State of the World's Forests
TK	traditional knowledge
TRIPS	Trade Related Aspects of Intellectual Property Rights
TroFCCA	Tropical Forest and Climate Change Adaptation Project
UNCCD	United Nations Convention to Combat Desertification
UNDP	United Nations Development Programme
UNFCCC	United Nations Framework Convention on Climate Change
VPA	Voluntary Partnership Agreement
WIPO	World Intellectual Property Organization

Executive summary

This ninth biennial issue of *State of the World's Forests* is being launched at the outset of 2011, the International Year of Forests. This Year aims to promote awareness and understanding of forests and forestry issues. The chapters assembled for this year's *State of the World's Forests* draw attention to four key areas that warrant greater attention during the International Year of Forests and beyond:

- regional trends on forest resources;
- the development of sustainable forest industries;
- climate change adaptation and mitigation; and
- the local value of forests.

Each of these themes has implications for the various upcoming assessments of progress towards sustainable development, including the Rio+20 Summit in 2012 and the Millennium Development Goals Review Conference in 2015.

Forests have unrecognized potential in furthering the development agenda. To maximize the contribution of forests to poverty eradication, this year's *State of the World's Forests* identifies some of the areas that can enhance or challenge the sustainability of people's livelihoods. Forest industries have the opportunity to maximize energy efficiency, spur innovation, create a reliable fibre supply and contribute to local economies. Negotiators designing climate change policies and actions recognize that, to be successful, efforts related to reducing emissions from deforestation and forest degradation and the role of conservation and enhancement of forest carbon stocks (REDD+) in developing countries must, at the same time, address poverty alleviation. They also recognize that the long-term implications of forest carbon tenure need to be examined more critically to ensure equitable benefit sharing and long-term management of local resources and rights.

The contribution of forests to local livelihoods also needs further consideration and research, for example on traditional forest-related knowledge, non-wood forest product (NWFP) governance, the non-cash value of forests, small and medium enterprises and community-based forest management (CBFM). Taken together, these themes can maximize the contribution of forests to the creation of sustainable livelihoods and alleviation of poverty.

This report is divided into four chapters, addressing the four key areas highlighted above.

Chapter 1: The state of forest resources: a regional analysis

The *Global Forest Resources Assessment 2010 – Main Report* (FAO, 2010a), which was released in October 2010, noted that the overall rate of deforestation remained alarmingly high, although the rate was slowing. Major trends in the extent of forests, and changes in the rates of forest loss, as well as the current state of productive and protective forests, show disparities between the six regions: Africa, Asia and the Pacific, Europe, Latin America and the Caribbean, the Near East and North America. The highest forest area worldwide was found in Europe, primarily because of the vast swaths of forest in the Russian Federation, while Latin America and the Caribbean had the highest net forest loss over the last decade.

Africa

Although continued forest loss was reported in Africa, the overall trend in net forest loss in the region slowed between 1990 and 2010. The area of planted forests was increasing in Africa, in particular in West and North Africa. Some forest planting programmes were established to combat desertification, while others were created in an effort to secure industrial wood and energy sources.

There were notable increases in the area designated for conservation of biodiversity, mostly as a result of changes in the designation of some forests in Central and East Africa. However, there were declines in productive forest areas.

Woodfuel removals jumped as a result of the rising population in the region. Nevertheless, Africa's share of global wood removals by value remained significantly lower than its potential. Nearly half a million people were employed in the primary production of forest goods, although countries in the region provided few data on employment, and particularly on informal sector activities where much employment occurs.

Asia and the Pacific

The extent of forests in Asia and the Pacific has changed dramatically over the past two decades. In the 1990s, the region experienced a net forest loss of 0.7 million hectares per year, while in the last decade the forest area increased by an average of 1.4 million hectares per year. The planted forest area also substantially increased through afforestation programmes, mainly as a result of programmes in China, India and Viet Nam.

The area of primary forests decreased in all Asia and the Pacific subregions in the last decade, despite the fact that the area designated for conservation of biodiversity increased in the same period. Mixed trends were observed in the subregions in the extent to which forests were set aside for soil and water protection.

With the exception of the South Asia and Oceania subregions, the area of productive forests declined over the last decade. Falling levels of wood removals were also observed throughout the region, largely as a result of the reduction in woodfuel removals. Employment in the primary production of forest goods was very high in the region when compared with the global total.

Europe

Europe contained the largest area of forests compared with other regions, totalling 1 billion hectares. Europe's forest area continued to grow between 1990 and 2000, although the overall rate of increase slowed during the last decade. The Russian Federation, which contained 80 percent of Europe's forest area, showed minimal declines in forest area after 2000. The rate of expansion

of planted forest area also decreased in the last decade when compared with global trends.

Europe had a relatively high percentage of forest area classified as primary forest (26 percent) when compared with the global primary forest area (36 percent). Over the last 20 years, forest area designated for conservation purposes doubled in the region. There were also positive trends in the areas designated for the protection of soil and water, mostly as a result of actions taken by the Russian Federation.

A greater proportion of forest area was designated for productive functions in Europe than in the rest of the world. The area designated for productive functions declined in the 1990s, although this trend reversed in the last decade. Wood removals in Europe also showed variable trends over the last 20 years and have declined as a result of the 2008–2009 recession in Europe, which lowered demand for wood. Finally, employment in the primary production of forest goods declined, and this trend is expected to continue in the near future.

Latin America and the Caribbean

Nearly half of the Latin American and Caribbean region was covered by forests in 2010. Forest area declined in Central and South America over the last two decades, with the leading cause of deforestation being the conversion of forest land to agriculture. Although the overall planted forest area was relatively small, it expanded at a rate of 3.2 percent per year over the last decade.

The region contained over half of the world's primary forests (57 percent), which was mostly located in inaccessible areas. The area of forest set aside for biodiversity conservation has increased by about 3 million hectares annually since 2000, with a vast amount of this area located in South America.

About 14 percent of all forest area in the region was designated primarily for production. Wood removals continued to rise with more than half removed for woodfuel. In common with other regions, it was difficult to quantify the extent and type of NWFPs removed in the Latin American and Caribbean region. Employment trends in the primary production of forest goods showed an upward swing of 30 percent in the first few years of the last decade.

The Near East

The Near East region has a small forest area, with 26 countries in the region categorized as low forest cover countries[1]. Although the region showed a net gain in forest area over the last decade, an analysis further back in time is constrained by changes in assessment methodologies over time in some larger countries in the region. Planted forest area increased by about 14 percent in the region in the last 20 years, particularly as a result of expansion of these areas in West Asia and North Africa.

During the last decade, the area of primary forests has remained largely stable, with Sudan containing the largest area of primary forest. There was an increase in area of forest for biodiversity conservation, with an additional 85 000 ha designated for this purpose each year (on average) in the last 10 years. The region also enlarged the area devoted to soil and water conservation over the last 20 years.

The Near East saw a decline in the area designated for productive functions in the 1990s, although the trend reversed slightly in the last decade. The region represented a very small portion of global wood removals. It was difficult to determine a trend for the annual value of wood products, as data were missing from some countries' submissions for the Global Forest Resources Assessment 2010 (FRA 2010).

North America

North America showed a slight increase in forest area between 1990 and 2010. The planted forest area also increased, and the region showed a relatively stable, positive trend in the level of biomass it contained. This region accounted for about 25 percent of global primary forests. The area of forest designated primarily for soil and water conservation was less than in other regions, as the management of these areas is largely embedded in national and local laws and other forest management guidance.

In contrast with other regions, a very small amount of wood (about 10 percent) was removed for woodfuel, with the remaining amount removed for industrial roundwood. Employment trends in the United States of America and Canada's forest sectors showed a decline over the last decade.

---

[1] Low forest cover countries are countries with less than 10 percent forest cover.

Chapter 2: Developing sustainable forest industries

Over the last decade, there has been little analysis of what constitutes a 'sustainable forest industry' and the drivers that affect this sustainability. Of the factors identified for this report, increasing population and economic growth, expansion of markets, and social trends related to social and environmental performance were found to be the most important drivers for the sustainability of the industry. However, some of the same factors also have the potential to negatively impact markets where the industry faces a greater level of complexity and competition for resources.

Governments and industry have responded to the opportunities and threats presented by these drivers by making strategic choices to improve the industry's sustainability. Many of these strategies include similar features such as: analyses of competitiveness, and strengths and weaknesses in the sector; measures to increase and cover costs for fibre supply; support for research, development and innovation; and development of new products (e.g. biofuels), which may signal a move to a 'greener' economy.

As a response to the economic downturn that began in 2008 and negatively affected most developed countries, industry has consolidated and restructured, reduced overcapacity and reconciled production in areas where countries were competitive. Typically, this has been done by innovating or creating new partnerships. Governments have also strengthened policies and regulations to improve social and environmental performance. FAO will continue to research these trends and will produce a more thorough research product on the theme of sustainable forest industries in 2011.

Chapter 3: Climate change mitigation and adaptation

Over the last few years, forestry has become a critical part of the international climate change agenda. Governments have already agreed on the potential importance of REDD+, and have provided large financial resources to initiate pilot activities. Nevertheless, the long-term sustainability of climate change and forestry activities will depend on a number of factors, including effective forest governance, secure forest carbon tenure and equitable benefit sharing, and integration of adaptation actions into climate change policies and projects, among others.

The UN Framework Convention on Climate Change (UNFCCC) highlighted REDD+ and adopted a decision on REDD+ in Cancún, Mexico in December 2010. The decision outlines the scope of REDD+, which includes reducing emissions from deforestation and forest degradation, and the conservation, sustainable management of forests and the enhancement of carbon stocks, as well as the principles and safeguards for REDD+. Further work on methodological issues, including on monitoring, reporting and verification, will continue throughout 2011 and perhaps beyond.

One of the most difficult aspects of ensuring the sustainability of REDD activities is defining the ownership of forest carbon rights. As this report shows, a number of countries in the Asia and the Pacific region have created legislation establishing property rights in carbon and formalizing carbon rights. Some have taken this measure a step further to establish carbon rights as a separate interest in the land. The cases presented in this report show the diversity of established guidelines and laws on forest carbon rights at the country level, and provide clear examples that have the potential to be replicated in other countries.

While the issue of REDD in the climate change mitigation debate is being addressed at the highest levels, the subject of adaptation has not been as widely discussed or integrated into policies and programmes. Adaptation is complex and requires actions at multiple scales. Current international agreements take adaptation into account to a limited extent, but lack appropriate mechanisms to incorporate adaptation and related forest activities in the context of REDD+. More work is needed to consider the role of forests in adaptation in climate change policies and actions.

Chapter 4: The local value of forests

Chapter 4 provides an introduction to the local value of forests, in preparation for further discussions on the theme 'Forests for People' during the International Year of Forests in 2011. To expand upon this theme, the topics of traditional knowledge, community-based forest management (CBFM), small and medium forest enterprises (SMFEs) and the non-cash value of forests are explored.

Traditional knowledge (TK) contributes to local incomes, typically through the use of commercialized products. While there is some protection of traditional knowledge in the international policy arena, further awareness and integration of traditional knowledge into policies is needed, particularly as REDD activities take shape.

Community-based forest management and SMFEs are important for the production and marketing of wood and NWFPs. The drivers of CBFM include decentralization, enabling policy frameworks, national poverty reduction agendas, rural development and emerging grassroots and global networks. Under favourable conditions, CBFM benefits can be seen over the long term and can lead to greater participation, reduced poverty, increased productivity and diversity of vegetation, and the protection of forest species. As forests become more productive, they can also lead to the development of SMFEs, which are known to have clear benefits for local livelihoods but require a sound enabling environment to attract continued flows of investment.

Non-wood forest products remain critical to the success of SMFEs. Legislation and regulation of NWFPs are increasing to ensure the sustainable use of these resources, through both international arrangements and domestic policies and laws. Despite the known cash values of NWFPs and their promotion through CBFM and SMFEs, the 'non-cash' values of forests also need to be further explored. Non-cash values often provide important support for households in or near forests and can sometimes make a larger contribution to households than cash income. Particularly in remote, rural areas, non-cash income is an essential part of sustainable livelihoods, especially for women and the rural poor.

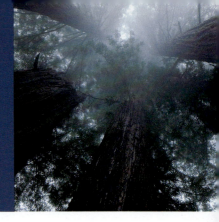

1 The state of forest resources – a regional analysis

The Food and Agriculture Organization (FAO), in cooperation with its member countries, has assessed the world's forests resources at 5 to 10 year intervals since 1946. These global assessments provide valuable information to policy-makers at the national and international levels, members of the public and other groups and organizations interested in forestry.

The Global Forest Resources Assessment 2010 (FRA 2010) was the most comprehensive assessment to date (FAO, 2010a). It examined the current status and trends for more than 90 variables related to the extent, condition, uses and values of all types of forests in 233 countries and areas for four points in time: 1990, 2000, 2005 and 2010. FRA 2010 told us that the world's total forest area was just over 4 billion hectares, corresponding to 31 percent of the total land area or an average of 0.6 ha per capita. The five most forest-rich countries (the Russian Federation, Brazil, Canada, the United States of America and China) accounted for more than half of the total forest area. Ten countries or areas had no forest at all and an additional 54 had forest on less than 10 percent of their total land area.

Figure 1: State of the World's Forests 2011 – subregional breakdown

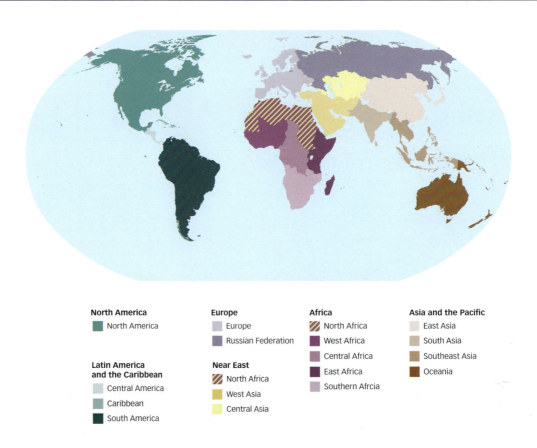

North America	Europe	Africa	Asia and the Pacific
North America	Europe	North Africa	East Asia
	Russian Federation	West Africa	South Asia
Latin America and the Caribbean		Central Africa	Southeast Asia
Central America	**Near East**	East Africa	Oceania
Caribbean	North Africa	Southern Afrcia	
South America	West Asia		
	Central Asia		

A key message from FRA 2010 was that, while the rate of deforestation and loss of forest from natural causes was still alarmingly high, it was slowing down. At the global level, it decreased from an estimated 16 million hectares per year in the 1990s to around 13 million hectares per year in the last decade. At the same time, afforestation and natural expansion of forests in some countries and areas reduced the net loss of forest area significantly at the global level. The net change in forest area in the period 2000–2010 was estimated at -5.2 million hectares per year (an area about the size of Costa Rica), down from -8.3 million hectares per year in the period 1990–2000. However, most of the loss of forest continued to take place in countries and areas in the tropical regions, while most of the gain took place in the temperate and boreal zones, and in some emerging economies.

Significant progress was made in developing forest policies, laws and national forest programmes. Some 76 countries issued or updated their forest policy statements since 2000, and 69 countries – primarily in Europe and Africa – reported that their current forest law has been enacted or amended since 2005. Close to 75 percent of the world's forests were covered by a national forest programme, i.e. a participatory process for the development and implementation of forest-related policies and international commitments at the national level.

More detailed results are presented in FRA 2010, according to seven key aspects of sustainable forest management: extent of forest resources; forest biological diversity; forest health and vitality; productive functions of forest resources; protective functions of forest resources; socio-economic functions of forests; and the legal, policy and institutional framework. For the purposes of this report, a few of the key findings related to these thematic elements will be discussed, providing an overview at the regional level.

Africa[2]
Extent of forest resources
According to FRA 2010, the estimated forest area in Africa[3] was close to 675 million hectares (Table 1), accounting for about 17 percent of global forest area and 23 percent of the total land area in the region. At the

Table 1: Forest area in Africa, 1990–2010[a]

Subregion	Area (1 000 ha)			Annual change (1 000 ha)		Annual change rate (%)	
	1990	2000	2010	1990–2000	2000–2010	1990–2000	2000–2010
Central Africa	268 214	261 455	254 854	-676	-660	-0.25	-0.26
East Africa	88 865	81 027	73 197	-784	-783	-0.92	-1.01
North Africa	85 123	79 224	78 814	-590	-41	-0.72	-0.05
Southern Africa	215 447	204 879	194 320	-1 057	-1 056	-0.50	-0.53
West Africa	91 589	81 979	73 234	-961	-875	-1.10	-1.12
Total Africa	749 238	708 564	674 419	-4 067	-3 414	-0.56	-0.49
World	4 168 399	4 085 063	4 032 905	-8 334	-5 216	-0.20	-0.13

a All tables and graphs showing trends are based on those countries which provided information for all points in time (1990, 2000, 2005 and 2010). More complete information on the status as of 2010 may be available for some variables. The annual change rate is the gain or loss in percent of the remaining forest area each year within the given period.

2   For the purposes of this review, countries and areas in Africa are grouped in the following subregions:
   - Central Africa: Burundi, Cameroon, Central African Republic, Chad, Democratic Republic of the Congo, Equatorial Guinea, Gabon, Republic of the Congo, Rwanda, Saint Helena, Ascension and Tristan da Cunha, Sao Tome and Principe
   - East Africa: Comoros, Djibouti, Eritrea, Ethiopia, Kenya, Madagascar, Mauritius, Mayotte, Réunion, Seychelles, Somalia, Uganda, United Republic of Tanzania
   - North Africa: Algeria, Egypt, Libyan Arab Jamahiriya, Mauritania, Morocco, Sudan, Tunisia, Western Sahara
   - Southern Africa: Angola, Botswana, Lesotho, Malawi, Mozambique, Namibia, South Africa, Swaziland, Zambia, Zimbabwe
   - West Africa: Benin, Burkina Faso, Cape Verde, Côte d'Ivoire, Gambia, Ghana, Guinea, Guinea-Bissau, Liberia, Mali, Niger, Nigeria, Senegal, Sierra Leone, Togo
3   The countries and areas forming part of the North Africa subregion (Algeria, Egypt, Libyan Arab Jamahiriya, Mauritania, Morocco, Sudan, Tunisia and Western Sahara) also appear in the Near East regional section. The inclusion of these countries and areas in both regions was intentional and necessary, as it reflects the categorization of countries within the FAO Regional Forestry Commissions.

subregional level, Central Africa accounted for 37 percent of the total forest area, Southern Africa for 29 percent, North Africa for 12 percent, and East and West Africa for 11 percent each.

The five countries with the largest forest area (Democratic Republic of the Congo, Sudan, Angola, Zambia and Mozambique) together contained more than half the forest area of the continent (55 percent). Countries reporting the highest percentage of their land area covered by forest were Seychelles (88 percent), Gabon (85 percent), Guinea-Bissau (72 percent), Democratic Republic of the Congo (68 percent) and Zambia (67 percent).

There was a reduction in the rate of net forest loss in the region, from 4.0 million hectares per year in the decade 1990–2000 to 3.4 million hectares per year during the period 2000–2010. A major difference was seen in parts of North Africa, where the net loss dropped from 590 000 ha per year to just 41 000 ha per year. The reduction was mostly a result of Sudan's recent efforts to gather annual data on actual changes taking place, which resulted in much lower figures for 2000–2010 than those estimated for 1990–2000, which were based on fairly old data. Southern Africa had the highest net loss at the subregional level over the last 20 years, although the rate has slowed in recent years.

Countries with large areas of forest also reported the most significant losses. In addition to the five countries with the largest forest area, Cameroon, Nigeria, the United Republic of Tanzania and Zimbabwe also reported large losses. The countries with the highest net

Table 2: Area of planted forest in Africa, 1990–2010

Subregion	Area (1 000 ha)			Annual change (1 000 ha)		Annual change rate (%)	
	1990	2000	2010	1990–2000	2000–2010	1990–2000	2000–2010
Central Africa	482	606	709	12	10	2.32	1.58
East Africa	1 184	1 258	1 477	7	22	0.61	1.62
North Africa	6 794	7 315	8 091	52	78	0.74	1.01
Southern Africa	2 316	2 431	2 639	12	21	0.49	0.82
West Africa	888	1 348	2 494	46	115	4.26	6.35
Total Africa	11 663	12 958	15 409	129	245	1.06	1.75
World	178 307	214 839	264 084	3 653	4 925	1.88	2.09

Table 3: Area of forest designated primarily for conservation of biodiversity in Africa, 1990–2010

Subregion	Area (1 000 ha)			Annual change (1 000 ha)		Annual change rate (%)	
	1990	2000	2010	1990–2000	2000–2010	1990–2000	2000–2010
Central Africa	7 463	8 243	9 711	78	147	1.00	1.65
East Africa	4 806	6 110	7 865	130	176	2.43	2.56
North Africa	13 325	12 597	12 769	-73	17	-0.56	0.14
Southern Africa	9 661	9 429	9 199	-23	-23	-0.24	-0.25
West Africa	14 672	14 972	15 328	30	36	0.20	0.24
Total Africa	49 927	51 351	54 873	142	352	0.28	0.67
World	270 413	302 916	366 255	3 250	6 334	1.14	1.92

loss in percentage terms were Comoros, Togo, Nigeria, Mauritania and Uganda. Ten countries reported a net gain in forest area between 1990 and 2010 with Tunisia, Côte d'Ivoire, Rwanda, Swaziland and Morocco topping the list.

Africa also had extensive areas of land classified as 'other wooded land', with scattered tree growth too sparse to be defined as forest. The total area was more than 350 million hectares, corresponding to 31 percent of the total area of other wooded land in the world, which declined by close to 1.9 million hectares per year (0.5 percent per annum) during the period 1990–2010. The largest losses occurred in Mali, Sudan, the United Republic of Tanzania, Nigeria and Madagascar.

Forest planting programmes were established in several countries for both productive and protective purposes. Africa's total area of planted forests was about 15 million hectares (or 2.3 percent of the total forest area), with the biggest area located in North Africa (Table 2). Sudan had by far the largest area with more than 6 million hectares including governmental, private and community planting schemes. South Africa had almost 2 million hectares of planted forest area of which almost three-quarters were privately owned (corporate growers and individual commercial farmers).

Growing stock and carbon storage were assessed to determine relevant trends related to climate change – while sustainable management, planting and rehabilitation of forests can conserve or increase forest carbon stocks, deforestation, forest degradation and poor management practices reduce them. The region contributed 21 percent of the global total of carbon in forest biomass, with Central Africa containing the largest amount of carbon in forest biomass (Figure 2). Côte d'Ivoire reported the highest level of carbon stock per hectare in the region (177 tonnes per hectare) followed by the Republic of the Congo. Except for North Africa, all the subregions experienced a decline in carbon stocks in forest biomass between 1990 and 2010 because of the loss of forest area.

Biological diversity and protective functions

Around 10 percent of the total forest area in the region was reported to be primary forest (i.e. composed of native species with no clearly visible indications of human activity and no disruptions to ecological processes). However, this figure may be an underestimate because Cameroon and the Democratic

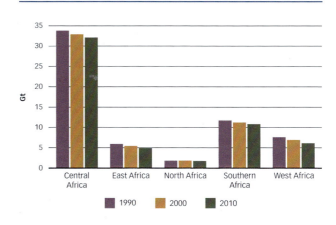

Figure 2: Carbon stock in forest biomass in Africa, 1990–2010 (Gt)

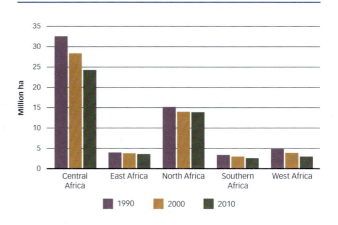

Figure 3: Area of primary forest in Africa, 1990–2010 (million ha)

Republic of the Congo, which together represented 26 percent of the total forest area in the region, did not report on this category. There was evidence of an overall decline in primary forest area in the region (Figure 3), with primary forests declining by more than half a million hectares per year over the period 2000–2010. The five countries that reported the largest primary forest area were Gabon, Sudan, Republic of the Congo, Madagascar and Central African Republic. The countries reporting the largest proportion of their forests as being primary (ranging from 65 to 24 percent) were (in descending order): Gabon, Réunion, Sao Tome and Principe, Republic of the Congo, Malawi and Madagascar. Gabon registered the largest annual loss of primary forest, an area of more than 330 000 ha per year, largely due to a reclassification of primary forests to 'other naturally regenerated forests' because of selective logging and other human interventions within the reporting period.

About 14 percent of the total forest area in Africa was designated for conservation of biological diversity (Table 3). Most of the countries in the region showed an increase in forest area designated for conservation or showed no change since 1990. Just six countries showed a negative trend (Mauritius, Mozambique, Republic of the Congo, Senegal, Sudan and Togo). At the regional level, there was a substantial increase during the last decade, particularly as a result of increases in Central and East Africa. However, Southern Africa showed a negative change because of the decrease in forest area reported by Mozambique.

Only about 3 percent of the forest area was designated primarily for protection of soil and water, compared with 8 percent at the global level. Mozambique reported the largest area (almost 9 million hectares) under this designation, corresponding to 22 percent of its total forest. In terms of percentage, Libyan Arab Jamahiriya reported that all of its forests were designated primarily for protection of soil and water, while Kenya listed 94 percent of its forest area under this category, which corresponded to all its natural forest. Comoros reported that two-thirds of its forest area was designated for soil and water conservation while Algeria and Egypt both recorded around 50 percent of their forest area under this designation; in Algeria most of this was inaccessible forest area, and in Egypt all of this was planted. Africa's total forest area designated for soil and water protection showed a net loss of 0.9 million hectares in the last decade, while globally this area increased by more than 27 million hectares over the same period (Table 4).

Productive and socio-economic functions

The extent of forests designated for production of wood and non-wood forest products (NWFPs) declined in Africa over the last 20 years (Table 5). As conservation areas

Table 4: Area of forest designated primarily for protection of soil and water in Africa, 1990–2010

Subregion	Area (1 000 ha)			Annual change (1 000 ha)		Annual change rate (%)	
	1990	2000	2010	1990–2000	2000–2010	1990–2000	2000–2010
Central Africa	342	752	662	41	-9	8.20	-1.27
East Africa	3 703	3 596	3 475	-11	-12	-0.29	-0.34
North Africa	4 068	3 855	3 851	-21	n.s.	-0.54	-0.01
Southern Africa	10 300	9 715	9 136	-59	-58	-0.58	-0.61
West Africa	2 297	2 529	2 417	23	-11	0.97	-0.45
Total Africa	20 709	20 447	19 540	-26	-91	-0.13	-0.45
World	240 433	271 699	299 378	3 127	2 768	1.23	0.97

Table 5: Area of forest designated primarily for production in Africa, 1990–2010

Subregion	Area (1 000 ha)			Annual change (1 000 ha)		Annual change rate (%)	
	1990	2000	2010	1990–2000	2000–2010	1990–2000	2000–2010
Central Africa	66 944	66 197	59 844	-75	-635	-0.11	-1.00
East Africa	34 330	31 127	27 957	-320	-317	-0.97	-1.07
North Africa	39 557	36 637	36 819	-292	18	-0.76	0.05
Southern Africa	36 950	34 834	33 199	-212	-163	-0.59	-0.48
West Africa	33 164	33 898	28 208	73	-569	0.22	-1.82
Total Africa	210 944	202 693	186 027	-825	-1 667	-0.40	-0.85
World	1 181 576	1 160 325	1 131 210	-2 125	-2 911	-0.18	-0.25

Figure 4: Volume of wood removals in Africa, 1970–2008 (million m³)

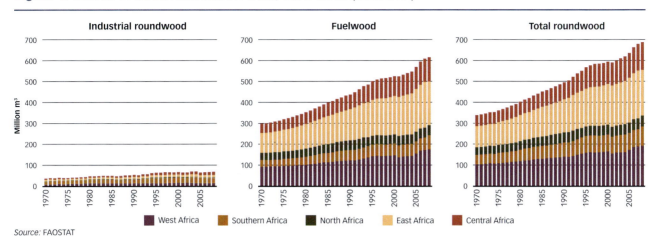

Source: FAOSTAT

increased, this may have caused the area of productive forests to decline. It may also be an indication that concessions were cancelled or productive forests were being cleared to convert the land to non-forest uses.

Central and West Africa's areas of forest designated primarily for productive functions fell considerably between 2000 and 2010. In Central Africa, the decrease was largely the result of a change in Gabon's forest legislation in 2001 and a reassignment of forest functions, which reduced the country's productive forest area by nearly one-half. In the same subregion, Cameroon showed the highest increase in forest area designated for production over the last ten years, due to recent designations of additional forest concessions, community and communal forests and hunting reserves. In West Africa, the biggest decreases took place in Liberia and Nigeria. In Liberia, the reported decline was caused by the cancellation of forest concessions after 2005.

Only 10 percent of wood removals in Africa were used as industrial roundwood, while the rest was used as fuelwood (Figure 4). Africa accounted for 33 percent of global fuelwood removals and only 5 percent of global industrial wood removals. However, there was considerable variation between the subregions, largely due to differences in access and the proportion of commercial species. Fuelwood removals increased in line with growing population and despite the decline in the area of forest designated for productive purposes. In the absence of information on annual allowable harvests, it was difficult to conclude whether current removals were sustainable. Since market demand and access were key determinants of the intensity of removal, easily accessible areas were more intensively logged than those that were remote.

Socio-economic trends in Africa were mixed and only 27 countries in the region – representing just 33 percent of Africa's forest area – reported on the value of forest products. The value of wood removals (fuelwood and industrial roundwood) increased in the region from US$2.6 billion in 1990 to about US$2.9 billion in 2005, although they declined in West Africa (Figure 5). However, Africa's share of the global value of wood removals remained significantly lower than its potential. In 2005, the value of industrial wood removals in the region was estimated at only 11 percent of the global value, while fuelwood removals made up nearly 50 percent of the value of global fuelwood removal. As limited information was available on this variable, it is likely these values are underestimated.

The value of wood products in the formal economic sector was concentrated in a small number of countries, and it was not possible to conclude how much of the

Figure 5: Value of wood removals in Africa, 1990–2005 (billion US$)

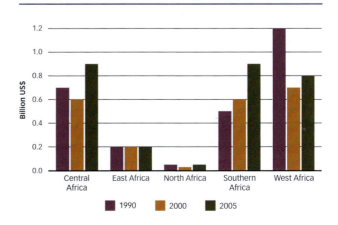

value was generated from legally harvested timber, NWFPs and subsistence removals, respectively, because of weak monitoring and reporting capacity in several key countries. Exudates, food and living animals were the most important NWFPs extracted from African forest areas. However, very little information was reported on this variable.

More than half a million people were reportedly involved in the primary production of goods in forests in Africa (Table 6). A number of countries reported growth in employment in the formal forest sector while others reported a decline. For instance, forestry employment in Algeria doubled from 2000 to 2005. Liberia noted a decrease in employment, however, mainly due to the 2003 sanctions imposed by the UN Security Council, which halted government revenues from logging thus affecting employment levels.

The scarcity of information on production and employment in the informal sector means that these reports do not provide an accurate picture of the importance of the sector for national economies. A significant proportion of wood production (fuelwood, in particular) and processing (e.g. pit-sawing, charcoal production, and collection and trade of NWFPs) took place in the informal sector and has not been adequately evaluated. Improvements in the understanding of the informal sector are needed to suggest better policies and practices for greater sustainability.

Asia and the Pacific[4]
Extent of forest resources

Forests cover slightly less than one-third of the total land area of the Asia and the Pacific region. Based on estimates for FRA 2010, the region's forested area was 740 million hectares in 2010, accounting for about 18 percent of the global forest area (Table 7). East Asia contained the largest forest area (255 million hectares), followed by Southeast Asia (214 million hectares),

Table 6: Employment in primary production of forest goods in Africa, 2005 (1 000 FTE)

Subregion	Employment in primary production of goods, 2005
Central Africa	30
East Africa	12
North Africa	209
Southern Africa	139
West Africa	181
Total Africa	571
World	10 537

Table 7: Forest area in Asia and the Pacific, 1990–2010

Subregion	Area (1 000 ha)			Annual change (1 000 ha)		Annual change rate (%)	
	1990	2000	2010	1990–2000	2000–2010	1990–2000	2000–2010
East Asia	209 198	226 815	254 626	1 762	2 781	0.81	1.16
South Asia	78 163	78 098	80 309	-7	221	-0.01	0.28
Southeast Asia	247 260	223 045	214 064	-2 422	-898	-1.03	-0.41
Oceania	198 744	198 381	191 384	-36	-700	-0.02	-0.36
Total Asia–Pacific	733 364	726 339	740 383	-703	1 404	-0.10	0.19
World	4 168 399	4 085 063	4 032 905	-8 334	-5 216	-0.20	-0.13

[4] For the purposes of this review, countries and areas in the Asia and the Pacific region are grouped into the following subregions:
- East Asia: China, Democratic People's Republic of Korea, Japan, Mongolia, Republic of Korea
- South Asia: Bangladesh, Bhutan, India, Maldives, Nepal, Pakistan, Sri Lanka
- Southeast Asia: Brunei, Cambodia, Indonesia, Lao People's Democratic Republic, Malaysia, Myanmar, Philippines, Singapore, Thailand, Timor-Leste, Viet Nam
- Oceania: American Samoa, Australia, Cook Islands, Federated States of Micronesia, Fiji, French Polynesia, Guam, Kiribati, Marshall Islands, Nauru, New Caledonia, New Zealand, Niue, Norfolk Island, Northern Mariana Islands, Palau, Papua New Guinea, Pitcairn, Samoa, Solomon Islands, Tokelau, Tonga, Tuvalu, Vanuatu, Wallis and Futuna Islands

Oceania (191 million hectares) and South Asia (80 million hectares). The five countries with the largest forested area (China, Australia, Indonesia, India and Myanmar) accounted for 74 percent of the forest in the region, with China and Australia alone accounting for almost half the forest area of the region. The Federated States of Micronesia reported that 92 percent of its land area was covered by forests while six countries reported that forests covered no more than 10 percent of their total land area. Two of these, Nauru and Tokelau, reported no forest at all.

In the Asia and the Pacific region as a whole, forests were lost at a rate of 0.7 million hectares per year in the 1990s but grew by 1.4 million hectares per year over the period 2000–2010. This was primarily due to large-scale afforestation efforts in China, where the forest area increased by 2 million hectares per year in the 1990s and by an average of 3 million hectares per year since 2000. Bhutan, India, the Philippines and Viet Nam also registered forest area increases in the last decade.

Despite the net increase in forest area reported at the regional level, deforestation continued at high rates in many countries. Southeast Asia experienced the largest decline in forest area in the region in the last ten years, with an annual net loss of forests of more than 0.9 million hectares. However, when compared with figures for 1990–2000 (-2.4 million hectares per year), this represented a significant drop. Oceania also experienced a negative trend, primarily because severe drought and forest fires in Australia have exacerbated the loss of forest since 2000 and caused it to register the largest annual loss of any country in the region between 2000 and 2010. Cambodia, Indonesia, Myanmar and Papua New Guinea also reported large forest losses in the last decade.

Planted forests (i.e. forests established through planting and/or deliberate seeding of native or introduced tree species) made up 16 percent of the forest area in the region. Planted forests experienced a substantial increase within the last ten years in the Asia and the Pacific region (Table 8). Most of the region's planted forests were established through afforestation programmes. China contributed the bulk of this growth through several large programmes that aimed to expand its forest resources and protect watersheds, control soil erosion and desertification, and maintain biodiversity.

China, India and Viet Nam have established targets for large-scale forest planting and also developed incentive programmes for smallholders to plant more trees. China plans a 50 million hectare increase in the area of its planted forests by 2020, with the aim of covering 23 percent of the total land area with forests, a target which may be reached by 2015 if current planting rates continue. India set a target to cover 33 percent of its land area with forests and tree cover by 2012. Based on figures supplied in FRA 2010, some 25 percent of India's land area was covered by forests, other wooded land or other land with tree cover in 2010. To this should be added an unknown area of line plantings and other 'trees outside forests'. The Government of Viet Nam aimed to restore forest cover to 43 percent by 2010 and, according to the information provided for FRA 2010, this target was achieved.

Growing stock and carbon storage were also important parameters in determining the relevant trends in the extent of forest resources. Total carbon stored in forest biomass was 44 Giga tonnes (Gt) in the Asia and the Pacific region as a whole. Carbon stocks in forest

Table 8: Area of planted forests in Asia and the Pacific, 1990–2010

Subregion	Area (1 000 ha)			Annual change (1 000 ha)		Annual change rate (%)	
	1990	2000	2010	1990–2000	2000–2010	1990–2000	2000–2010
East Asia	55 049	67 494	90 232	1 244	2 274	2.06	2.95
South Asia	6 472	7 999	11 019	153	302	2.14	3.25
Southeast Asia	10 059	11 737	14 533	168	280	1.56	2.16
Oceania	2 583	3 323	4 101	74	78	2.55	2.12
Total Asia–Pacific	74 163	90 553	119 884	1 639	2 933	2.02	2.85
World	178 307	214 839	264 084	3 653	4 925	1.88	2.09

biomass decreased by an estimated 159 million tonnes annually during the period 2000–2010, despite an increase in the forest area in the region. The decreasing trend occurred because the forest converted to other uses contained more biomass and carbon than the newly established forests. East Asia and South Asia registered a positive trend in forest carbon stocks over the period 1990–2010, while Southeast Asia and Oceania experienced a net loss (Figure 6).

Figure 6: Carbon stock in forest biomass in Asia and the Pacific, 1990–2010 (Gt)

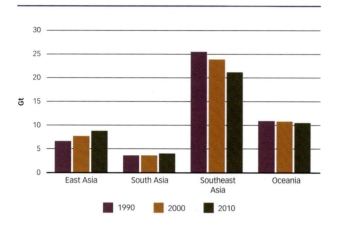

Figure 7: Area of primary forest in Asia and the Pacific, 1990–2010 (million ha)

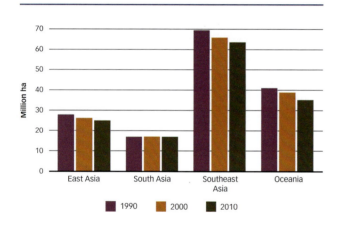

Biological diversity and protective functions

Primary forests accounted for 19 percent of the total forest area of the region. Data indicated that the area of primary forests decreased in all the Asia and the Pacific subregions. Southeast Asia experienced a loss of primary forests, but the trend slowed in recent years. In Oceania, the decline in primary forest accelerated since the 1990s (Figure 7). The data collected did not allow for an analysis of the proportion of net loss of primary forest that was caused by deforestation and conversion compared with the opening of primary forests to selective logging or other human activities, which would move the forest to the class 'other naturally regenerated forest' in the FRA 2010 classification system.

The area of forest designated primarily for conservation of biodiversity accounted for 14 percent of the total forest area. Since 2000, this area has increased by almost 14 million hectares in the Asia and the Pacific region as a whole (Table 9). Oceania registered a small contraction in the area designated for conservation of biodiversity since 2000. The area of forest within formally established protected areas represented 22 percent of the forest area in the region. Southeast Asia reported the highest percentage of forest within protected areas in the region (32 percent) while Oceania reported the lowest (16 percent).

Nineteen percent of the forest area in the region was primarily designated for the protection of soil and water

Table 9: Area of forest designated primarily for conservation of biological diversity in Asia and the Pacific, 1990–2010

Subregion	Area (1 000 ha)			Annual change (1 000 ha)		Annual change rate (%)	
	1990	2000	2010	1990–2000	2000–2010	1990–2000	2000–2010
East Asia	10 167	10 798	14 889	63	409	0.60	3.26
South Asia	15 037	15 530	22 191	49	666	0.32	3.63
Southeast Asia	32 275	35 475	38 655	320	318	0.95	0.86
Oceania	7 196	8 412	8 234	122	-18	1.57	-0.21
Total Asia–Pacific	64 675	70 215	83 969	554	1 375	0.83	1.80
World	270 413	302 916	366 255	3 250	6 334	1.14	1.92

resources. The area of forest assigned for protective functions increased by 17 million hectares in the 1990s and by 26 million hectares between 2000 and 2010 primarily because of large-scale planting in China (Table 10). An odd trend was observed in Southeast Asia, where forest areas with a protective function increased from 1990 to 2000 and then fell again from 2000 to 2010 because of the heterogeneous situation within the subregion. There was a steady increase in forest cover with a protective function in the Philippines and Thailand, while the opposite trend was observed in Indonesia, Lao People's Democratic Republic and Timor-Leste. The area of protective forest increased over the period 1990–2000 in Malaysia, Myanmar, Viet Nam and Oceania, although it fell in these areas throughout the next decade.

Productive and socio-economic functions

In the Asia and the Pacific region, 32 percent of the total forest area was designated primarily for production

of wood, fibre, bioenergy and/or NWFPs. The area designated for production has fallen since 2000 in the region as forests were designated for other management purposes such as conservation of biodiversity and protection of soil and water. Only South Asia and Oceania showed an increasing trend for this category (Table 11).

Wood removed from forests and other wooded land constituted an important component of the productive function of forests. For the Asia and the Pacific region as a whole, total removals declined by 10 percent from 1.16 billion m^3 in 1990 to 1.04 billion m^3 in 2010 (Figure 8). Reductions in fuelwood removals accounted for the bulk of this fall. Removals of industrial roundwood in the region remained quite stable (approximately 280 million m^3 per year) over the past two decades. Roundwood supply remained unchanged despite partial logging bans and log export restrictions in some

Table 10: Area of forest designated primarily for protection of soil and water in Asia and the Pacific, 1990–2010

Subregion	Area (1 000 ha)			Annual change (1 000 ha)		Annual change rate (%)	
	1990	2000	2010	1990–2000	2000–2010	1990–2000	2000–2010
East Asia	24 061	38 514	65 719	1 445	2 721	4.82	5.49
South Asia	12 125	12 296	12 760	17	46	0.14	0.37
Southeast Asia	43 686	45 636	43 741	195	-190	0.44	-0.42
Oceania	1 048	1 078	888	3	-19	0.28	-1.92
Total Asia–Pacific	80 920	97 524	123 108	1 660	2 558	1.88	2.36
World	240 433	271 699	299 378	3 127	2 768	1.23	0.97

Table 11: Area of forest designated primarily for production in Asia and the Pacific, 1990–2010

Subregion	Area (1 000 ha)			Annual change (1 000 ha)		Annual change rate (%)	
	1990	2000	2010	1990–2000	2000–2010	1990–2000	2000–2010
East Asia	126 936	119 592	94 711	-734	-2 488	-0.59	-2.31
South Asia	18 255	18 684	19 713	43	103	0.23	0.54
Southeast Asia	96 554	109 973	104 526	1 342	-545	1.31	-0.51
Oceania	7 241	11 180	11 569	394	39	4.44	0.34
Total Asia–Pacific	248 986	259 429	230 519	1 044	-2 891	0.41	-1.17
World	1 181 576	1 160 325	1 131 210	-2 125	-2 911	-0.18	-0.25

Figure 8: Volume of wood removals in Asia and the Pacific, 1970–2008 (million m³)

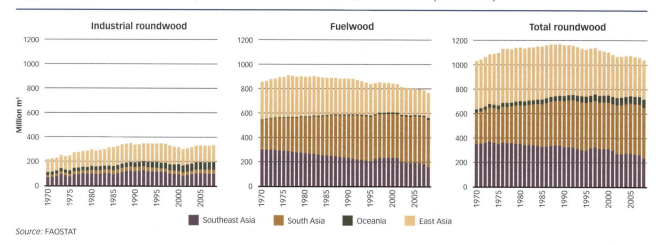

Source: FAOSTAT

countries (China, Indonesia, Malaysia and Thailand) because the increased supply of wood from planted forests (not covered by the restrictions) and imports replaced supply from natural forests.

The value of wood and NWFP removals is an indicator of the contribution of forests to national economies and of socio-economic benefits of forests. The value of total wood removals (including roundwood and fuelwood) in 2005 was around US$29 billion in the Asia and the Pacific region as a whole. Subregional trends in the value of wood removals between 1990 and 2005 fluctuated and only Oceania reported an increasing trend in the value of wood removals since 1990 (Figure 9). Forests in the region also provided a large variety of NWFPs collected mainly for home consumption, which had an important economic value that was only partially accounted for. Data on the value of these removals were reported by 16 countries, accounting for 70 percent of the forest area of the

region. NWFP removals reached a total reported value of US$7.4 billion in the region as a whole.

The level of employment in forestry is also an indicator of both the social and economic value of the sector to society. Table 12 shows employment in the primary production of forest goods and related services, (i.e. excluding the processing of wood and NWFPs). The reported level of employment in the region was very high (8.2 million) compared with the world total (10.5 million), as a result of the inclusion of people employed to establish forest plantations and other part-time jobs. Conversely, most countries' statistics did not include people collecting fuelwood and NWFPs for subsistence purposes, although some provided partial estimates of subsistence employment. Employment in forestry declined slightly from 1990 to 2005, mainly as a result of China's partial logging ban in the late 1990s and general increases in labour productivity (e.g. increased mechanization of harvesting operations).

Figure 9: Value of wood removals in Asia and the Pacific, 1990–2005 (billion US$)

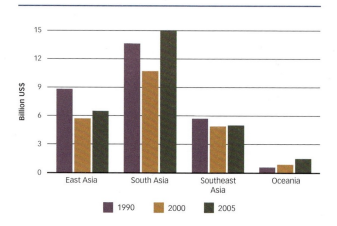

Table 12: Employment in primary production of forest goods in Asia and the Pacific, 2005 (1 000 FTE)

Subregion	Employment in primary production of goods, 2005
East Asia	1 293
South Asia	6 396
Southeast Asia	457
Oceania	27
Total Asia–Pacific	8 172

Europe[5]

Extent of forest resources

The region of Europe consists of 50 countries and areas with a total forest area of just over 1 billion hectares or about 25 percent of the global forest area. Based on statistics from FRA 2010, forests covered about 45 percent of total land area in Europe, ranging from 0 in Monaco to 73 percent in Finland. Forest area in Europe was dominated by the Russian Federation, which contained the largest forest area in the world. The country reported a forest area of almost 810 million hectares or over 80 percent of Europe's forest area and one-fifth of the global forest area. For practical reasons, this report provides the figures for Europe, Europe excluding the Russian Federation, and the Russian Federation separately.

Europe's forest area continued to grow between 1990 and 2010, although the rate of increase slowed over the period analysed (Table 13). The expansion of forest area was a result of new forest planting and natural expansion of forests onto former agricultural land. In the last decade, the annual net increase in forest area was just under 700 000 ha per year, down from close to 900 000 ha per year during the 1990s. In comparison with other regions, Europe was the only region with a net increase in forest area over the entire period 1990–2010. The forest area in the Russian Federation was virtually stable, with a small increase in the 1990s and a small decline in the period 2000–2010. This slight fluctuation was insignificant in statistical terms given the large forest area. The reported forest area for Europe excluding the Russian Federation was 196 million hectares in 2010.

The net increase in forest area in Europe over the period 2000–2010 was due in large part to a few countries, led by Spain (118 500 ha per year) and Sweden (81 400 ha per year), followed by Italy, Norway, France and Bulgaria. However, the apparent increase in forest area in Sweden between 2000 and 2005 was largely the result of a change in assessment methodology rather than an actual change. The largest percentage increases in the last decade were reported by countries with low forest cover: Iceland (5.0 percent per year) and the Republic of Moldova (1.8 percent per year). Estonia, Finland and the Russian Federation were the only European countries to report a net loss of forest area over the period 2000–2010, together accounting for an average decrease of 51 000 ha per year; however, this amounted to less than a 0.01 percent loss per year.

The increases in the area of planted forests in Europe also slowed in the last decade, when compared with the global trend over the same time period (Table 14). Close to 7 percent of the region's forest area was composed of planted forests in 2010. About half of the net increase in forest area over the past 20 years was a result of an increase in the area of planted forests. About half of the net increase in forest area over the last 10 years was due to afforestation, with the balance of the increase resulting from the natural expansion of forests mainly onto former agricultural land.

Table 13: Forest area in Europe, 1990–2010

Region	Area (1 000 ha)			Annual change (1 000 ha)		Annual change rate (%)	
	1990	2000	2010	1990–2000	2000–2010	1990–2000	2000–2010
Russian Federation	808 950	809 269	809 090	32	-18	n.s.	n.s.
Europe excluding Russian Federation	180 521	188 971	195 911	845	694	0.46	0.36
Total Europe	989 471	998 239	1 005 001	877	676	0.09	0.07
World	4 168 399	4 085 063	4 032 905	-8 334	-5 216	-0.20	-0.13

---

[5] Countries and areas included in this regional section for the purposes of this review are: Albania, Andorra, Austria, Belarus, Belgium, Bosnia and Herzegovina, Bulgaria, Croatia, Czech Republic, Denmark, Estonia, Faroe Islands, Finland, France, Germany, Gibraltar, Greece, Guernsey, Holy See, Hungary, Iceland, Ireland, Isle of Man, Italy, Jersey, Latvia, Liechtenstein, Lithuania, Luxembourg, Malta, Monaco, Montenegro, Netherlands, Norway, Poland, Portugal, Republic of Moldova, Romania, Russian Federation, San Marino, Serbia, Slovakia, Slovenia, Spain, Svalbard and Jan Mayen Islands, Sweden, Switzerland, The Former Yugoslav Republic of Macedonia, Ukraine, United Kingdom.

In Europe, the total carbon stock in forest biomass was estimated at 45 Gt or almost 16 percent of the world total (Figure 10). Europe excluding the Russian Federation accounted for almost 13 Gt and here the annual increase was about 145 tonnes per year in 2000–2010 compared with 135 tonnes per year in the 1990s. In the Russian Federation the carbon in forest biomass was relatively stable with a minor decrease in the 1990s and a slight increase over the last decade.

Biological diversity and protective functions

About 26 percent of Europe's forest area was classified as primary forest, compared with 36 percent of the world as a whole. The large majority of this area was located in the Russian Federation. Excluding the Russian Federation, less than 3 percent of Europe's forests were classified as primary forest. The data indicated a slightly increasing trend in primary forests in Europe excluding the Russian Federation (Figure 11). The Russian Federation reported a decrease of 1.6 million hectares per year in the 1990s, which reversed to show a gain of 164 000 ha per year in the period from 2000 to 2010. This change was mainly the result of a modification in the classification system introduced in 1995 rather than actual changes in primary forest area. A number of countries reported an increase in the area of primary forest, which can occur when countries set aside natural forest areas in which no intervention should take place. With time, these areas evolve into forests in which there are no clearly visible indications of human activity and the ecological processes are not significantly disturbed, thus meeting the definition of primary forest as used in the FRA process. It should be noted that information was missing from some forest rich countries such as Finland.

Throughout the 1990s and 2000s there was a positive global trend in the extent to which forest ecosystems were designated for the conservation of biological diversity, with the total increase over 20 years approaching 100 million hectares, equivalent to a 35 percent rise in conservation area. In Europe, the forest area designated primarily for conservation of biological diversity doubled over the same period (Table 15). Most of this increase occurred in the 1990s, but the area continued to grow

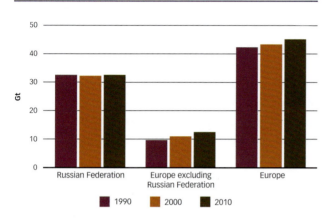

Figure 10: Carbon stock in forest biomass in Europe, 1990–2010 (Gt)

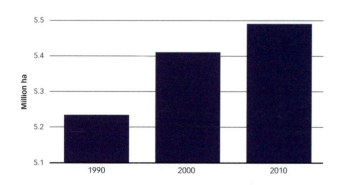

Figure 11: Area of primary forest in Europe excluding the Russian Federation, 1990–2010 (million ha)

Table 14: Area of planted forests in Europe, 1990–2010

Region	Area (1 000 ha)			Annual change (1 000 ha)		Annual change rate (%)	
	1990	2000	2010	1990–2000	2000–2010	1990–2000	2000–2010
Russian Federation	12 651	15 360	16 991	271	163	1.96	1.01
Europe excluding Russian Federation	46 395	49 951	52 327	356	238	0.74	0.47
Total Europe	59 046	65 312	69 318	627	401	1.01	0.60
World	178 307	214 839	264 084	3 653	4 925	1.88	2.09

between 2000 and 2010 at just over 2 percent per year. Some 10 percent of the forest area in Europe (excluding the Russian Federation) was designated for biodiversity conservation, compared with a global average of 12 percent. In the Russian Federation, the forest area designated for conservation increased from 1.5 percent in 1990 to 2.2 percent of total forest area in 2010, largely due to national policies that strengthened nature conservation.

In Europe, 4 percent of the total forest area was located within formally established protected areas. Excluding the Russian Federation, this figure rose to 12 percent. Over the last decade, the annual increase in the area of forest within a protected area system was almost 560 000 ha per year, compared with about 910 000 ha per year in the previous decade (1990–2000).

The forest area primarily designated for protection of soil and water accounted for 9 percent of the total forest area in the region. A large increase in this area was recorded in the decade from 1990 to 2000 (Table 16). The Russian Federation was mainly responsible for this significant

increase and, although a similar trend was observed in Europe excluding the Russian Federation, it was less pronounced.

The positive trends in forest area designated primarily for protection of soil and water indicate that countries in Europe have recognized the importance of protective forest functions. Concern about maintaining the protective functions of forests were the driving force behind the forest laws in many countries, notably in mountainous regions. Although considerable research has been carried out on the benefits of forest protection, they are difficult to quantify because they are rarely valued in markets and tend to be highly site-specific.

Productive and socio-economic functions

In Europe, 52 percent of the total forest area was designated primarily for production (57 percent excluding the Russian Federation), compared with a global average of 30 percent. The area of Europe's forests designated primarily for production declined significantly in the 1990s, but increased slightly over the last decade (Table 17). Country data suggested an

Table 15: Area of forest designated primarily for conservation of biological diversity in Europe, 1990–2010

Region	Area (1 000 ha)			Annual change (1 000 ha)		Annual change rate (%)	
	1990	2000	2010	1990–2000	2000–2010	1990–2000	2000–2010
Russian Federation	11 815	16 190	17 572	438	138	3.20	0.82
Europe excluding Russian Federation	6 840	13 203	19 407	636	620	6.80	3.93
Total Europe	18 655	29 393	36 979	1 074	759	4.65	2.32
World	270 413	302 916	366 255	3 250	6 334	1.14	1.92

Table 16: Area of forest designated primarily for protection of soil and water in Europe, 1990–2010

Region	Area (1 000 ha)			Annual change (1 000 ha)		Annual change rate (%)	
	1990	2000	2010	1990–2000	2000–2010	1990–2000	2000–2010
Russian Federation	58 695	70 386	71 436	1 169	105	1.83	0.15
Europe excluding Russian Federation	18 237	20 403	21 559	217	116	1.13	0.55
Total Europe	76 932	90 788	92 995	1 386	221	1.67	0.24
World	240 433	271 699	299 378	3 127	2 768	1.23	0.97

increase in the total growing stock in many countries, especially in areas of central Europe. The net result at the regional level has been an increase in total growing stock in cubic metres and in cubic metres per hectare over the last 20 years.

Wood removals provide another indicator of the productive functions of forest. During the early 1990s, total wood removals in Europe declined because of the collapse of the eastern European economies (Figure 12). Although removals rebounded slightly in later years, they once again dropped sharply in conjunction with the 2008–2009 recession in Europe as a result of declining demand for wood. The value of wood removals in Europe excluding the Russian Federation also dipped at the end of the 1990s, and rose again between 2000 and 2005 (Figure 13). Excluding the Russian Federation, Europe accounted for 24 percent of the world's industrial roundwood removals, but only 5 percent of the world's forest area. Including the Russian Federation, Europe accounted for 32 percent of global industrial roundwood removals. With Europe's

forest area and growing stock expanding, it would seem that a high level of wood removal for production is not incompatible with sustainable forest management in countries with relatively developed economies and stable institutions. The volume of wood harvested in Europe's forests was increasing, yet remained considerably below increment (UNECE/FAO, 2007).

A substantial quantity of NWFPs were harvested for self-consumption in Europe, although they rarely entered markets or were recorded in national statistics. NWFPs have an important economic value. Data on the quantity and value of NWFP removals were reported by 29 countries despite the fact that comprehensive data were limited in most countries. Some countries submitted data on a limited number of products. The reported total value of NWFP removals reached US$8.4 billion in Europe, which is still considered to be an incomplete estimate. Globally, the reported value of NWFP removals amounted to US$18.5 billion in 2005.

Figure 12: Wood removals in Europe, 1970–2009 (million m³)

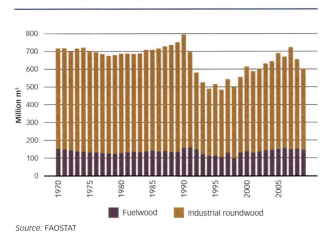

Source: FAOSTAT

Figure 13: Value of wood removals in Europe excluding the Russian Federation (billion US$)

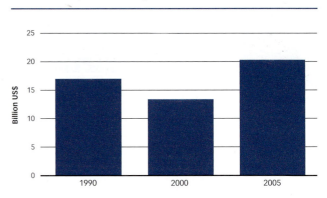

Table 17: Area of forest designated primarily for production in Europe, 1990–2010

Region	Area (1 000 ha)			Annual change (1 000 ha)		Annual change rate (%)	
	1990	2000	2010	1990–2000	2000–2010	1990–2000	2000–2010
Russian Federation	446 679	411 437	415 791	-3 524	435	-0.82	0.11
Europe excluding Russian Federation	111 363	111 229	108 829	-13	-240	-0.01	-0.22
Total Europe	558 042	522 666	524 620	-3 538	195	-0.65	0.04
World	1 181 576	1 160 325	1 131 210	-2 125	-2 911	-0.18	-0.25

Some 1.1 million people were employed in the primary production of forest goods in Europe (Table 18). However, employment levels declined significantly over the period 1990–2005. As noted in UNECE/FAO (2005), "labour productivity has been rising faster than production, so total employment in the forest sector has been steadily falling". The effect of the recession in Europe was also likely to result in a drop in employment after late 2008.

Latin America and the Caribbean[6]
Extent of forest resources

The region of Latin America and the Caribbean has abundant forest resources, with almost 49 percent of its total land covered by forest in 2010. With an estimated 891 million hectares, it accounted for around 22 percent of the world's forest area. Brazil was one of the five most forest-rich countries in the world with 13 percent of the global forest area and was the country with the largest extent of tropical forest. The five countries with the largest forest area in the region (Brazil, Peru, Colombia, the Plurinational State of Bolivia and the Bolivarian Republic of Venezuela) represented 84 percent of the total forest area of the region.

Forest area continued to decline in Central and South America, with the leading cause of deforestation being the conversion of forest land to agriculture and urbanization. Within the region, the largest decline in

Table 18: Employment in primary production of forest goods in Europe, 2005 (1 000 FTE)

Region	Employment in primary production of goods, 2005
Russian Federation	444
Europe excluding Russian Federation	665
Total Europe	1 109
World	10 433

forest area continued to be in South America, although this has slowed and in percentage terms remained stable since 1990 (Table 19). The largest percentage loss of forest area continued to take place in Central America, although the rate has fallen in this subregion since 2000. Chile, Costa Rica and Uruguay were among the countries that increased their forest areas. Forest area also increased in the Caribbean, mainly through natural expansion of forest onto abandoned agricultural land. The total area of other wooded land in the region accounted for 187 million hectares or 10 percent of the total land area. In Central America and the Caribbean the area of other wooded land was stable, while in South America there was a reduction of more than half a million hectares per year between 1990 and 2010.

Table 19: Forest area in Latin America and the Caribbean, 1990–2010

Subregion	Area (1 000 ha)			Annual change (1 000 ha)		Annual change rate (%)	
	1990	2000	2010	1990–2000	2000–2010	1990–2000	2000–2010
Caribbean	5 901	6 433	6 932	53	50	0.87	0.75
Central America	25 717	21 980	19 499	-374	-248	-1.56	-1.19
South America	946 454	904 322	864 351	-4 213	-3 997	-0.45	-0.45
Total Latin America and the Caribbean	978 072	932 735	890 782	-4 534	-4 195	-0.47	-0.46
World	4 168 399	4 085 063	4 032 905	-8 334	-5 216	-0.20	-0.13

[6] For the purposes of this report, Latin American and Caribbean countries and areas are grouped into the following subregions:
- Central America: Belize, Costa Rica, El Salvador, Guatemala, Honduras, Nicaragua, Panama
- South America: Argentina, Bolivia (Plurinational State of), Brazil, Chile, Colombia, Ecuador, Falkland Islands (Malvinas), French Guiana, Guyana, Paraguay, Peru, Suriname, Uruguay, Venezuela (Bolivarian Republic of). It should be noted that a dispute exists between the Government of Argentina and the United Kingdom of Great Britain and Northern Ireland concerning sovereignty over the Falkland Islands (Malvinas).
- Caribbean: Anguilla, Antigua and Barbuda, Aruba, Bahamas, Barbados, Bermuda, British Virgin Islands, Cayman Islands, Cuba, Dominica, Dominican Republic, Grenada, Guadeloupe, Haiti, Jamaica, Martinique, Montserrat, Netherlands Antilles, Puerto Rico, Saint Kitts and Nevis, Saint Lucia, Saint Martin (French part), Saint Vincent and the Grenadines, Saint Barthélemy, Trinidad and Tobago, Turks and Caicos Islands, United States Virgin Islands

Globally, planted forests comprised about 7 percent of total forest area. In Latin America and the Caribbean they made up less than 2 percent of total forest area and the region accounted for less than 6 percent of the global area of planted forests. However, planted forests have expanded at a rate of about 3.2 percent per year in the region over the last decade (Table 20). Brazil, Chile, Argentina, Uruguay and Peru showed the largest increase in the area of planted forest between 2000 and 2010.

It was estimated that in Latin America and the Caribbean the total carbon stored in forest biomass was 104 Gt and it decreased by an estimated 424 million tonnes annually during the period 1990–2010 (Figure 14). Central and South America registered a net loss over the period 1990–2010, while the Caribbean showed an overall gain in carbon in forest biomass.

Biological diversity and protective functions

Primary forests in Latin America and the Caribbean accounted for 75 percent of the total forest area and the region held 57 percent of the world's primary forests. Most of the primary forest was located in inaccessible or protected areas. Despite this, there was a significant loss of primary forest outside protected areas, particularly in South America. Caribbean countries reported that the area of primary forest had been stable since 1990. Central America increased its net loss from 54 000 ha per year in the decade 1990–2000 to 74 000 ha annually from 2000 to 2010 (Figure 15). The data collected did not allow for an analysis of the proportion of this net loss that was caused by deforestation and conversion to other uses, compared with that resulting from the opening up of primary forests to selective logging or other human activities,

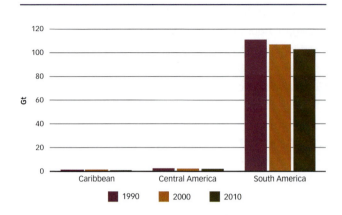

Figure 14: Carbon stock in forest biomass in Latin America and the Caribbean, 1990–2010 (Gt)

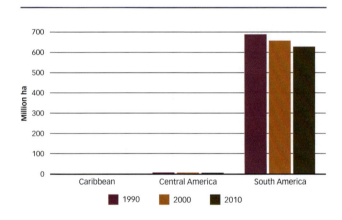

Figure 15: Area of primary forest in Latin America and the Caribbean, 1990–2010 (million ha)

which would mean that the forest was reclassified as 'other naturally regenerated forest' in the FRA 2010 classification system.

Table 20: Area of planted forest in Latin America and the Caribbean, 1990–2010

Subregion	Area (1 000 ha)			Annual change (1 000 ha)		Annual change rate (%)	
	1990	2000	2010	1990–2000	2000–2010	1990–2000	2000–2010
Caribbean	391	394	547	n.s.	15	0.09	3.34
Central America	445	428	584	-2	16	-0.37	3.14
South America	8 276	10 058	13 821	178	376	1.97	3.23
Total Latin America and the Caribbean	9 111	10 880	14 952	177	407	1.79	3.23
World	178 307	214 839	264 084	3 653	4 925	1.88	2.09

In Latin America and the Caribbean, 14 percent of the forest area was designated primarily for the conservation of biological diversity. This area has increased by more than 3 million hectares annually (or 4.5 percent per year) since 2000 (Table 21) with the vast majority of this increase in South America. A total of 18 percent of the total forest area in the region was located in formally designated protected areas.

The forest area designated for protection of soil and water resources represented 7 percent of the total forest area in the region, compared with 8 percent globally. This area increased slightly between 1990 and 2010 (Table 22), with virtually all of the increase being in the Caribbean. The countries with the highest proportion of their forest area designated for protective functions were (in descending order): Cuba, Chile, Ecuador, Trinidad and Tobago, and Honduras.

Productive and socio-economic functions

In 2010, about 14 percent of all forest area in the region was designated primarily for production, compared with a global average of 30 percent. Latin America and the Caribbean contained 10 percent of the total worldwide forest area designated for productive purposes. Guyana reported the largest proportion of forest area designated primarily for production (97 percent), followed by Uruguay (64 percent), Haiti (54 percent), the Bolivarian Republic of Venezuela (49 percent) and Chile (46 percent). While the forest area designated for productive functions fell at the global level, it grew in Latin America and the Caribbean, primarily in South America (Table 23).

Wood removals in the region showed continued growth over the past two decades. Fuelwood accounted for slightly more than half (57 percent) of total wood removals

Table 21: Area of forest designated primarily for conservation of biodiversity in Latin America and the Caribbean, 1990–2010

Subregion	Area (1 000 ha)			Annual change (1 000 ha)		Annual change rate (%)	
	1990	2000	2010	1990–2000	2000–2010	1990–2000	2000–2010
Caribbean	617	671	711	5	4	0.85	0.58
Central America	4 337	4 023	3 677	-31	-35	-0.75	-0.90
South America	40 683	52 548	84 222	1 187	3 167	2.59	4.83
Total Latin America and the Caribbean	45 637	57 243	88 610	1 161	3 137	2.29	4.47
World	270 413	302 916	366 255	3 250	6 334	1.14	1.92

Table 22: Area of forest designated primarily for protection of soil and water in Latin America and the Caribbean, 1990–2010

Subregion	Area (1 000 ha)			Annual change (1 000 ha)		Annual change rate (%)	
	1990	2000	2010	1990–2000	2000–2010	1990–2000	2000–2010
Caribbean	869	1 106	1 428	24	32	2.44	2.58
Central America	124	114	90	-1	-2	-0.90	-2.33
South America	48 656	48 661	48 549	1	-11	n.s.	-0.02
Total Latin America and the Caribbean	49 650	49 881	50 066	23	19	0.05	0.04
World	240 433	271 699	299 378	3 127	2 768	1.23	0.97

in the region. In Central America and the Caribbean, by far the majority of wood removed from forest was for fuelwood (90 percent), while in South America removals were equally distributed between industrial roundwood and fuelwood (Figure 16).

Very limited information was reported on NWFPs so it was difficult to draw any conclusions about these removals. The reports indicated that food products, live animals and exudates were the principal NWFPs extracted from the forests in Latin America and the Caribbean. NWFP collection was mainly practised by forest-dependent people and was generally not registered in official trade statistics.

Wood removals in the region were estimated to be worth about US$6.8 billion or 7 percent of the world total in 2005. Regional trend analysis (based on those countries that provided information for all the reporting years) showed a drop in the value from

1990 to 2000, which rebounded between 2000 and 2005 (Figure 17). Information on the value of fuelwood continued to be scarce. Most of the countries in Latin America and the Caribbean noted that quantitative data related to the extraction of fuelwood both for domestic and industrial purposes was very limited or non-existent.

More than 350 000 full-time jobs were reported in the primary production of goods from forests (the figures exclude employment in wood processing industries) (Table 24). Global employment in forestry declined over the period 1990–2005, but in Latin America and the Caribbean there was an upward swing of 3.4 percent from 2000 to 2005. Suriname and Brazil nearly doubled the number of full-time jobs related to forestry over the last five years. Honduras, Nicaragua and El Salvador also showed a rising trend. Most other countries in the region did not present sufficient data to report a trend.

Figure 16: Volume of wood removals in Latin America and the Caribbean, 1970–2008 (million m³)

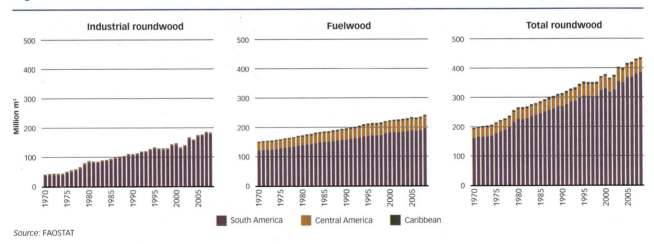

Source: FAOSTAT

Table 23: Area of forest designated primarily for production in Latin America and the Caribbean, 1990–2010

Subregion	Area (1 000 ha)			Annual change (1 000 ha)		Annual change rate (%)	
	1990	2000	2010	1990–2000	2000–2010	1990–2000	2000–2010
Caribbean	879	860	1 028	-2	17	-0.21	1.80
Central America	1 743	1 620	1 522	-12	-10	-0.73	-0.62
South America	70 857	75 866	80 827	501	496	0.69	0.64
Total Latin America and the Caribbean	73 478	78 346	83 378	487	503	0.64	0.62
World	1 181 576	1 160 325	1 131 210	-2 125	-2 911	-0.18	-0.25

Figure 17: Value of wood removals in Latin America and the Caribbean (billion US$)

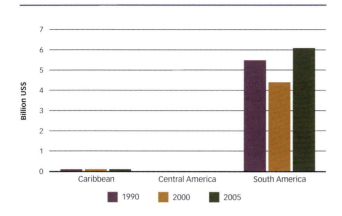

Table 24: Employment in primary production of forest goods in Latin America and the Caribbean, 2005 (1 000 FTE)

Subregion	Employment in primary production of goods, 2005
Caribbean	41
Central America	83
South America	239
Total Latin America and the Caribbean	363
World	10 537

The Near East[7]
Extent of forest resources

Although the Near East[8] accounted for close to 16 percent of the world's land area, it represented only 3 percent of the world's forest area as of 2010. Of the 33 countries and areas included in this region, 26 are 'low forest cover countries' where forest occupied less than 10 percent of the land area; one country (Qatar) reported no forest at all. According to FRA 2010, the total forest area in the region in 2010 was 122 million hectares or 6 percent of the land area.

North Africa contained the greatest share (65 percent) of the region's forest area, followed by Western Asia (22 percent) and Central Asia (13 percent) (Table 25). In the Near East, the trend in forest area shifted from a net loss of 518 000 ha per year in the 1990s to a net gain of 90 000 ha per year over the last decade. However, this trend should be viewed as a general estimate, as few countries could provide reliable data from comparable assessments over time. Trends in Central and Western Asia were quite stable: forest area declined slightly in some countries and increased slightly in others, with the exception of Turkey, which experienced rapid gains over the period 1990–2000. In North Africa, however, the trends fluctuated and the data suggested that a net loss of more than half a million hectares of forest per year in the 1990s became a net gain in the last decade. This was at least partly a result of a change in assessment methodology in Sudan.

Table 25: Forest area in the Near East, 1990–2010

Subregion	Area (1 000 ha)			Annual change (1 000 ha)		Annual change rate (%)	
	1990	2000	2010	1990–2000	2000–2010	1990–2000	2000–2010
Central Asia	15 901	15 980	16 016	8	4	0.05	0.02
North Africa	85 123	79 224	78 814	-590	-41	-0.72	-0.05
Western Asia	25 588	26 226	27 498	64	127	0.25	0.47
Total Near East	126 612	121 431	122 327	-518	90	-0.42	0.07
World	4 168 399	4 085 063	4 032 905	-8 334	-5 216	-0.20	-0.13

[7] For the purposes of this report, the Near East countries and areas are grouped into the following subregions:
- Western Asia: Afghanistan, Bahrain, Cyprus, Israel, Iran (Islamic Republic of), Iraq, Jordan, Kuwait, Lebanon, Occupied Palestinian Territory, Oman, Qatar, Saudi Arabia, Syrian Arab Republic, Turkey, United Arab Emirates, Yemen
- Central Asia: Armenia, Azerbaijan, Georgia, Kazakhstan, Kyrgyzstan, Tajikistan, Turkmenistan, Uzbekistan
- North Africa: Algeria, Egypt, Libyan Arab Jamahiriya, Mauritania, Morocco, Sudan, Tunisia, Western Sahara
[8] The countries and areas forming part of the North Africa subregion (Algeria, Egypt, Libyan Arab Jamahiriya, Mauritania, Morocco, Sudan, Tunisia and Western Sahara) also appear in the Africa regional section. The inclusion of these countries and areas in both regions was intentional and necessary, as it reflects the categorization of countries within the FAO Regional Forestry Commissions.

Forest established through planting or seeding made up 12 percent of the forest area of the region. This was mainly composed of native species (95 percent). The area of planted forest showed an increase in all subregions in the last 20 years (Table 26).

It was estimated that the forests of the Near East stored 3.5 Gt of carbon in biomass in 2010 and that this amount had increased over the last 10 years. Only North Africa's carbon stock declined in the last 20 years, mainly because of the reduction of forest area (Figure 18).

Biological diversity and protective functions

Primary forests accounted for 14 percent of the total forest area in the Near East, with more than 80 percent of the region's primary forest being located in Sudan. The area of primary forest declined by some 100 000 ha per year in the 1990s, but has since remained largely stable (Figure 19).

The forest area designated for biodiversity conservation in the Near East has increased by 85 000 ha annually

over the last ten years and by 2010 accounted for close to 13 percent of the total forest area in the region. Most of this increase took place in Central Asia (Table 27). Overall, 16 percent of the forests in the region were within legally established protected areas, with the highest percentage being found in North Africa (18 percent).

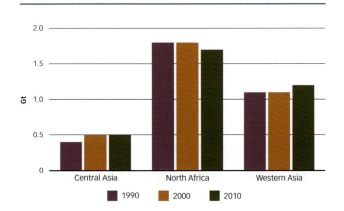

Figure 18: Carbon stock in forest biomass in the Near East, 1990–2010 (Gt)

Table 26: Area of planted forests in the Near East, 1990–2010

Subregion	Area (1 000 ha)			Annual change (1 000 ha)		Annual change rate (%)	
	1990	2000	2010	1990–2000	2000–2010	1990–2000	2000–2010
Central Asia	1 470	1 771	1 918	30	15	1.89	0.80
North Africa	6 794	7 315	8 091	52	78	0.74	1.01
Western Asia	3 208	3 926	5 073	72	115	2.04	2.60
Total Near East	11 471	13 012	15 082	154	207	1.27	1.49
World	178 307	214 839	264 084	3 653	4 925	1.88	2.09

Table 27: Area of forest designated primarily for conservation of biological diversity in the Near East, 1990–2010

Subregion	Area (1 000 ha)			Annual change (1 000 ha)		Annual change rate (%)	
	1990	2000	2010	1990–2000	2000–2010	1990–2000	2000–2010
Central Asia	795	1 039	1 566	24	53	2.71	4.19
North Africa	13 325	12 597	12 769	-73	17	-0.56	0.14
Western Asia	915	1 056	1 208	14	15	1.45	1.35
Total Near East	15 035	14 692	15 544	-34	85	-0.23	0.56
World	270 413	302 916	366 255	3 250	6 334	1.14	1.92

Fourteen percent of the forest area in the region was designated primarily for the protection of soil and water resources. Collectively, the region increased these areas by some 60 000 ha annually over the last 20 years (Table 28). At the subregional level, the rate of increase in forest area designated for protection in Central Asia dropped over the last ten years in comparison with the previous decade. Gains were made here in the second half of the 1990s largely because Georgia changed the designation of a part of its forest from social services to soil protection and water regulation. Western Asia's area of protective forest by contrast expanded in the last decade, mainly as a result of Turkey's increasing attention to soil erosion problems that caused the country to dedicate a larger portion of its forests to the conservation of soil and water.

Productive and socio-economic functions

In the Near East region 38 percent of the forest area was primarily designated for the production of wood and NWFPs. After the overall area of productive forest dropped in the 1990s, it remained stable from 2000 onwards. At the subregional level, the trend in area designated primarily for production was quite heterogeneous: Central Asia registered a positive trend, which accelerated in the last ten years; North Africa's productive forest area fell over the period 1990–2000 and rose slightly between 2000 and 2010; and in Western Asia, the area increased in the 1990s and then decreased again in the last ten years (Table 29).

Figure 19: Area of primary forest in the Near East, 1990–2010 (million ha)

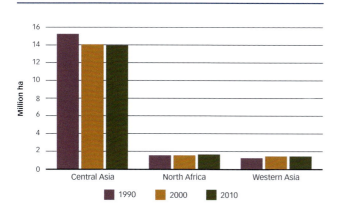

Table 28: Area of forest designated primarily for protection of soil and water in the Near East, 1990–2010

Subregion	Area (1 000 ha)			Annual change (1 000 ha)		Annual change rate (%)	
	1990	2000	2010	1990–2000	2000–2010	1990–2000	2000–2010
Central Asia	10 361	10 974	10 983	61	1	0.58	0.01
North Africa	4 068	3 855	3 851	-21	n.s.	-0.54	-0.01
Western Asia	1 861	2 086	2 685	22	60	1.15	2.56
Total Near East	16 290	16 914	17 520	62	61	0.38	0.35
World	240 433	271 699	299 378	3 127	2 768	1.23	0.97

Table 29: Area of forest designated primarily for production in the Near East, 1990–2010

Subregion	Area (1 000 ha)			Annual change (1 000 ha)		Annual change rate (%)	
	1990	2000	2010	1990–2000	2000–2010	1990–2000	2000–2010
Central Asia	27	28	90	n.s.	6	0.36	12.37
North Africa	39 557	36 637	36 819	-292	18	-0.76	0.05
Western Asia	9 539	9 657	9 439	12	-22	0.12	-0.23
Total Near East	49 123	46 323	46 348	-280	3	-0.59	0.01
World	1 181 576	1 160 325	1 131 210	-2 125	-2 911	-0.18	-0.25

Figure 20: Volume of wood removals in the Near East, 1970–2008 (million m³)

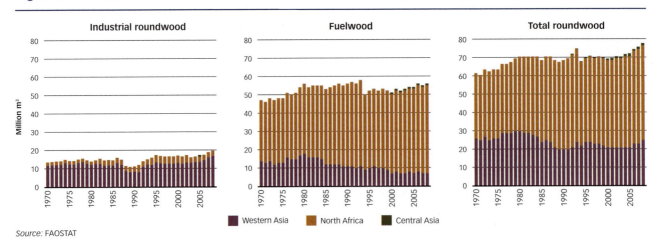

Source: FAOSTAT

The region accounted for only 2 percent of global wood removals, more than 70 percent of which was used as fuelwood (Figure 20). Turkey was the only country in the region where industrial roundwood removals were significant (14 million cubic metres) and played an important role as a source of raw material for wood industries. Approximately 296 000 people were employed in 2005 in the primary production of goods in the region (Table 30). Of these, 209 000 were in North Africa.

Information on the value of NWFPs was provided by only 13 countries in the region, with a total value of US$126 million as of 2005. The reported annual value of wood products in the Near East region was close to US$2 billion in 2005. However, information was missing from most of the countries in Central Asia, so the true value is likely to be considerably higher. In Western Asia, Jordan and Turkey recorded a sharp drop in the value of wood products between 1990 and 2000, which was only partly recovered during the period 2000–2005 (Figure 21).

North America[9]
Extent of forest resources

In 2010 forests covered 34 percent of North America's land area and accounted for 17 percent of the global forest area. In the North American region, the forest area in 2010 was estimated to be slightly larger than in 1990 (Table 31). While Canada reported no change in forest area, Mexico registered a decreasing rate of loss over the last 20 years, which was outweighed by a net gain in forest area in the United States of America.

Globally, planted forest made up about 7 percent of the world's total forest area. In North America, a total of 6 percent of the forest area (more than 37 million hectares) was planted forest, accounting for 14 percent of the world total (Table 32). In Canada, planted forests represented 3 percent of the total forest area, in Mexico, 5 percent and in the United States of America, 8 percent. The area of planted forest in the three countries continued to increase.

Table 30: Employment in primary production of forest goods in the Near East, 2005 (1 000 FTE)

Subregion	Employment in primary production of goods, 2005
Central Asia	38
North Africa	209
Western Asia	49
Total Near East	296

Figure 21: Value of wood removals in the Near East, 1990–2005 (billion US$)

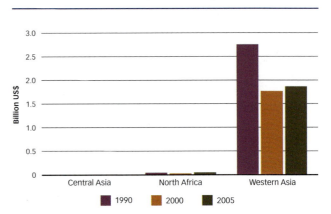

9   For the purposes of this report, North America includes Canada, Mexico and the United States of America (excluding US territories in the Caribbean).

Canada, Mexico and United States of America all reported on carbon in forest biomass (Figure 22) with a positive overall trend for the region.

Biological diversity and protective functions

North America accounted for 25 percent of global primary forest in 2010, which corresponded to 41 percent of the forest area in the region. In Canada and Mexico, 53 percent of the countries' forest area was classified as primary forest, while in the United States of America it made up 25 percent. The area of primary forest in the region overall increased slightly in the last decade (Figure 23). This can occur when countries set aside natural forest areas in which no intervention should take place.

North America designated 15 percent of its forest for the conservation of biological diversity compared with 12 percent at the global level. At a national level, the United States of America classified 25 percent of its forest under this designation, the highest in the region,

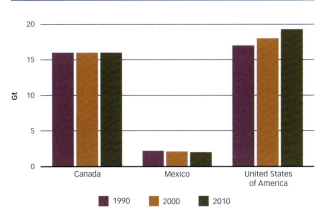

Figure 22: Carbon stock in forest biomass in North America, 1990–2010* (Gt)

* The figures presented for Canada are FAO estimates as Canada only reported carbon in forest biomass of 'managed forests' in accordance with reporting requirements for the UNFCCC.

followed by Mexico (13 percent) and Canada (5 percent). Canada showed no change over the period analysed, while the area in Mexico rose and in the United States of America the area decreased (Table 33). Nine percent

Table 31: Forest area in North America, 1990–2010

Region	Area (1 000 ha)			Annual change (1 000 ha)		Annual change rate (%)	
	1990	2000	2010	1990–2000	2000–2010	1990–2000	2000–2010
Canada	310 134	310 134	310 134	0	0	0	0
Mexico	70 291	66 751	64 802	-354	-195	-0.52	-0.30
United States of America	296 335	300 195	304 022	386	383	0.13	0.13
Total North America	676 760	677 080	678 958	32	188	n.s.	0.03
World	4 168 399	4 085 063	4 032 905	-8 334	-5 216	-0.20	-0.13

Table 32: Area of planted forest in North America, 1990–2010

Region	Area (1 000 ha)			Annual change (1 000 ha)		Annual change rate (%)	
	1990	2000	2010	1990–2000	2000–2010	1990–2000	2000–2010
Canada	1 357	5 820	8 963	446	314	15.67	4.41
Mexico	350	1 058	3 203	106	215	-	11.71
United States of America	17 938	22 560	25 363	462	280	2.32	1.18
Total North America	19 645	29 438	37 529	979	809	4.13	2.46
World	178 307	214 839	264 084	3 653	4 925	1.88	2.09

Figure 23: Area of primary forest in North America, 1990–2010 (million ha)

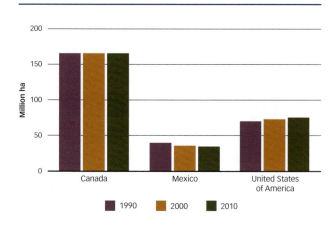

of the forest area in the region falls within a protected area system, ranging from 8 percent of the forest area in Canada to 13 percent of the forest area in Mexico.

In North America, the protection of soil and water are embedded in forest legislation, policy and guidance on sound forest management practices. The protection of soil and water are primary considerations in the development of forest plans and practices. While legislation, regulations and policy exists to guide where forest areas must be set aside, these areas are not legally defined and captured on land use maps. As a result, forest areas that are set aside for the purposes of soil and water conservation are included in the multiple use primary designated function.

Productive and socio-economic functions

About 14 percent of the forest area in North America was designated primarily for production in 2010, compared with 30 percent at the global level (Table 34). The vast majority of this area (93 percent) was located in the United States of America, where 30 percent of the forest area was designated primarily for productive purposes, compared with only 5 percent of Mexico's forest area and 1 percent of Canada's. An additional 68 percent of the forest area in the region was designated for multiple use – in most cases including the production of wood and NWFPs. There was

Table 33: Area of forest designated primarily for conservation of biological diversity in North America, 1990–2010

Region	Area (1 000 ha)			Annual change (1 000 ha)		Annual change rate (%)	
	1990	2000	2010	1990–2000	2000–2010	1990–2000	2000–2010
Canada	15 284	15 284	15 284	0	0	0	0
Mexico	4 547	4 457	8 488	-9	403	-0.20	6.65
United States of America	69 980	72 878	75 277	290	240	0.41	0.32
Total North America	89 811	92 619	99 049	281	643	0.31	0.67
World	270 413	302 916	366 255	3 250	6 334	1.14	1.92

Table 34: Area of forest designated primarily for production in North America, 1990–2010

Region	Area (1 000 ha)			Annual change (1 000 ha)		Annual change rate (%)	
	1990	2000	2010	1990–2000	2000–2010	1990–2000	2000–2010
Canada	3 928	3 928	3 928	0	0	0	0
Mexico	0	1 058	3 203	106	215	-	11.71
United States of America	76 632	82 520	90 007	589	749	0.74	0.87
Total North America	80 560	87 506	97 138	695	963	0.83	1.05
World	1 181 576	1 160 325	1 131 210	-2 125	-2 911	-0.18	-0.25

Figure 24: Volume of wood removals in North America, 1970–2009 (million m³)

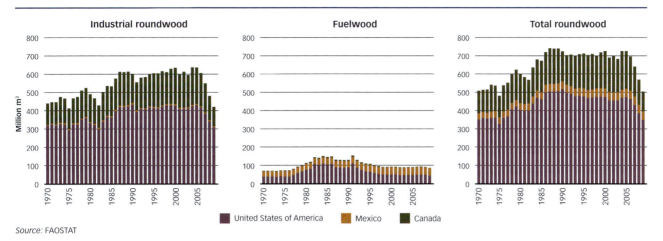

Industrial roundwood   Fuelwood   Total roundwood

United States of America   Mexico   Canada

Source: FAOSTAT

a large variation in the proportion of forest for multiple use within the region with values ranging from 46 percent in the United States of America to 87 percent in Canada. A combination of the two areas (production plus multiple use) may thus provide a better picture of the area available for wood supply in this region.

Only 10–15 percent of the wood removed in North America was used as fuelwood. The remainder was industrial roundwood consumed by wood processing and pulp industries. The long-term trends (Figure 24) show that in North America (the United States of America and Canada in particular), wood removals fluctuated widely over the past four decades. This suggests that forest owners and managers were quick to adjust wood supply depending on the level of demand for forest products and prices. The recent economic and housing crises in

the United States of America led to a sharp decline in industrial roundwood removals (about 30 percent). The information available on NWFPs at the regional level was insufficient to draw conclusions or to identify trends. The principal reported products were Christmas trees, maple products, resins, hides and skins, and fruit. The value of wood products increased steadily between 1990 and 2005 (Figure 25), but has since fallen sharply.

Countries were requested to report on paid employment in terms of full-time equivalents involved in primary production of forest goods (Table 35). Mexico did not provide data for this variable. The United States of America showed a continuous decrease in employment from 1990 to 2005. Canada's figures indicated that the employment level rose by 18 percent between 1990 and 2000 and then declined by 20 percent between 2000 and 2005.

Figure 25: Value of wood products in North America (billion US$)

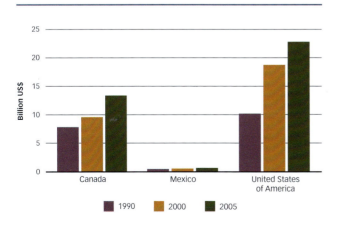

1990   2000   2005

Table 35: Employment in primary production of forest goods in the United States of America and Canada, 1990–2005 (1 000 FTE)

	Employment in primary production of goods		
	1990	2000	2005
Canada	73	87	70
United States of America (paid employment only)	103	98	84

2 Developing sustainable forest industries

This chapter describes current trends in the forest industry and shows how the industry is contributing to sustainable development. The analysis does not attempt to comprehensively measure the sustainability of the industry (although relevant statistics and other information are presented where available). Rather, the purpose of the analysis is to describe the factors affecting profitability and sustainability in the industry over the last 10–15 years and show how the industry is responding to the challenges they pose.

The analysis draws upon the recent work of FAO and others in outlook studies, policy analysis and forest resource assessment, but attempts to go beyond the measurement and forecasting of trends by combining and analysing these results within a strategic planning framework. It is hoped that this approach will present a new perspective on the trends and outlook for the sector that were originally presented in *State of the World's Forests 2009* to understand how sustainability might be improved.

The text is divided into two main sections. The first section describes some of the main external and internal forces affecting forest industry development. The second section outlines a number of different possible strategies to respond to these forces and current initiatives by governments and industry to improve sustainability in the sector. This is followed by a brief summary of the results and conclusions.

Driving forces affecting forest industries

The earliest references to the phrase 'sustainable industry' appeared at the start of the 1990s, in various articles about the activities of forestry companies (e.g. Renner, 1991). Although there is no commonly accepted definition of 'sustainable forest industry', papers such as this noted that sustainable industries should aim to make improvements in areas such as energy efficiency; lower waste production processes and resource conservation; the use of safe and environmentally compatible materials; safe working conditions; and human resource capacity. Economic sustainability must be a core part of these considerations because continual improvements

Table 36: Summary assessment of the main forces affecting forest industry development

	Positive forces	Negative forces
External forces	**Opportunities** • demographics in low and middle-income countries • economic growth • globalization • social trends	**Threats** • demographics in high-income countries • competing materials • competition for resources • changes in forest ownership, control and management
Internal forces	**Strengths** • environmental attributes of product • adaptability and management of raw material supply • potential for innovation	**Weaknesses** • existing industry structure • labour costs and working conditions • social and environmental performance and perceptions • maturity of existing product markets • end use issues (durability, regulations, etc.)

in productivity and profitability are fundamental requirements for the economic viability of the industry in the long-run.

Table 36 outlines the external and internal forces affecting the sector and categorizes them into potentially positive and negative influences. This is a very generalized assessment of the influences because they vary from country to country and between sectors of the industry. In addition, some forces (such as globalization) may be viewed as a positive force in some places, but as a threat in others. For the forest industry to continue contributing to sustainable development, the industry will need to consider the impact of the driving forces shown in Table 36, develop appropriate responses to overcome potentially negative impacts and take advantage of positive driving forces.

External driving forces

The main external forces affecting the forest industry are trends in economies, society and the environment. The two most fundamental forces are population demographics and economic growth. These have a major impact on forest product demand and may also influence industry development on the supply side through related changes such as increased globalization. Related to this, social trends also change with rising incomes, as people become less focused on meeting basic needs and demand a broader range of goods and services.

The other major driving force is changes in competing sectors as they also adapt and respond to the same trends. The competitive environment for forest products is constantly changing, often in unpredictable ways. Furthermore, linkages between the forest industry and the energy, chemicals and food sectors are becoming more evident, while policies that drive renewable energy, climate change mitigation and food security all influence the forest industry, both directly and indirectly.

Demographics and economic growth

As noted in *State of the World's Forests 2009* (FAO, 2009a), global population and the size of the global economy are expected to increase in the next few decades at similar rates to those seen in the past. Although global economic growth slowed in the recession of 2008–2009, this was more significant in developed countries. It is likely that most countries will return to a more normal growth trajectory in the coming years (see Box 1). Some of the main features of the long-term demographic and economic trends are outlined below.

The global population increased by 1.3 percent per annum from 5.3 billion in 1990 to 6.9 billion in 2010 and is projected to increase by 0.9 percent per annum to 8.2 billion in 2030. In the next two decades, the largest increases in population will occur in Africa (+235 million) and Asia and the Pacific (+255 million), which will increase their share of the global population (to 18 percent and 53 percent respectively). In contrast, Europe's population is expected to fall by 17 million over the period due to falling numbers in some significant countries.

Box 1: Uncertainties in the economic recovery

Following the decline in global economic growth to 1.7 percent in 2008 and −2.1 percent in 2009, the World Bank has projected economic growth of 3.3 percent in 2010 and 2011 and 3.5 percent in 2012, bringing growth back in line with the long-term trend expected in the future. However, two factors continue to cause uncertainty about the strength of the recovery. The first is the speed at which fiscal policies are tightened to control public debt in the (mostly developed) countries that were most affected by the recession of 2008–2009. The second is the risk of a default or a requirement for major restructuring of government debt in one or more of the weaker European countries. Should these uncertainties persist, global economic growth could be somewhat lower due to weaknesses in credit markets and lower government spending (especially in Europe). As an alternative, lower forecast, the World Bank projects growth of 3.1 percent (in 2010), 2.9 percent (in 2011) and 3.2 percent in 2012.

Developing countries were less affected by the recession of 2008–2009 and are expected to continue to grow rapidly as a result of higher productivity growth and fewer difficulties in their government finances and banking sectors. The World Bank is projecting growth of over 6.0 percent over the three years (2010–2012) or 5.9 percent under the alternative low growth scenario, although it is noted that a sovereign debt crisis in Europe could weaken international capital flows to some developing regions where European banks are major operators (e.g. parts of Eastern Europe, Western Asia, Latin America and the Caribbean).

Source: World Bank, 2010.

Figure 26: Global economic growth is shifting to the east and the south

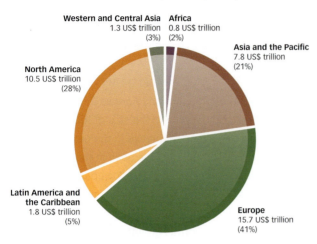

GDP in 1990 (at 2010 prices)

Western and Central Asia
1.3 US$ trillion
(3%)

Africa
0.8 US$ trillion
(2%)

Asia and the Pacific
7.8 US$ trillion
(21%)

North America
10.5 US$ trillion
(28%)

Latin America and
the Caribbean
1.8 US$ trillion
(5%)

Europe
15.7 US$ trillion
(41%)

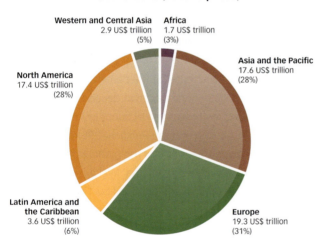

GDP in 2010 (at 2010 prices)

Western and Central Asia
2.9 US$ trillion
(5%)

Africa
1.7 US$ trillion
(3%)

Asia and the Pacific
17.6 US$ trillion
(28%)

North America
17.4 US$ trillion
(28%)

Latin America and
the Caribbean
3.6 US$ trillion
(6%)

Europe
19.3 US$ trillion
(31%)

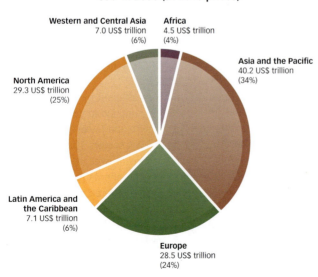

GDP in 2030 (at 2010 prices)

Western and Central Asia
7.0 US$ trillion
(6%)

Africa
4.5 US$ trillion
(4%)

Asia and the Pacific
40.2 US$ trillion
(34%)

North America
29.3 US$ trillion
(25%)

Latin America and
the Caribbean
7.1 US$ trillion
(6%)

Europe
28.5 US$ trillion
(24%)

Sources: World Bank, 2010 and EIU, 2010.

The age-structure of populations will continue to change towards a higher proportion of older people in the total population and, in some cases, a decline in the workforce. This trend has already started to appear in some developed countries and will increase over the next 20 years. For example, in 2030, the size of the workforce in Japan, the Republic of Korea and most European countries will be less than it is today. Even in China, it is projected to peak in 2015 and then start to gradually fall. The main exceptions to this trend are Africa, South and Southeast Asia and Latin America, where the workforce is expected to continue to grow rapidly.

Global gross domestic product (GDP) increased in real terms by 2.5 percent per annum from about US$38 trillion in 1990 to US$63 trillion in 2010 (at 2010 prices and exchange rates). It is projected to grow by 3.2 percent per annum to US$117 trillion in 2030, with relatively higher growth rates projected for less developed regions. The result of this will be a continued shift in the regional shares of global GDP away from developed regions such as Europe and North America towards other regions such as Asia and the Pacific (Figure 26).

Globalization

The trends described above have contributed to increased globalization in recent years. For example, in some countries with large and rapidly growing populations, low labour costs have combined with other factors (such as investments in education, communications and infrastructure) to stimulate rapid growth in domestic markets and higher production for exports. Other countries have become more closely linked into the global economy for other reasons, such as domestic political and market reforms, international trade liberalization, and the expansion of regional trade agreements. The result of these changes has been a rapid expansion in international flows of capital, goods and services since 1990 (Figure 27), which is expected to continue in the future.

In addition to these supply-side impacts, globalization has also led to some homogenization of markets. For example, with the expansion of multinational corporations, many products and services are now delivered to consumers in a similar way across the world and consumers are now aware of trends, tastes and fashions in other parts of the world. These developments present opportunities to increase efficiency in the delivery of products and services across a much larger global marketplace, but they also enable firms to gain competitive advantage through local market knowledge, product differentiation and the development of local market niches.

Figure 27: Increasing globalization of the world economy

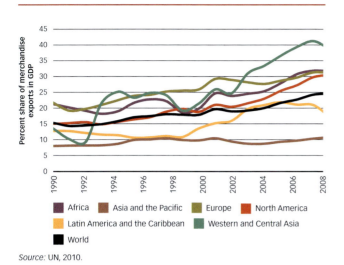

Africa
Asia and the Pacific
Europe
North America
Latin America and the Caribbean
Western and Central Asia
World

Source: UN, 2010.

Competing materials

The major end uses of forest products include media and communications materials, packaging, personal care products, construction (including home decoration) and furniture. In most of these markets, forest products compete with other goods and services and this competition has increased in recent years.

Demand for media and communications materials tends to increase when a significant proportion of the population earns incomes above subsistence levels (i.e. a middle-class develops). When this occurs, rising incomes result in more expenditure on leisure activities and the development of a service sector that relies very heavily on communication with customers. In these markets, speed, ease of use and cost are the major factors that affect competition between alternative forms of media. For many years, these markets relied heavily on newsprint, printing and writing paper to serve customers' needs, but advances in electronic media (i.e. increased availability and reduced costs) have resulted in strong competition in recent years. For example, paper books will continue to dominate this market for quite some time, but a gradual change is starting to occur as younger generations (who are more familiar with new technologies) shift the balance in demand towards electronic media, such as mobile phones and electronic books. More recently, the deregulation and, in particular, the expansion of internet connections (especially high-speed connections) have radically altered the way that companies and individuals communicate.

Packaging and personal care products (tissue paper and related products) account for the majority of other paper and paperboard consumption. Demand for these products increases rapidly once a certain level of economic development is reached. The demand for packaging materials is largely driven by growth in manufacturing, with cost, recyclability, weight, durability and ease of use being the main factors affecting their competitiveness. Plastic and, to a lesser extent, glass (in liquid packaging) and metal are the main materials competing with paper in these markets. Thus, energy and raw material costs are important factors affecting the cost competitiveness of the different materials. In most cases, paper products have maintained their share of this rapidly expanding market and, in some, have even improved it. This has largely been a result of investments in technology that have kept costs down and improved durability. In addition, the industry continues to innovate to produce packaging products that meet a wider range of customer needs, including product information or user instructions (Box 2).

In the markets for personal care products, paper products meet specific niches that are not so vulnerable to competition from other materials. Opportunities to increase revenue come from improvements in product quality and product innovations that meet new customer needs. In addition, sales of these products are not as strongly affected by business cycles and can remain profitable even during recessions, ensuring that this remains one of the most profitable sectors of the industry.

For solid wood products (i.e. sawnwood and wood-based panels) construction is the major end use in most countries and regions. The fundamental drivers of this market are population growth and economic growth, but expansion tends to slow (in relation to economic growth) at higher levels of income. Similar to packaging, construction meets basic functional needs, so cost, durability and ease of use are key factors determining the competitiveness of different materials.

The competitiveness of wood as a construction material varies quite a lot between countries and regions, partly for historical reasons. Countries with significant forest resources and forest processing industries tend to have a much longer history of wood use in construction and more familiarity with the potential of wood as a building material. In other countries, wood use for construction lags far behind its potential. For example, timber frame construction accounts for over 90 percent of house construction in

As noted by Wagberg (2007), many of the markets for paper products have suffered in recent years from fragmentation and increased competition from new media. For example, in Norway, the market for media has multiplied by a factor of 25 since 1980, but the different avenues for advertising have increased from five main segments in 1980 to over 40 today. In response to these developments, paper manufacturing and utilizing industries are using a number of different strategies to maintain demand for their products. Newspaper companies, for example, are switching from a focus on paid newspapers to a range of products that includes free smaller newspapers and internet services. At a broader level, paper companies are differentiating more between high-volume, low cost products (driven by technology developments) and more complex, high-value niche products (developed with greater understanding of customer needs and habits).

The packaging sector is also developing new products to remain competitive by meeting existing and future customers' needs better. Paper packaging products are being designed with new functionality to improve logistics and storage capabilities, with features such as automatic tamper discovery, improved traceability, authentication and encryption, and chemical and temperature monitoring. Other advanced examples of 'smart paper' are also being developed, including the incorporation of Radio Frequency Identification technology into paper (to improve product tracking and logistics) as well as the integration of other electronic devices into paper to perform a variety of different functions (e.g. display devices and batteries).

Source: Wagberg, 2007; Moore, 2007.

North America, Australia and Nordic countries, but only about 45 percent in Japan and less than 10 percent in some West European countries (Palmer, 2000). Metal, plastic and concrete are the main competing materials, and energy and raw material costs become important factors in determining the selection of construction materials. On the whole, wood has remained competitive in construction markets, with the notable exception of external doors and windows, for which plastic (PVC) alternatives have taken market share because of their cost and durability advantages.

The other significant end use of solid wood products is furniture manufacturing. Unlike construction and packaging, furniture is mostly sold directly to the public, so personal disposable income is a major driver of demand. As with personal care products, rising incomes present opportunities to increase revenues and profitability through quality improvements, innovations and marketing of higher value products more generally.

Demand for wooden furniture is affected in part by its cost competitiveness in comparison with furniture manufactured from other materials (mostly plastic, metal, glass and aluminium, but also bamboo, rattan and other fibrous plants). Consumer tastes and product quality also play important roles in determining the demand for wooden furniture, particularly at higher levels of income. Across a broader part of the market, many furniture manufacturers also now produce or sell matching home décor and accessories. By doing this, manufacturers are no longer simply selling furniture to meet functional needs, but are encouraging redecoration or renovation of existing furniture. Often these additional items also have higher profit margins than the furniture itself, which increases the value-added and profitability of the business as a whole. Furniture manufacturers are adopting much more sophisticated marketing techniques than producers of other wood products to maintain competitiveness and profitability.

In general, wooden furniture has maintained a share of about 45 percent of the total furniture market and consumption has risen in line with increasing incomes. Globally, cost competitiveness has been maintained by relocating production to countries with lower labour costs while, at the same time, the industry has generally maintained its reputation for quality.

Social trends

Social trends are changes in public opinions, attitudes and lifestyles that occur when incomes rise. For example, as incomes increase, people move beyond trying to meet basic needs and start to seek new products and services that will improve their quality of life, according to their tastes and preferences. Other wealth related factors also affect consumption, such as increases in home ownership (including second homes), trends towards larger homes and greater leisure time, as well as changes in the amount of time spent at home.

As incomes increase, consumers' perceptions of products also move beyond consideration of their costs and functional attributes to include more intangible factors (e.g. quality, status and fashion) that meet different needs. People become more aware of environmental and social issues, leading to demands for more sustainable products and lifestyles. These trends affect the demand for forest products and may affect the industry in other ways, such as government attempts to improve environmental and social standards through incentives and regulation.

Some of these trends are also magnified by increased education levels and much better communication between consumers. For example, social networking sites and other internet sites enable consumers to become much more knowledgeable about companies and their products through online product reviews and discussion forums. These may also include information or discussions about the sustainability of different products.

Competition for resources

The driving forces described above mostly affect the demand for forest products. On the supply side, the main driving force affecting the forest industry is the increased competition for resources (land, labour and capital) that occurs when populations and economies expand. In particular, in the case of the forest industry,

competition for land or, more specifically, competition for access to forest resources, is a major driving force that affects development. Competing demands for land are now sometimes referred to as the '5-Fs' - food; (animal) feed, forest (for conservation), fibre and fuel – and there is growing interest in how these demands will be met in the future (see, for example, OECD, 2009).

Although there is considerable scope to improve productivity, demand for land for food production continues to increase with population growth and this seems likely to continue for many years. More recently, with higher income levels in countries such as India and China, diets have started to change to include more meat and animal products. This has led to increased demand for animal feed, which is likely to reinforce the overall trend of increasing demand for agricultural land.

The rising demand for land to grow biofuel crops as a result of bioenergy policies is another emerging trend. Although the impacts of these policies remain uncertain and some policies are currently being revised, it seems likely that these developments will result in significant new demands for land and wood fibre that could stimulate forest conversion (Table 37).

These impacts are further complicated by the increased globalization of agriculture, so that higher demand in

Table 37: Potential expansion of biofuel crops onto other land uses by 2030 (in million hectares)

Region	Types of land likely to be used for expansion of biofuel crops						Total
	Mostly within agriculture		Degraded land	Possible forest conversion			
	Sugar beet and cereals	Oil crops	Jatropha, cassava, sorghum	Biomass energy crops	Sugar cane	Oil crops	
Net importers of biofuels							
North America	11.5	6.3		10			27.9
Europe	8.9	15.2		15			39.2
Asia and the Pacific	1.0	5.2	12.7		1.8	3.5	24.3
Net exporters of biofuels							
Latin America and Caribbean					4.3	8.0	12.3
Africa			1.4		1.3	2.8	5.5
World	21.5	26.8	14.2	25	7.4	14.2	109.1

Source: Cushion, Whiteman and Dieterle, 2010.

one part of the world leads to major (and unpredictable) changes in the demand for land in other regions. The potential impact of climate change also creates uncertainty, especially for water availability, which could affect demand for land or require changes in forest management.

Changes in forest ownership, control and management

Within the forestry sector, economic growth continues to increase the demand for wood while the social trends noted earlier are also leading to greater demands for forest conservation and changes in the way that forests are managed. These changes suggest that access to wood supply could become more complicated, with more fragmented forest ownership, more diverse forest management objectives and more forest areas excluded from wood production. Demand may have to be met by improving the management of forest resources and by relying more on other supply sources. For example, trees outside forests are already a major supply source in some densely populated Asian countries.

Internal forces

In addition to the forces described above, there are a number of other forces affecting industry development that can be more easily controlled by the industry or by others with an interest in the sector (e.g. governments). These forces appear throughout the production chain (i.e. from fibre supply to end product) and many are related to the way in which the industry operates. Other internal forces concern the industry's relationships with other stakeholders (including the general public), and these are more complicated and difficult to manage.

Industry structure and investment

In response to forces such as globalization, raw material supply and regional differences in economic growth, the structure of the forest industry is changing, but some features of the industry present challenges for future development.

In most countries, the forest sector is quite small especially in comparison with competing industries (e.g. cement) and others based on natural resources. The forest industry is also often fragmented and spread out across a country, for example where firms are located close to forests. The small size of the industry restricts the development of suppliers, subcontractors, service providers and other supporting infrastructure, and fragmentation makes it difficult to achieve economies of scale and other efficiency gains. Some countries have achieved economies of scale through industry consolidation (e.g. in pulp and paper and wood-based panel production), but sawmilling and, in particular, forest harvesting remain fragmented in many places.

The industry is also generally slow to adopt new technology. This is partly related to its small size and fragmentation: it is not viable for technology suppliers to serve countries where the market is fragmented or simply too small. Other factors play a part, too: market imperfections, a lack of knowledge or skills to operate and benefit from new technology, raw material supply insecurity, and the informal nature of the industry in some places all result in slower adoption. In some countries the forest industry continues to compete without much new technology by simply relying on good access to raw materials and using existing assets that are mostly depreciated.

In many countries it is also difficult for the forest industry to raise capital. For example, in many tropical countries, firms rely heavily on internal funds (e.g. retained profits) and unconventional sources of finance due to their small size and the difficulty for investors to assess risks (Canby, 2006). In many temperate countries, forest industry investments are relatively unattractive because of the lack of scale and the perception that the industry is a low-risk, low-return industry.[10] Other financing issues include the long-term nature of investments, the highly cyclical markets for products such as pulp and paper, and risks associated with fibre supply and regulation. The result is that many technologies exist that could improve profitability and sustainability, but many firms do not have the incentives or funding to invest in these technologies.

Labour costs and working conditions

In almost all countries, there is a trend towards mechanization, but much of the industry is still quite labour intensive, especially in harvesting and small-scale processing. In addition, the public have a very poor

---

[10] One exception is the Russian Federation, where there is considerable potential for large-scale investment in the sector. Unfortunately, this has not yet materialized due to the perceptions of high investment risk in the country and the more attractive investment opportunities currently available in other natural resource industries.

perception of employment in the forest industry, with many believing that most jobs involve repetitive, low skill tasks with little chance for innovation and career progression. The one contrasting view is that some parts of the industry (e.g. furniture and papermaking) offer opportunities for creativity and innovation in design and marketing (EC, 2002).

With rising labour costs, ageing populations and higher expectations from employment, this situation makes it increasingly difficult to hire and retain workers in the industry (see Box 3). It also increases the need for mechanization (putting further strains on the industry's ability to raise capital) and encourages relocation towards countries where working conditions and labour costs are lower (with further consequences for the sustainability and public perceptions of the industry).

Social and environmental performance

The increased interest in social and environmental issues (noted previously) presents a unique challenge to the forest industry, because of its reliance on forests for much of its raw material supply. Forest harvesting is very different from other industries, in that it occurs over relatively large areas and has an impact on large numbers of people. Not only is this impact relatively large, but it involves a broad and complex set of environmental and social issues that are often difficult to mitigate. It is also complicated by the diversity of views held about these issues and the failure (in many cases) to resolve the different and often conflicting interests of stakeholders.

These factors have had a number of impacts on the forest industry. First, they have placed new demands on forest harvesting operations, requiring forest managers to

---

Box 3: Trends in employment

Trends in employment indicate that mechanization in the sector is increasing. For example, the value-added per employee in forestry increased by almost 50 percent from 1990 to 2006 (see Figure A) and much of this increase can be attributed to the mechanization of harvesting in the sector. In the wood industry (sawnwood and wood-based panels), labour productivity has also increased by around one-third since 1990. The paper industry is already capital intensive, which is reflected in the much higher level of value-added per employee (roughly twice the level of the other two parts of the forestry sector).

However, there are still significant differences in the levels of mechanization between countries (see Figure B). As might

be expected, Europe and North America generally have the highest levels of labour productivity in the sector (particularly in processing). With ageing populations in both developed and many developing countries it is likely that further investments in mechanization will be required in the future.

For example, there are already automated plants in the furniture and flooring industries, where industrial robots are used in the same way as in the car industry. Many modern paper machines can also be operated from outside the mill premises and some machinery manufacturers provide this service, which increases their earnings and reduces the labour requirement in the mill.

Source: Lebedys, 2008.

Figure A: Value added per employee in US$ (at 2010 prices and exchange rates)

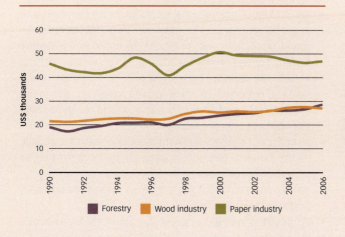

Figure B: Value-added per employee in 2006, by subsector and region (at 2010 prices and exchange rates)

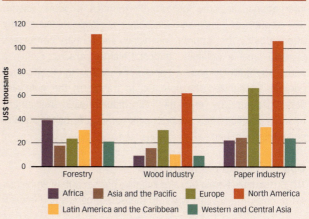

consider more social and environmental aspects of their activities. To some extent, this has increased production costs and may have reduced supply where companies have – either voluntarily or because of regulation – set aside forest areas for conservation and restoration (see Box 4). However, these measures are not always costly and a good deal of ignorance remains about how some improvements in harvesting can be profitable, as well as supportive of other forest benefits. Thus, it is important to improve communication about the forest industry's contributions to sustainable development, educate the public about forest industry operations, and promote the benefits of using wood as a renewable resource that contributes to sustainable forest management.

A second impact is the generally poor perception of wood products that has developed over many years in some countries. In response to consumer demand, some parts of the forest industry do meet high environmental and social performance standards, but other parts of the industry have seen less need to respond to these issues. As a result of this uneven performance, the industry as a whole has not yet managed to overcome these negative perceptions.

Since 2002 leading forest stakeholder organizations from the NGO community, companies, resource owners and managers, intergovernmental organizations, universities and labour have used The Forests Dialogue (http://environment.yale.edu/tfd/) platform and process to address pressing forestry issues with the aim of

building consensus and agreement across social and environmental fracture lines. Multi-stakeholder dialogues have focused on certification, forest biodiversity, the role of intensively managed forests, illegal logging and corruption. Current dialogue streams are on forests and climate (REDD+), investing in locally controlled forestry and "free, prior and informed" consent of indigenous peoples and local communities.

Maturity of existing product markets

In addition to factors affecting the industry, forest products themselves have a number of characteristics that affect developments in the sector. One of these characteristics is the concentration of demand in a few end uses, some of which are mature markets. For example, as noted previously, construction, printing and publishing grow rapidly in the early stages of economic development, but growth slows when countries reach a high level of development and these markets mature. Currently, the largest markets for these products (i.e. in developed countries) are already mature and growing relatively slowly. Although demand in developing economies is growing rapidly, it is also likely to diminish in these countries when their markets mature.

Related to this, it is quite difficult for the sector to advance through product innovation in mature markets. For example, there have been many innovations in markets for solid wood products, but they have often substituted one wood product for another rather than

Box 4: Case study – Sustainable Forest Mosaics Initiative

In late 2007, the Sustainable Production and Biodiversity Conservation in Forest Mosaics Initiative (or Sustainable Forest Mosaics Initiative) was launched by Kimberly-Clark, Conservation International, and the Instituto BioAtlântica to work toward the creation of sustainable landscape mosaics. Joined shortly afterwards by The Nature Conservancy and forestry companies Suzano Papel e Celulose, Veracel Celulose, Aracruz Celulose and Votorantim Celulose e Papel (now jointly Fibria), initiative partners recognized the potential to transform the pulp and paper industry by promoting an industry-wide movement towards practices that are both environmentally beneficial and economically sound.

Objectives and results to date
The Sustainable Forest Mosaics Initiative has set out an ambitious set of objectives against which to measure progress and impact.

Among the results expected from a fully-implemented initiative at the end of the five-year period are:
- 250 000 ha of natural ecosystems on forest company land in Northeast Brazil under more effective and scientifically-sound protection, and restoration to enhance the Central Atlantic Forest Corridor (CAFC);
- 4 000 ha owned by companies in Northeast Brazil formally protected as new private reserves, and more than 13 000 ha of forest company private reserves using management effectiveness tools in the CAFC;
- an additional 400 000 ha of natural ecosystems in the Atlantic Forest owned by forestry companies or their suppliers under protection or restoration;
- 200 000 ha of biodiversity priority areas in forestry landscapes worldwide identified for conservation;
- 20 percent of new global forest plantations/managed forests of participating companies set aside for conservation.

expanding the total market for wood products. Some notable examples of this include:

- the replacement of sawnwood and plywood used in construction by other types of wood-based panels and engineered wood products;
- the replacement of sawnwood produced from natural and semi-natural forests in the north by finger-jointed sawnwood manufactured from plantation wood grown in the southern hemisphere;
- the increasing competition between laminate flooring made from medium and high density fibreboard (MDF, HDF) and traditional solid wood flooring;
- the competition between laminated veneer lumber (LVL) and glue-laminated beams.

Where markets are mature, radical and disruptive technologies and innovations are usually required to boost growth in the sector above the more normal (relatively slow) growth trends. Product innovations in the forest industry in recent years have tended to be more incremental with relatively modest impacts on growth, although recent developments in bioenergy and biomaterials may present some opportunities for a radical reorientation of the sector.

The maturity of many forest product markets means that it is difficult to increase product value, value-added and profitability through product innovation, especially when many wood products meet basic functional needs and the products are relatively simple. This suggests that the industry should try to look beyond traditional end uses and explore the potential for expanding into new markets that may present new opportunities for growth.

Other end use issues

Forest products are natural materials that can vary in quality and reliability, which means that they may have less durability and higher lifetime 'costs of ownership' than competing non-wood alternatives. These factors are particularly important in some end uses of solid wood products (e.g. construction), where reliability and durability are crucial factors in the purchasing decision.

Related to this, the complexity of building codes, environmental regulations and other measures can make it difficult for forest products to enter new market segments. Not only are such codes complicated, but they often vary from country to country, making it more difficult to develop export markets. In addition, in some countries forest products are excluded from some end uses simply because they are not recognized at all in such regulations.

The forest industry continues to invest significant resources in product development, testing and awareness-raising to address these issues, but perceptions and practical barriers remain that limit the expansion of forest products into new end uses. Product development is not always sufficient to overcome such problems, as the costs of addressing systemic and regulatory bottlenecks may outweigh the benefits of product improvements.

Environmental attributes of forest products

In contrast to the problems noted above, wood products – as natural materials – have environmental attributes that may be preferred over other competing materials. Forest products are renewable materials that can be relatively easily recycled. Furthermore, most solid wood products are produced with relatively little use of energy (see Box 5). This results in a low 'carbon footprint' from their production and use, which is further enhanced by the fact that carbon is stored in wood products. Pulp and paper production is more energy intensive, but is coming under increased pressure to reduce its energy intensity and carbon emissions by adopting better technology (see Box 6).

Improvements in communications with consumers, architects and material specifiers have been achieved in the area of timber certification, and tools such as environmental scorecards in retail outlets have been effective in attracting consumers' attention. Lessons can be learned from these efforts for communicating other environmental benefits of wood products (such as their lower energy intensity and emissions of greenhouse gases during manufacturing), but improved information (with rigorous scientific proof) will be required to convince professional buyers.

Adaptability and management of the raw material supply

Most forest products are manufactured from a relatively small number of inputs. By far the most important input is the fibre itself, followed by energy and then a variety of chemical inputs (glues, preservatives, fillers, etc., depending on the product). While this simplicity may limit the scope for product innovation, it does benefit the sector in other ways.

First, the overwhelming importance of fibre as a raw material means that the sector has become adept at using fibre from a wide variety of sources, such as wood from trees outside forests, recycled paper, wood residues, recovered wood products and non-wood fibres

Box 5: Energy intensity in the forest industry

Energy intensity can be measured in a number of ways, such as the amount of energy used to produce a given weight or volume of a product, or the amount used to produce one dollar of value-added.

Table A shows how much energy is used to produce one cubic metre (m³) of sawnwood and wood-based panels and one metric tonne (MT) of paper and paperboard. For sawnwood and panels, energy use is about 2 400 megajoules (MJ) per m³, with some considerable variation between the different regions. It is also increasing in some major regions such as Europe and North America. This can be explained by the shift in production towards reconstituted panels, because the amount of energy used to produce a given amount of particleboard and fibreboard is higher

than that used to make sawnwood. Taking this into account, the energy used to make each type of product has probably not increased at all and may have decreased.

For paper and paperboard, energy use is about 19 300 MJ per MT, with less variation between the regions. Much more information is available about energy use in this industry, so these figures are more representative of the sector as a whole. The figures also show that energy intensity has declined slightly in recent years at the global level and in most regions.

The energy intensity per unit of value-added is shown below. The energy intensity of sawnwood and panel production is slightly higher than in the economy as a whole. However, the service sector (included in the latter) has a very low energy intensity and,

Table A: Energy use by product volume or weight, 2002 to 2007

Region	Sawnwood and wood-based panels				Paper and paperboard			
	Data availability		Energy use		Data availability		Energy use	
	2007 (%)	2002–2007 (%)	MJ/m³ in 2007	Annual change 2002–2007 (%)	2007 (%)	2002–2007 (%)	MJ/MT in 2007	Annual change 2002–2007 (%)
Africa	0	25	n.a.	4.1	0	79	n.a.	0
Asia and the Pacific	67	67	1 686	-6.7	87	97	14 299	-0.9
Europe	75	79	1 806	3.4	90	90	16 831	0.1
Latin America and Caribbean	1	6	3 120	-2.1	88	95	24 752	-1.4
North America	63	98	4 167	5.1	97	100	25 091	-1.1
Western and Central Asia	0	88	n.a.	5.8	37	45	18 832	12.3
World	61	74	2 443	1.4	90	95	19 304	-0.7

Note: Data availability is shown as the total production of countries with information about energy use divided by the total production (of all countries) in each region. Statistics for partial energy use (e.g. electricity only) are not included in the figures for 2007, but are included in the calculations of trends (annual change), so data availability is higher for the latter.

Box 6: Benchmarking CO_2 emissions in the European pulp and paper industry

The European Commission and member states are currently in the process of defining carbon dioxide (CO_2) emission trading benchmarks for industrial sectors in Europe, including the pulp and paper sector. These benchmarks will provide the basis for allocating emission rights among the pulp and paper mills in Europe after 2012. Benchmarks will be based on performance

levels of the best 10 percent of mills, with different benchmarks for different product groups. If a mill emits more than the benchmark value they will have to buy additional credits from the market or at government auctions. The Confederation of European Paper Industries (CEPI) is involved as a key stakeholder in the process.

compared with many other manufacturing activities, sawnwood and panel production has a relatively low energy intensity. In contrast, pulp and paper production has a high energy intensity and the sector is one of the five most energy intensive industries when measured in this way.

Table B also shows that energy intensity is increasing slightly, due to the increasing energy use in sawnwood and panel production and declining value-added (per MT of production) in the pulp and paper sector. In the case of pulp and paper, this is partly a result of the business cycle (where value-added has been declining in recent years). For example, a longer time series on energy use and value-added is available for Europe and this shows that, since 1990, energy intensity has increased by about one percent per year rather than the 6.1 percent seen between 2002 and 2006.

The use of renewable energy is a further important factor in the evaluation of energy intensity in the sector. Only partial information exists, but statistics show, for example, that renewable energy accounts for almost 40 percent of the energy used in sawnwood and panel production in much of Europe. For pulp and paper production, renewable energy accounts for about 30 percent of consumption in Europe and Japan, 45 percent in North America and over 60 percent in South America. Most of this energy is produced from waste wood, so the use of fossil fuels in the sector is much lower than suggested by the tables.

Comparisons with other materials usually take into account a wider range of energy inputs in the production and use of products using life cycle analyses (LCA). Consequently, LCA studies vary considerably in terms of their methodologies and results (see, for example, Hammond and Jones, 2008 and Alcorn, 2003). In general, they show that, for a given weight, sawnwood and panel products tend to have similar or slightly higher energy intensities than bricks, cement, concrete and plaster, while the energy intensities of metals are 3–5 times higher and plastics up to 10 times higher than wood. However, comparisons in use also have to take into account the different amounts of materials needed for any specific purpose to lower energy use overall.

Sources: data derived from EIA, 2010; EUROSTAT, 2010; FAO, 2010b; and IEA, 2010.

Table B: Energy use by US$ of value-added, 2002 to 2006

Region	Energy intensity (MJ per US$ of value-added)				
	Sawnwood and panels		Pulp and paper		Whole economy
	MJ per US$ in 2006	Annual change 2002–2006 (%)	MJ per US$ in 2006	Annual change 2002–2006 (%)	MJ per US$ in 2006
Africa	n.a.	1.9	n.a.	4.7	14.6
Asia and the Pacific	17.8	-6.0	39.1	-2.5	14.2
Europe	8.8	3.2	36.3	6.1	8.6
Latin America and Caribbean	12.3	-5.5	52.9	5.8	11.8
North America	15.2	5.5	46.7	-0.7	8.4
Western and Central Asia	n.a.	1.8	19.7	9.2	20.6
World	13.4	1.9	41.6	1.0	10.7

(see Box 7). Furthermore, to deal with the diffuse and fragmented supply sources in many countries, some companies have developed considerable expertise in transport and logistics and have become excellent managers of their fibre supply chains.

Second, waste products from one production process can often be used in other processes or other parts of the industry either as fibre inputs or for energy. Complex wood fibre supply chains and linkages have already developed in many countries with well developed forest industries and these are gradually being expanded to accommodate growing demands for bioenergy. The industry is also continuing to examine ways in which more wood fibre can be extracted from the forest resource base through, for example, the use of forest harvesting residues and the use of forest resources previously considered to be uneconomic.

The fibre used to manufacture sawnwood, panels and paper comes from a wide – and increasing – variety of sources. In 2005, the fibre required to produce these products was equal to 2.6 billion m³ of roundwood, yet industrial roundwood production only amounted to 1.7 billion m³. The remaining fibre requirement (equal to 900 million m³ or about 35 percent of the total) was met through the use of recovered paper (550 million m³), non-wood fibre sources, and unrecorded sources such as wood residues from sawnwood and plywood manufacturing and recovered (waste) wood products.

Figure A shows the trend in the use of these other fibre sources from 1990 to 2005 and projections to 2030 from FAO's global outlook study (FAO, 2009a). It shows that the importance of these other sources has increased from 21 percent of fibre requirements in 1990 to 37 percent in 2010 and is projected to increase to almost 45 percent in 2030. Recovered paper is the most important of these other sources, but increased collection of waste wood products (demolition waste, used furniture, etc.) is also increasing rapidly.

As the problem of waste disposal increases in many countries, the ability of the forest industry to recycle waste fibre into new

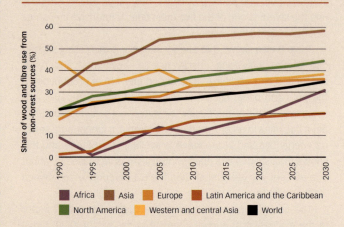

Figure A: Trends in use of recycled, recovered and non-wood fibre sources, 1990 to 2030

Legend: Africa · Asia · Europe · Latin America and the Caribbean · North America · Western and central Asia · World

forest products will help the industry to meet its growing fibre requirements as well as reduce the environmental impact of growing consumer demands.

Sources: data derived from FAO, 2009a and 2010b.

Recently, the World Business Council for Sustainable Development's Vision 2050 project – looking at the future role of global business in achieving a sustainable, carbon and natural resource constrained world – has articulated a forest 'pathway' based on significantly improving the bio-capacity of intensively managed forests to supply expanding fibre needs for wood, paper and bio-energy products, and the regeneration and conservation of natural forest systems for their ecosystem services, starting with carbon market incentives and payments.[11]

Potential for innovation

Despite some of the challenges described earlier, the forest industry has shown that it is capable of innovation. This is demonstrated by the advances the industry has made in harvesting and logistics, processing technologies and the steady progress in extracting more product from each unit of fibre input. There have also been a number of successful product innovations in engineered wood products and paper products. The increased attention given to patents and licensing

Table 38: Possible strategic responses to driving forces affecting the forest industry

	Strengths (S)	**Weaknesses (W)**
Opportunities (O)	**S-O Strategies** • green building and green packaging initiatives • bioenergy and biomaterials development	**W-O Strategies** • industry restructuring for investment and expansion • industry clusters and partnerships • measures to strengthen fibre supply
Threats (T)	**S-T Strategies** • product and process innovation • diversification of fibre sources • life cycle analyses (LCA) • collaboration to secure fibre supplies	**W-T Strategies** • industry restructuring for cost savings • product focus and product differentiation • development of technical standards and information • mechanization of operations and human resource development

Note: The strengths, weaknesses, opportunities and threats shown in Table 38 are those identified in Table 36 on page 30 (i.e. strengths – environmental attributes, adaptability and management of raw material supply, innovation; weaknesses – industry structure, labour costs and working conditions, social and environmental performance, maturity of existing product markets, end use issues; opportunities – demographics (low and middle-income countries), globalization and economic growth, social trends; threats – demographics (high-income countries), competing materials, competition for resources, changes in forest ownership). Each strategy identified in Table 38 responds to a different combination of strengths, weaknesses, opportunities and threats, as discussed in the text.

[11] http://www.wbcsd.org/Plugins/DocSearch/details.asp?DocTypeId=25&ObjectId=MzczOTc

to protect intellectual property and increase revenue provides an indication of the importance of innovation in the forest industry.

Strategic choices for the future of the forest industry

The driving forces described above will affect developments in the forest industry for many years to come. They will directly influence markets for both raw materials and forest products, and are also likely to affect government policies and regulation of the sector.

As part of their long-term planning, industries and governments need strategies to respond to these forces. Table 38 lists some of the different strategies that the forest industry has already developed – often in collaboration with governments, end users and other stakeholders – to strengthen the long-term profitability and sustainability of the forest industry in the future. Some of these strategies focus on increasing the profitability and competitive advantage of individual firms (e.g. industry restructuring and mechanization), so it is appropriate that they have mainly been implemented by individual firms. However, where there are benefits for the industry as a whole or benefits from a more co-ordinated approach, strategies may be developed and implemented at the sectoral level, usually with a lead from industry or government.

Traditional government support for industrial development declined in the 1980s and 1990s in many countries with changes in the political landscape, privatization of nationalized industries and an emphasis on deregulation of economies. This free-market approach to economic development prevailed for many years, but there has recently been a reversal in some countries and some parts of the economy. This reversal can be explained by a number of factors, such as the impact of globalization on industrial competitiveness and growing interest in the development of a more sustainable 'green economy'. More recently, the recession of 2008–2009 has caused a number of countries to re-examine their economic policies and to support stronger, more sustainable economic growth in the future.

In line with these trends, support for the development of forest industries has increased over the last few years in almost all developed countries. For example, the European Union (EU) examined the competitiveness of the European forestry sector in 2007 (IIASA, 2007) as part of the EU Forest Action Plan and currently

provides support through initiatives such as the Forest Technology Platform. A number of Canadian provinces have recently examined the competitiveness of their forest industries and, at the federal level, Canada has recently launched a major initiative to support innovation in the sector (the 'Transformative Technologies Program'). Other recent initiatives to examine industry competitiveness and support industry development can be found in Australia (DAFF, 2009) and New Zealand (MAF, 2009). Many countries have also started to provide considerable support for the development of biofuels and bioenergy, which is partly directed towards the forestry sector.

Most of these initiatives have some similar features, including analyses of competitiveness, strengths and weaknesses in the sector; measures to increase supply and lower the costs of fibre; support for research, development and innovation; and development of new products (especially biofuels and new wood-based products and materials). Although they differ in scale and emphasis, they indicate that many governments believe the forest industry has a viable future, especially as part of the emerging 'green economy'. Some of these initiatives are relatively new (e.g. bioenergy developments) or have suddenly grown in recent years (e.g. wood promotion activities) and greater demands for sustainability are part of the reason for this. A review of some of these initiatives, below, shows how the industry is responding to the driving forces described above.

Wood promotion initiatives

The promotion of forest products (e.g. through advertising and communication) is a core function of the forest industry; individual companies and industry associations have been promoting their products for many years. However, over the last decade these activities have expanded considerably and have become much broader than simply advertising and marketing of products. Significant, well-organized and co-ordinated wood promotion initiatives currently operate in Australia, New Zealand, North America and most western European countries. Industry associations in a number of emerging economies (e.g. Brazil, Ghana and Malaysia) are intensifying their wood promotion initiatives.

In most cases, these initiatives are industry-led and have developed as specific projects initiated by forest industry associations (or groups of associations). Government agencies may be involved (especially where state forests are used for wood production) or, in some cases, provide funding or technical assistance. Most initiatives focus on domestic markets, but a number of regional or multi-country wood promotion initiatives have also started (e.g. Pro:Holz in Austria has been very active in collaborating to establish wood promotion initiatives in other countries).

Public demands for sustainability have been a driving force behind these new initiatives, so many of them have gone far beyond the traditional promotional activities of trade fairs, product literature and business directories. In particular, they show how forest products can contribute to more sustainable lifestyles and, based on this, try to develop a stronger wood-using culture. Initiatives have developed a wide range of information materials and resources, including:

- case studies on the design and sustainability aspects of wood product use;
- literature about the technical properties of wood products;
- information about environmental aspects of wood product manufacturing;
- tools and models to assess the environmental impacts of wood use;
- discussion forums and mechanisms to provide technical advice;
- seminars and training in wood use;
- competitions in design and sustainable use of wood;
- directories of suppliers and other service providers and experts.

Most of these wood promotion initiatives have three common features: linkages to green building initiatives; development and provision of information about technical standards; and examples of life cycle analysis of wood products or wood product use.

Green building initiatives

Most of the countries with well-developed wood promotion initiatives also have green building initiatives. Some of these are industry-led, but many are governed by boards or committees that include other stakeholders with an interest in sustainable construction. In a few places (e.g. United States of America) there are a number of green building initiatives that may compete or collaborate with each other.

Green building initiatives exist to promote sustainable construction rather than one material over another or the construction industry more generally. They tend to focus on the development and implementation of tools, models

and methodologies for assessing the sustainability of buildings and often administer certification or rating schemes for companies that want to demonstrate their environmental performance. Green building initiatives are largely voluntary, although some aspects of green building (e.g. standards for energy efficiency) may be included in building regulations.

To assess the sustainability of buildings, the efficiency of resource use (e.g. energy, water and other natural resources) is examined throughout a building's life cycle from location to design, construction, operation, maintenance, renovation and demolition. It also takes into account waste, pollution and environmental degradation associated with a building project, as well as aspects of building use such as indoor air quality and employee health and safety.

Wood is just one of a range of materials used in building construction, and the environmental impact of manufacturing forest products compares favourably with many other materials. Thus, the emphasis on green building within wood promotion initiatives is a useful strategy that builds upon the strength of the environmental attributes of forest products. However, many green building systems are still in the early stages of development and a number of problems remain for promoting wood within such systems.

For instance, most schemes do not adequately consider LCA in material specification, which puts wood at a disadvantage compared with other materials because wood generally scores favourably (UN, forthcoming). Furthermore, scoring systems often give a relatively low weighting to material selection (where wood performs well) compared with other factors such as energy efficiency and sourcing of local materials. Some systems such as the Leadership in Energy and Environmental Design (LEED) in the United States of America and the Green Building Council in Australia have chosen to recognize only forest product certification by the Forest Stewardship Council, effectively barring other certified wood products from their systems (UN, forthcoming).

Green packaging

At present, wood promotion initiatives focus mostly on green building, but interest in green packaging is also increasing. This has been largely driven by retailers and consumer goods companies, which are much closer to consumers and more directly affected by the growing public interest in environmental issues. As with the green

The European Directive 94/62/EC on Packaging and Packaging Waste, adopted in 1994, was one of the earliest attempts to increase the sustainability of packaging. This focused on minimizing the use of packaging and the hazardous materials it contained, and on encouraging the reuse and recycling of packaging materials. Most other countries outside the EU have not so far followed a regulatory approach towards increased sustainability in the packaging sector. However, sustainable packaging initiatives have been developed by a number of industry groups, non-governmental and government agencies, and large individual companies.

The objectives of many of these initiatives are similar to the EC Directive: to reduce the total amount of packaging used and increase the reuse and/or recycling of packaging materials, increase the content of recycled materials and reduce the use of hazardous materials. Some go even further and examine other aspects, such as greenhouse gas emissions from packaging production, the use of resources (water, energy, land, etc.) in packaging production, and transport distances along the supply chain.

Many of these initiatives are voluntary, but some are backed by major companies which expect their suppliers to improve performance in packaging sustainability (e.g. the Wal-Mart Packaging Scorecard). These initiatives offer various tools to help companies assess and minimize their environmental impact, including scorecards for assessing overall impacts, design guidelines, LCA tools and other design tools (Five Winds International, 2008).

Although reducing packaging is a major objective of many of these initiatives, they can also encourage changes in the types of packaging materials used. For example, as a result of the Wal-Mart Packaging Scorecard, paper cartons have replaced metal cans for some products in ASDA supermarkets in the United Kingdom. Further research and development in the paper industry on issues such as tamper-proof mechanisms and temperature monitoring ('smart paper') could enable more paper products to replace less environmentally-friendly packaging materials and contribute to these efforts.

building initiatives described previously, sustainable or green packaging initiatives (Box 8) are likely to present opportunities for the forest industry to contribute to more sustainable lifestyles.

Technical standards and information

Many wood promotion initiatives include activities to explain and provide information about technical aspects of wood use (especially in construction) to businesses and professionals, as well as to the general public. This complements the promotion of wood in green building and aims to overcome one of the weaknesses of wood promotion, which is the lack of information about the properties of wood products, or the perception that they are less reliable than products made of other materials.

In addition to raising awareness, wood promotion activities in many countries also include active participation in the development of technical standards and codes. Although such standards are, quite rightly, administered by public agencies, contributions and expertise provided by the forest industry are often useful for their development and revision, especially when the industry develops new products. In some cases, these consultations occur at an international level, as in the case of the Canada–US–Japan Building Experts Committee.

Life cycle analysis

Most wood promotion initiatives also include case studies, tools and models to calculate and demonstrate the environmental impacts of substituting wood for other materials. With the high public interest in climate change, many of these focus on the effects of product substitution on energy use and carbon emissions, but some go further and examine a broader range of environmental impacts such as those evaluated in green building initiatives (as noted above). This strategy complements efforts to promote wood in green building, by addressing the threat of competing materials and quantifying the environmental benefits of using forest products.

Collaborative business practices

The development of more collaborative business practices in many sectors and industries is an increasing trend in recent years. For many years firms in many industries have collaborated closely along the production chain with suppliers and end users to improve product quality and develop new markets, but new approaches to collaboration aim to address some of the specific weaknesses in the forest industry.

Collaboration to secure fibre supplies

Greater collaboration offers a response to the threats of increased competition for fibre supplies, changes in forest ownership, control and management, and the fragmented nature of forest ownership in many countries. This takes the form of both collaboration among forest owners, and between owners and the industry to secure fibre supplies and encourage wood production from forest areas that would previously have been considered uneconomic or unsuitable for harvesting. Such collaborative strategies build on the strengths of the forest industry to organize and manage fibre supplies and (in some cases) transfer some of these skills to small private forest owners.

Collaboration between forest owners (in cooperatives and associations) has occurred for many years in some countries (e.g. in parts of Europe and North America), but has expanded in recent years to become an important force in wood supply. For example, private forest owners' organizations in 23 European countries are members of the Confederation of European Forest Owners (CEPF). A recent survey of 11 of these countries indicated that members of the national organizations accounted for 11 percent of all private forest owners, 42 percent of the area of private

forests and 22 percent of total roundwood production (CEPF, 2008). There is also evidence of the expansion of forest owners' organizations in other countries such as Mexico and the United States of America.

The expansion of cooperatives and forest owners' organizations has occurred for a number of reasons. With the transfer of state forests to private owners in Eastern Europe in the 1990s, a number of forest owners' organizations emerged to assist the new private forest owners with forest management and harvesting (e.g. in the three Baltic States, Czech Republic, Hungary and Slovakia). In some places, opportunities for forest certification have been a motivation for better organization of forest owners (e.g. see Ota (2007) for a description of recent activities in Japan). Other examples of improved collaboration include the use of internet tools to manage forests and market forest products such as the 'myForest' service in the United Kingdom (see Box 9).

Box 9: The use of internet technology to develop wood supply from small forest owners

For many years, roundwood supply from the private sector in the United Kingdom has been well below its potential because of the large number of small forest owners and the very variable (or unknown) quality of wood resources in many of these forests. Recent developments in renewable energy policy and incentives have substantially increased the demand for wood with lower quality requirements to meet the needs of the energy sector. In response to this, a number of organizations have been examining ways of increasing wood supply. One example is the 'myForest' service developed by the Sylva Foundation.

The service provides a web-based map that allows wood users to link up with local wood producers. Forest owners can identify their forest on the map and store inventory information for each forest compartment. This is complemented by a forest management module that can be used to prepare forest management plans in the format required by the Forestry Commission in grant and licence applications.

The third module is a national map where forest owners and other forestry businesses can advertise their products and services and display where wood is available or required (see Figure A). Other features include a forum for discussion about forestry issues and links to other resources of interest to forest owners and managers.

During the 18 months it took to develop the service (which was launched in April 2010), 100 businesses and 50 forest owners registered to use the service. The Sylva Foundation is currently actively promoting this free service to other potential users.

Source: Sylva Foundation, 2010.

Figure A: Businesses registered with 'myForest', June 2010

The development of outgrower schemes is another form of collaboration to secure fibre supplies. In this format, the forest industry supports tree planting by private forest owners in order to increase wood supply and develop local capacity for plantation establishment and management. Outgrower schemes appeared in the 1990s and now exist in at least 13 developing countries (Brazil, Colombia, Ghana, India, Indonesia, Papua New Guinea, Philippines, Solomon Islands, South Africa, Thailand, Vanuatu, Viet Nam and Zimbabwe) as well as some developed countries (e.g. Australia, New Zealand and Portugal).

Forestry outgrower schemes vary tremendously in size and the scope of their activities, as well as the distribution of costs and benefits between the forest owners and industry. With the growing interest in such schemes, organizations such as FAO and the Center for International Forestry Research (CIFOR) have analysed the strengths and weaknesses of different types of partnerships and developed guidelines to enable them to continue contributing to sustainable development of the sector in the future (FAO, 2002).

Industry clusters and partnerships

Industry clusters occur where firms and other related institutions (e.g. research facilities) are closely located or strongly linked together in other ways. Sometimes these clusters develop spontaneously as a result of the accumulation of technical expertise over a long time (e.g. some of the furniture industry clusters in Italy) or they may occur based on the location of resources (e.g. forest industry clusters in areas with significant forest resources). More recently, a number of countries have stimulated the formation of industry clusters through public policies and carefully located investments in research and technology.

Industry clusters usually include core businesses within the industry, plus a number of suppliers, end users, related service industries and, sometimes, training, research and development facilities. Clusters can potentially increase the competitive advantage of firms within the cluster by increasing productivity, stimulating innovation and assisting the development of new businesses in the industry (Porter, 1990).

Although some forest industry clusters have existed for many years, interest in their development has increased in the last couple of decades and significant forest industry clusters now exist in parts of most developed countries (Australia, Europe, Japan, New Zealand and North America). For example, according to the Harvard Business School Cluster Mapping Project (www.isc.hbs.edu/cmp), one-third of forest industry employment in 2007 occurred in just five states of the United States of America (and over half in just ten states). The development of forest industry clusters has also been actively supported by governments and industry in Europe, where around 200 clusters now exist, linking together firms in the forest industry and other related sectors such as construction, renewable energy and green technology (European Cluster Observatory, 2010).

A few notable forest industry clusters exist in emerging economies (e.g. pulp and paper clusters in Brazil, India and Thailand; furniture clusters in Brazil, Malaysia and Viet Nam). In addition to these, small-scale village clusters have developed for activities such as handicrafts, bamboo and rattan manufacturing and small-scale wood processing in India, Lao People's Democratic Republic, Thailand and Viet Nam (Anbumozhi, 2007). Collection and processing of NWFP is also well organized (with arrangements similar to clustering) in a number of places (e.g. the collection and processing of shea butter in Ghana and Brazil nuts in Bolivia).

The strategy of forest industry cluster development often aims to take advantage of the opportunities for market growth presented by economic growth and globalization, by addressing weaknesses in the industry such as the maturity of some existing end use markets, fragmentation of the industry (and low levels of technology adoption) and increasing competition from newly industrializing regions. Alternatively, new partnerships can occur to build upon the strengths of different partners to meet an emerging market demand.

For instance, forest product companies have entered the markets for liquid biofuels and other biomaterials, through the development of 'biorefineries'. At present, these developments are being driven by the growing demand for biofuels, but many companies working in this field eventually aim to expand and diversify production into a much wider range of chemicals and materials based on biomass. The largest and best known of these include the joint ventures between Weyerhaeuser and Chevron, Stora Enso and Neste Oil, and UPM, Andritz and Carbona, but others are developing at the level of individual facilities.

Product and process innovations

Innovation is the process of developing new goods or services, new markets, new supply sources, better processes or better ways of organizing production to increase productivity and generate profits and wealth (Schumpeter, 1934). Innovation can occur gradually (evolutionary innovations) or suddenly (revolutionary innovations) and may disrupt existing industries and markets by supplying new products and services in ways that the market does not expect (typically by lowering prices or meeting the needs of a different set of consumers). Revolutionary innovations are often, but not always, disruptive. In addition, contrary to common perceptions, efforts by end users to modify products or use them in new and more useful ways may be a more important source of innovation than the actions of manufacturers (von Hippel, 1988).

Despite the relatively low levels of technology adoption in some parts of the forest industry (and slow rate of technology adoption generally), the forest industry has innovated in many areas throughout the supply chain from harvesting to end user and continues to support innovation through public and industry research and development activities. Some examples of forest industry innovations are outlined below.

Evolutionary innovations

Evolutionary innovations occur when gradual improvements are made to existing processes and products to increase productivity, lower costs or expand quantity or quality of production to meet an existing market need. In forest harvesting, there have been numerous evolutionary innovations, such as the development and implementation of log grading systems; the gradual move from manual to mechanized harvesting; and the use of low-impact harvesters that reduce soil compaction, and enable year-round harvesting and access to softer soils. These innovations are quite common now in most countries with a modern forest industry. More recently innovation to improve real-time communication between harvesters, transport operators and processing facilities (using global positioning system (GPS) and optimization software) allows just-in-time deliveries of roundwood and reduces the amount of working capital tied up in raw material stocks.

Processing technologies have also improved in numerous ways with developments such as scanning and optimization of product recovery in sawnwood and plywood production, improvements in stress grading, kiln drying and treatments, development of adhesives technologies, as well as higher levels of automation and gradually faster operating speeds in processing facilities to increase labour productivity. Process innovations in the pulp and paper sector have focused in particular on environmental performance in recent years, with reductions in water, bleaching chemicals and energy use (and greater use of bioenergy), plus changes to processes (speed, fibre pre-treatment, etc.) and adoption of abatement technologies to reduce emissions of water and atmospheric pollutants.

Revolutionary innovations

Revolutionary innovation occurs when there is a radical improvement in processes or products to meet an existing or new market need. Whereas evolutionary innovations often occur as a result of learning from existing processes and uses of existing products and services, revolutionary innovations more often occur as a result of research and development programmes. A number innovative forest harvesting machines have been developed and introduced in recent years to supply wood for the expanding bioenergy market. These include combined industrial roundwood and bioenergy wood harvesters and forest processor–harvester machines for extracting forest residues. The use of acoustic tools fitted to harvester heads to improve and automate strength grading of standing trees at the time of harvest is a revolutionary innovation currently being tested (Mochan, Moore and Connolly, 2009).

Revolutionary innovations are less common in forest processing. One notable example, however, is the development of the rubberwood processing industry in Malaysia. Until the late 1970s, most rubberwood was used as fuelwood for drying and smoking sheet-rubber, curing tobacco, making bricks and producing charcoal. Malaysia has since become the world leader in the processing and utilization of rubberwood, with the value of its processing currently estimated at a little under US$2 billion per year.

Revolutionary innovations in the forest industry are more common in product markets and numerous examples exist. New types of panel products (e.g. oriented strand board and MDF) have substituted for more expensive sawnwood and plywood. The development of engineered wood products for structural applications (laminated veneer lumber, building components and I-Joists) followed panel innovations. A key feature of structural innovations has been the combination of solid wood pieces, reconstituted panels and non-wood materials in novel and useful ways that either reduce costs or improve the strength and durability of these composite products compared to previously utilized materials.

Low-end disruptive innovations

Disruptive innovations occur when an innovation leads to new products, new markets or new market segments that meet existing or new customer needs. Disruptive innovations can be evolutionary or revolutionary and occur infrequently in most manufacturing industries (although they can be quite common in the service and high-technology industries). Low-end disruptive innovations tend to occur gradually over time, when new products and processes capture first the bottom end of a market, then move upwards to displace other existing high-value products.

One example of this type of innovation in the forest industry is the use of low-cost particleboard with a variety of overlays and finishes for manufacturing some types of furniture (e.g. kitchen and bedroom furniture). This started with the emergence of cheap, ready-to-assemble furniture in the 1970s and 1980s, which replaced expensive solid wood furniture, the only alternative available at the time. Gradually, with improvements in quality, design and marketing, this type of furniture has moved into higher-end markets so that it is now by far the most common type of furniture available in these market segments in many countries.

Other examples of low-end disruptive innovations are the substitution of wood-based panels (e.g. oriented strand board and MDF), glue-edged panels and finger-jointed wood products for sawnwood and plywood in some applications. These are following the same pattern of development as that described above and are even starting to compete in the high-end furniture markets previously captured by particleboard, such as the use of MDF as a higher-quality base material for the production of kitchen cabinet doors.

New market disruptive innovations

The other main type of disruptive innovation is new market disruptive innovation. This occurs when an innovation satisfies new consumer needs or presents a radically different way of production or service delivery. New market disruptive innovations are often revolutionary and can appear quite quickly in an industry.

The rapid expansion in the use of wood pellets in the energy sector provides an example of a new market disruption. Renewable energy policies have created rapid growth in demand for wood energy that will require large amounts of fuelwood to be moved within and between countries. Wood pellets are an entirely new way of delivering fuelwood to end users that partly overcomes one of the main costs of traditional fuelwood supply (the cost of transportation), by reducing water content and increasing the energy content (or energy density) of the fuelwood. Other benefits of wood pellets include the greater ease of handling (e.g. by using existing equipment available at ports for grain handling), the more consistent properties of wood pellets as a fuel (i.e. more predictable energy content) and the greater ability with wood pellets to automate and regulate the feeding of the fuel into generating equipment such as boilers.

Measures to strengthen fibre supply

Measures to strengthen fibre supply include a number of policies and activities to promote good forest management through supply-chain initiatives, trade measures and procurement policies. The rationale for these strategies is very clear: they aim to address the weakness of poor social and environmental performance in the harvesting sector in some parts of the industry so that the opportunities for promoting forest products as 'green' products can be fully realized.

Activities to improve social and environmental performance in harvesting start with basic requirements such as the development and implementation of harvesting codes, forest management plans and health and safety legislation. These are then reinforced by reliable and robust tracking systems (e.g. chain-of-custody tracing systems) so that wood from well-managed forests can be clearly identified throughout the supply chain. Finally, some sort of certification, labelling or verification scheme can be used to differentiate forest products from well-managed forests from other products to gain competitive advantage in the marketplace.

Although many of the measures to strengthen fibre supply have been led by governments and/or NGOs, there is growing awareness and recognition within the forest industry that these measures may deliver benefits to individual firms as well as the industry as a whole. However, some considerable challenges remain, including:

- the lack of technical capacity in some countries to develop and implement improved harvesting practices;
- the administrative burden and costs of compliance for governments, producers and end users wishing to demonstrate improved performance;
- the complexity caused by the lack of standardization and varying procedures and requirements in different

countries and between different verification and certification schemes;

- the difficulty of translating improved performance into competitive advantage in countries and end uses where environmental concerns are not a major concern for consumers.

There are numerous examples of different measures being developed and implemented to strengthen fibre supply around the world. For a long time these focused on supply-side measures, but a more recent development has been the use of trade and procurement policies to stimulate demand for wood products that meet high social and environmental standards. A very brief summary of some of these initiatives is given below.

Supply-side measures

Supply-side measures to strengthen social and environmental performance in forest harvesting include a wide range of activities to develop and implement improved harvesting practices, such as codes and best practice guidelines for harvesting, forest management planning, and consultation with local communities; research, development and training in reduced impact logging; activities to support forest law enforcement; industry-led voluntary initiatives to source legal raw material; and the development of chain-of-custody and similar tracking schemes.

The basic requirements for sustainable forest harvesting (set out in codes, guidelines, etc.) have existed for many years now in most developed countries. In developing countries many international agencies (e.g. FAO and the International Tropical Timber Organization (ITTO)) and bilateral donors have provided technical support for the development of such materials. Most countries with significant forest industries should now have the codes and guidelines necessary to implement sustainable harvesting. However, what appears to be lacking is dissemination and training in the application of these codes and guidelines, as well as implementation and monitoring in the field. For example, a recent study to examine the monitoring of harvesting codes in the Asia and the Pacific region revealed that many aspects were only partially implemented and monitored and some aspects were not monitored at all (Pescott and Wilkinson, 2009).

Initiatives to support forest law enforcement

As noted above, supply-side measures to improve performance will have little impact if they are not implemented and monitored or there is no mechanism to differentiate between the social and environmental performance of different producers and reward those that meet higher standards. One such demand-side mechanism is to verify that forest products come from forests that are managed according to all local laws and regulation (legal verification).

Initiatives to strengthen forest law enforcement started about a decade ago with several international conferences to discuss the problems of illegality in the forestry sector and propose possible mechanisms to deal with this issue. Since then a number of different strategies have been adopted, including the following:

- Amendment of the Lacey Act (of 1900) in the United States of America. The Lacey Act originally prohibited the transportation of illegally captured or prohibited animals across state lines. It has been amended several times since 1900, with the latest amendment (in 2008) making it unlawful to import, export, transport, sell, receive, acquire, or purchase in interstate or foreign commerce any plant in violation of the laws of the United States of America, a State, an Indian tribe, or any foreign law that protects plants (and their products, including timber, derived from illegally harvested plants). The purpose of the amendment is to prevent trade in roundwood and wood products from illegally harvested trees. Different wood products are gradually phased in to comply with the Act, and the associated penalties are enforced more stringently to tangibly influence trade practices.
- The European Union has used a number of different approaches to combat illegal activities in the forestry sector, including: procurement policies (see below); a regulation entitled 'Obligations of Operators who Place Timber and Timber Products on the Market' (which will take some time to implement); and the development of Voluntary Partnership Agreements (VPAs) between the EU and other countries to support the EU's Forest Law Enforcement, Governance and Trade process. The first VPAs with Cameroon, Ghana and Republic of the Congo came into effect in 2009, so the first VPA licensed timber could arrive in the EU in 2011. VPA negotiations are proceeding with a number of other countries.
- When implementing these initiatives, both the United States of America and the EU encourage wood industries and traders to apply 'due care' and 'due diligence' in their procurement practices to avoid the entry of illegal wood products into their supply chains.
- Several countries have issued government procurement policies banning the use of forest

Table 39: Government procurement policies to stop the use of illegal forest products

Country	Year of enactment	Requirements for public procurement
Netherlands	1997 (revised in 2005)	Legal and preferably sustainable timber
Germany	1998 (revised in 2007)	Sustainable timber
Denmark	2003	Legal and preferably sustainable timber
UK	2004	Legal and preferably sustainable timber
New Zealand	2004 (mandatory in 2006)	Legal and preferably sustainable timber
France	2005	Legal and/or sustainable timber
Mexico	2005	Preferably sustainable timber
Belgium	2006	Sustainable timber
Japan	2006	Legal timber (sustainability as factor for consideration)
Norway	2007	Tropical timber excluded

Source: Lopez-Casero, 2008.
Note: some other countries are considering similar measures (e.g. Australia).

products harvested illegally and/or encouraging the use of forest products from sustainably managed sources (see Table 39).

- In addition to the demand-side measures above, international and bilateral agencies have continued to support activities to strengthen forest law enforcement in producer countries through technical assistance for policy and legal reform, training in law enforcement, development of chain-of-custody and other monitoring systems and other capacity building activities.

Forest product certification

Forest product certification was developed during the 1990s as a mechanism to identify forest products that come from sustainably managed forests. Four main elements of the certification process are: the development of agreed standards defining sustainable forest management; auditing of forest operations and issuance of certificates to companies that meet those standards; auditing of the chain-of-custody to ensure that a company's products come from certified forests; and the use of product labels so that certified products can be identified in the marketplace. There are presently more than 50 certification programmes in different countries around the world, many of which fall under the two largest umbrella organizations: the Forest Stewardship Council (FSC) and the Programme for the Endorsement of Forest Certification (PEFC). The area of certified forests covered by the two main organizations has steadily increased since the 1990s to reach about 350 million hectares in 2010.

A number of barriers to more widespread adoption of certification have been identified. Two of the most important of these are the costs of certification (especially for small forest owners) and the lack of a price premium for certified forest products in the marketplace. Although the latter has been noted in almost all developed country markets for forest products, one benefit of certification is that it facilitates entry to those markets, where prices generally may be higher than in countries where there is no demand for certified forest products.

Although forest certification has so far failed to stimulate widespread changes in forest management and harvesting practices in all parts of the world, it remains an important tool for companies in the forest industry to demonstrate their commitment to meeting high social and environmental performance standards. Indeed, many of the largest forest products companies are certified and can use this to gain competitive advantage by differentiating their products and communicating their superior performance to consumers. One question that remains unanswered is whether the net benefits from certification are sufficient to counter the generally negative perceptions of the industry that have developed in some places over the last couple of decades.

Industry restructuring

One of the major weaknesses of the forest industry in recent years has been the failure to translate the improvements in material efficiency (output of products per cubic metre of wood used) into higher value-added.

Value-added in the forestry sector comprises value-added from forestry (mostly industrial roundwood production), value-added in woodworking (production of sawnwood and wood-based panels) and value-added in pulp and paper manufacturing. Table A shows how value-added per cubic metre of industrial roundwood production can be calculated.

In 2006, about 1.5 billion m³ of industrial roundwood was produced, with a total value-added of US$100 billion (US$72 per m³). About 1 billion m³ (60 percent) was used for sawnwood and panel production, generating value-added of US$146 billion. This is equal to US$146 per m³ of wood used or US$89 per m³ of wood harvested (taking into account that only 60 percent is used for sawnwood and panels). Pulp and paper production uses three main fibre inputs (pulpwood, non-wood fibre and recovered paper) and, based on their shares in production, value-added from pulpwood use is US$180 per m³, or US$71 per m³ of wood harvested. In addition, the use of recovered paper (which originally comes from wood fibre) generates an additional US$47 per m³ of total production. Thus, each cubic metre of wood harvested generates a total of US$279 in value-added in the sector as a whole.

The figure below shows the global trend in value-added per cubic metre of industrial roundwood production since 1990. The value-added in forestry and woodworking have both increased slightly over the period (by about 8 percent in total), but value-added in pulp and paper manufacturing has declined

Figure A: Value-added per cubic metre of industrial roundwood production (in US$ at 2010 prices and exchange rates)

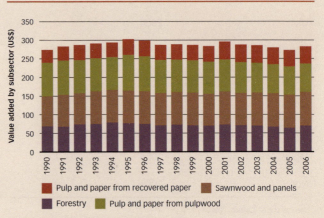

Sources: based on FAO, 2010b and Lebedys, 2008.

by about 4 percent (resulting in a total increase of 2 percent). Thus, although the sector has made considerable improvements in increasing the volume of products manufactured from each cubic metre of wood (see Box 7), it has been much less successful in translating this into increases in value-added.

Sources: based on FAO, 2010b and Lebedys, 2008.

Table A: Value-added by forestry operations, sawnwood and panels, and pulp and paper manufacturing

Global production and value added in 2006 (at 2006 prices and exchange rates)	Forestry	Sawnwood and panels	Pulp and paper		
			Pulpwood	Non-wood fibre	Recovered paper
Wood production/consumption (million m³)	1 519	998	644	n.a.	n.a.
Gross value-added (US$ billion)	110	146	116	10	78
GVA per m³ used (US$)	n.a.	146	180	n.a.	n.a.
GVA per m³ harvested (US$)	72	89	71	n.a.	47

For example, Box 7 on page 42 shows that the use of recovered and recycled fibre has almost doubled since 1990, but the total value-added per cubic metre of wood used has only increased by 2 percent over the same period (Box 10). Furthermore, some parts of the industry suffer from overcapacity and continue to expand production despite level or declining product demand. This is less of a problem for the sawnwood and panel industry where innovation has, perhaps, enabled companies to maintain or improve product prices, but it

is a major problem in the pulp and paper industry (Box 11 on page 54).

There are two main routes to consolidation in the forest industry: first by closing old and inefficient mills, and second through mergers and acquisitions. Consolidation through mill closures and extended downtime started before the current financial crisis, but accelerated during 2008 and 2009. For example, seven pulp and paper mills were closed in Finland in

2008, followed by three more in 2009. Employment was cut by 9 000 jobs and industrial roundwood use fell by 20 percent. When market pulp prices increased in early 2010, two pulp mills were restarted, but the other mills had either been refurbished and converted to other uses or dismantled and the equipment shipped to emerging economies.

Mergers and acquisitions usually remain at a low level until growth prospects improve and the potential benefits of such deals become more obvious. Following the 2008–2009 downturn it may take another two years before large-scale restructuring through mergers and acquisitions resumes in developed regions. However, interest in mergers and acquisitions remains high in some emerging economies. For example, Chinese companies are active in Viet Nam and the Lao People's Democratic Republic and may be seeking stronger collaboration with other countries in the region. Latin American firms are also exploring opportunities for restructuring. Aracruz and Votorantim have already merged their activities to form Fibria and other high-profile mergers are expected. Stora Enso and UPM (from Europe) also have some significant investments in Latin America and plan additional expansion in the next two to three years.

The desire to acquire or secure raw material supplies is also driving interest in mergers and acquisitions. Chilean giants Arauco and CPMP are looking for opportunities in Brazil and Uruguay, in response to domestic roundwood supply constraints. Stora Enso and Arauco also bought ENCE's forest plantations in Uruguay in 2009 (130 000 ha, plus an additional 6 000 ha of leased forest plantations) to add to the 250 000 ha of forests that they already own in Uruguay. On a smaller scale, an interesting acquisition was the purchase of most of Sabah Forest Industries in Malaysia by Ballarpur Industries of India. Wood supply is a major constraint for India's forest industry and this acquisition included a 289 000 ha concession (to the year 2094), which was an important motivation for the deal.

The country reports for FAO's 51st Advisory Committee on Paper and Wood Products (FAO, 2010c) provide further evidence of how some of the 'old' producer countries are starting to restructure their forest industries. Two examples of the strategies for restructuring, and the scale and impact of mill closures, are given below.
- Canada has closed or halted production at its predominantly old pulp and paper mills with the result that 39 000 jobs were lost in 2009. Falls were reported

in shipments of newsprint (down 27 percent), graphic paper (21 percent) and market pulp (10 percent). Under its 'BioPathways' project, the forest industry is examining the potential to develop new sawnwood and building systems, new value-added wood products and to transform pulp and paper mills into biorefineries that can produce bioenergy, valuable chemicals and high-performance fibres for advanced applications.
- In Germany, the paper industry is undergoing restructuring in three ways. The first is a shift in production away from graphic papers (which are oversupplied) towards the more attractive packaging, speciality papers and personal care (tissue) segments. The second is a move towards increasing competitiveness in the small and medium-sized industries, which must either focus on market niches or expand scale. The third is through the different impacts of climate change policies and trading systems (e.g. the EU Emissions Trading Scheme) on companies that have or have not invested in low carbon technologies such as biomass boilers. Carbon costs for biomass-based plants will be lower than for fossil fuel plants, especially those that use coal. In terms of more general trends in Europe, CEPI reported that newsprint output fell by 12 percent, woodfree graphic papers by 15 percent, mechanical papers by 19 percent and packaging grades by 6 percent in 2009. Chemical pulp output also decreased by 11 percent.

In addition to the emphasis on cutting costs and production during periods of consolidation, the forest industry needs to change the predominant business model towards one that will provide a more sustainable future for the industry. In particular, the current focus on low-cost, high volume commodity production has to change and move towards multiple products with higher value-added, greater flexibility and more resilience to market fluctuations.

The current financial crisis is limiting investment in many of the countries where forest industry consolidation is needed most desperately. However, as the examples above and in previous sections have shown, it appears that both governments and industry are now interested in a transformation to a more profitable and sustainable forest industry, with innovation as a major driver of future competitiveness. It is to be hoped that this interest will be maintained when economies fully recover, and that the industry will be able to implement such a transformation as part of future consolidation.

Changes in total value-added in the forest industry can be divided into three main components: changes in the quantity of production, price changes, and cost changes. Using national account statistics (where available) and production statistics (from FAOSTAT), trends in these three components of value-added were examined for the period since 2000 to identify changes in the competitiveness of different countries.

Sawnwood and wood-based panel production

Table A shows the average annual increase in total gross value-added for a number of countries, with the countries grouped into different combinations of output, cost and price changes. The first row shows the countries where both costs and prices are improving in the sector (i.e. falling costs and rising prices). In the countries on the left, output is also increasing, so value-added is increasing in all of these countries. Output is declining in the countries on the right, most likely due to scarcity of, or increasing competition for resources. However, with the exception of Japan, total value-added is also increasing in these countries.

The second row shows countries where the combination of cost and price changes is favourable. In other words, prices are increasing faster than costs (e.g. Finland) or costs are falling faster than prices (e.g. Canada). Again, the countries that have also been able to expand output (on the left) have increased total value-added. Some of the countries on the right may be constrained by resource availability (e.g. Estonia), but in a number of cases it is likely that declining output has been the result of deliberate measures to reduce production and cut costs or focus on higher value-added markets (e.g. Canada and Finland).

The third row shows the countries where cost and price changes have been unfavourable. In all of these countries except Chile, costs have increased and prices have either fallen or not increased by enough to cover the increased costs. On the left, Chile and Turkey are the only countries that have been able to increase total value-added (despite the unfavourable cost and price trends) by simply increasing production (by over 5 percent per year in both cases). In all of the other countries, total value-added has fallen at the same time that production has increased. All of the countries on the right have cut production but not sufficiently to improve competitiveness.

These figures show that the majority of countries remain competitive in sawnwood and wood-based panel production. The countries in the first row and left-hand side of the second row have managed to increase the value-added per unit of output and, in most cases, increase output as well. A second group of countries are increasing the value-added per unit of output

Table A: Average annual increase in total gross value-added in sawnwood and wood-based panel production since 2000

Countries with:	Increasing output		Decreasing output	
Costs and prices improving	Viet Nam	+32.0%	Indonesia	+5.4%
	China	+26.4%	Latvia	+4.0%
	Ukraine	+16.8%	Belgium	+2.6%
	India	+16.3%	Netherlands	+1.6%
	Russian Federation	+14.1%	United Kingdom	+1.1%
	Romania	+5.6%	Japan	-2.3%
	Brazil	+5.4%		
	Lithuania	+4.6%		
	Sweden	+3.4%		
Favourable cost and price changes	Republic of Moldova	+17.7%	Estonia	+0.7%
	Bulgaria	+13.3%	Portugal	0.0%
	Poland	+6.1%	Mexico	-0.4%
	South Africa	+5.9%	Finland	-1.6%
	Czech Republic	+3.6%	Canada	-1.6%
	Switzerland	+2.7%		
	Austria	+2.6%		
	New Zealand	+2.0%		
	Ireland	+1.5%		
	Republic of Korea	+0.8%		
Unfavourable cost and price changes	Chile	+1.1%	Spain	-0.5%
	Turkey	+0.8%	Norway	-1.2%
	Australia	-0.1%	Italy	-2.2%
	Hungary	-0.8%	United States of America	-3.0%
	Malaysia	-0.8%	France	-3.3%
	Germany	-2.1%		
	Argentina	-6.4%		
	Greece	-8.3%		

(i.e. 'favourable costs and price changes') by reducing production (e.g. Canada and Finland) or are increasing total value-added by producing more (e.g. Chile and Turkey). The countries facing the most problems are those in the third row where the cost and price trends are unfavourable and the industry has been unable to cut or refocus production to increase value-added.

Pulp and paper production

Table B shows the same information for the pulp and paper sector. This shows that both costs and prices are improving in four countries and production is increasing in another four countries where the combined cost and price trends are favourable. Production is declining in Australia and Hungary, but the cost and price trends are favourable and these countries have increased total value-added. As in the sawnwood and wood-based panel industry, Canada has also achieved improvements in value-added per unit of output (through significant cost reductions), but total output and total value-added have both fallen significantly.

In contrast to the sawnwood and wood-based panel industry, a large number of countries appear in the third row, including many of the largest pulp and paper producing countries. In almost all of these countries, prices are falling and costs increasing, resulting in declining value-added per unit of output. A few countries have managed to increase total value-added in the industry by increasing production, but many more have not increased total value-added. Furthermore, the majority of countries that have started to cut production have not yet managed to restructure their industries into a position where value-added can be improved.

To some extent the figures below could reflect cyclical changes in the industry, but this is unlikely to be a major factor in these results. For example, over each of the three previous decades, most of these countries managed to increase both total value-added and value-added per unit of output. A particular concern is that falling prices (due to reductions in demand) are a major cause of the declining value-added, yet the majority of countries are increasing production, putting further downward pressure on prices. Existing overcapacity in developed countries combined with rapid increases in capacity in some emerging economies suggest that significant industry restructuring and reorientation will be required to overcome the currently unfavourable trends in costs and prices.

Sources: based on FAO, 2010b and Lebedys, 2008.

Table B: Average annual increase in total gross value-added in pulp and paper production since 2000

Countries with:	Increasing output		Decreasing output	
Costs and prices improving	Viet Nam	+26.5%	Indonesia	+5.4%
	China	+18.4%	Latvia	+4.0%
	Argentina	+17.9%	Belgium	+2.6%
	Bulgaria	+15.2%	Netherlands	+1.6%
			United Kingdom	+1.1%
			Japan	-2.3%
Favourable cost and price changes	Indonesia	+11.8%	Hungary	+2.1%
	Romania	+8.1%	Australia	+1.4%
	Poland	+6.1%	Canada	-2.6%
	Turkey	+5.5%		
Unfavourable cost and price changes	Estonia	+7.1%	Netherlands	-2.5%
	Lithuania	+6.0%	United States of America	-2.7%
	Latvia	+2.9%	Greece	-2.8%
	Mexico	+2.7%	Japan	-3.2%
	Brazil	+1.3%	France	-5.5%
	India	+0.2%	United Kingdom	-5.7%
	Ukraine	+0.1%	Norway	-8.9%
	Germany	0.0%		
	Czech Republic	-0.5%		
	Chile	-0.7%		
	Switzerland	-0.8%		
	Spain	-0.9%		
	South Africa	-1.2%		
	Austria	-2.3%		
	Italy	-2.8%		
	Belgium	-3.4%		
	Portugal	-4.0%		
	Malaysia	-5.1%		
	Sweden	-6.6%		
	Russian Federation	-7.5%		
	Finland	-7.6%		
	Ireland	-7.6%		

Summary and conclusions

The preceding analysis has described the ways in which different driving forces are shaping developments in the forest industry, with consequences for the sustainability of the industry now and in the future. Many of the driving forces have diverse and sometimes contradictory impacts. For example, economic growth stimulates demand for forest products, but also increases competition for resources; and forest products have positive environmental attributes but environmental performance (or perceptions of performance) remains weak in parts of the industry. However, some of the most important forces are largely negative (e.g. industry structure and the maturity of some product markets) and can only be addressed by changes within the industry.

A number of aspects of forest industry sustainability were noted in the introduction (including energy efficiency, reduced waste production and resource conservation, environmentally compatible materials and safe working conditions) and current trends in these aspects are largely positive. Energy efficiency is generally improving in most regions and most parts of the industry. Resource efficiency and recycling are also improving and the industry is making progress in promoting wood products as more environmentally-friendly than alternative materials. However, these trends are only improving when they are measured in physical terms (i.e. volumes of production). When measured in terms of value-added, the trends are much less positive and are, in some cases, declining. This is due to the generally poor performance of the industry in recent years to increase the value-added per unit of output.

In some respects, the forest industry is facing challenges that have already been seen in other manufacturing sectors. In developed regions, the industry has significant capital assets and large domestic markets, but production costs are relatively high and markets are growing quite slowly, or even declining. In contrast, markets in emerging economies are growing rapidly and production costs are generally lower, with the result that much new investment is being directed towards these countries (further increasing their competitiveness). The result of this is overcapacity in many emerging economies and a generally negative outlook for prices, profitability and value-added both globally and especially in many developed countries.

As other industries have discovered, the solution to this challenge is consolidation and restructuring, to reduce overcapacity and reorient production into areas where each country is most competitive. The industry has been aware of the need for this for some time but, with the recent financial crisis, it seems at last to be moving in this direction. Innovation and the development of new partnerships with firms outside the industry appear to be important features of current restructuring efforts. Product innovation creates new markets that help to reduce overcapacity in existing markets and help to reduce the dependence of the industry on a few end uses. Some of the emerging partnerships are also bringing a number of benefits, such as improved access to finance, risk-sharing and new marketing opportunities. The main strength that the forest industry brings to these partnerships is its ability to manage and develop the raw material supply.

Governments are trying to improve sustainability in the forest industry in a number of ways. They continue to encourage the industry to improve its social and environmental performance, with a strong emphasis on policies and regulations related to wood supply and industrial emissions. Governments are also assisting the industry to improve competitiveness by funding research and development, facilitating the formation of industry clusters and partnerships, and providing support for wood promotion activities.

The overall outlook for the forest industry is one of continued growth with some significant changes in the future. The existing structure and location of the industry are not in line with the main economic driving forces, so new investment and production will continue to shift towards emerging economies. In the countries that can no longer compete with these emerging economies, restructuring of the industry is likely to be a major change. Although the outlook is uncertain, this is likely to result in a greater focus on products that meet high environmental performance standards and new products such as bioenergy, biochemicals and biomaterials. It is promising that a number of companies and countries are already actively pursuing these opportunities.

The role of forests in climate change adaptation and mitigation

orests play a crucial role in climate change mitigation and adaptation. Under the Kyoto Protocol,[12] forests can contribute to emissions reductions of Annex B countries (which are generally developed countries) to the Kyoto Protocol. Developing countries may participate in afforestation and reforestation activities under the Kyoto Protocol's Clean Development Mechanism (CDM)[13] to offset global emissions. Further mitigation options related to reducing emissions from deforestation and forest degradation (REDD) and enhancing forest stocks are proposed in a possible future agreement under the UN Framework Convention on Climate Change (UNFCCC). This chapter considers forest-related issues as they relate to countries' efforts to meet their commitments under the Kyoto Protocol, as well as further developments under the UNFCCC.

The use of forests for climate change mitigation also poses a number of unique problems. For instance, the ownership of forest carbon is recognized as an important issue that countries need to address. Concerns have emerged over the long-term financial benefits, and ownership of these benefits by the communities involved in forest mitigation activities. Unclear or inequitable forest carbon ownership or land tenure can constrain the implementation of climate change policies and actions. The latest trends in forest carbon law and policy, and mechanisms for defining carbon ownership and the transfer of carbon rights are presented in this chapter.

Adaptation measures in the forestry sector are essential both to climate change mitigation and for underpinning sustainable development. Without adaptation measures, the impacts of climate change are likely to affect forest dependent people in poorer countries more severely than the populations of developed countries. This chapter also discusses ways in which adaptation measures can – and should – be more closely integrated into climate change policies and actions.

Never before have forests and the forestry sector been so politically prominent. This is a unique moment in time. The forestry sector and the billions of people who depend on forests for their livelihoods have much to gain by using existing political support and emerging financial opportunities to take appropriate action.

Forests in the Kyoto Protocol

The world's forests store an enormous amount of carbon – more than all the carbon present in the atmosphere. The inclusion of forests, and of land use, land-use change and forestry (LULUCF) in the Kyoto Protocol was the subject of intense debate throughout negotiations on the Protocol. Indeed, forests and LULUCF were not definitively addressed until 2001 under the Marrakesh Accords.[14] These forest functions in the carbon balance are addressed by three Kyoto Protocol activities: afforestation/reforestation; deforestation; and forest management. Countries report on the changes to carbon stocks in managed forests that result from these three types of activities.

---

[12] According to the United Nations Framework Convention on Climate Change (UNFCCC), "the Kyoto Protocol is an international agreement linked to the UNFCCC. The major feature of the Kyoto Protocol is that it sets binding targets for 37 industrialized countries and the European Community for reducing greenhouse gas (GHG) emissions. These amount to an average of five per cent against 1990 levels over the five-year period 2008–2012". (http://unfccc.int)

[13] According to the UNFCCC, "the Clean Development Mechanism (CDM), defined in Article 12 of the Protocol, allows a country with an emission-reduction or emission-limitation commitment under the Kyoto Protocol (Annex B Party) to implement an emission-reduction project in developing countries. Such projects can earn saleable certified emission reduction (CER) credits, each equivalent to one tonne of CO_2, which can be counted towards meeting Kyoto targets". (http://unfccc.int)

[14] The Marrakesh Accords, according to the UNFCCC, include rules for LULUCF activities consisting of three main elements: "A set of principles to govern LULUCF activities; definitions for Article 3.3 activities (forest sinks) and agreed activities under Article 3.4 (additional human-induced activities); and a four-tier capping system limiting the use of LULUCF activities to meet emission targets". (http://unfccc.int)

In 2010, Annex B Parties of the Kyoto Protocol submitted their annual data on greenhouse gas emissions (GHG) for the year 2008 (Table 40). These data provide a clear indication of the role of forests in the carbon cycle and also of the new financial value that forests have through carbon markets. The data also indicate that forests in the Russian Federation absorb almost half a billion tonnes of CO_2 equivalent per year, primarily through forest management activities. Japan's forests offset over 29 million tonnes of CO_2 equivalent. If all of this could be sold on the market, assuming a price of US$20 per tonne of CO_2 equivalent, it would be worth a total of US$600 million per year.

The value of forests in developed countries (Annex B Parties to the Kyoto Protocol) is an indication of the potential magnitude of emissions offsets if all the world's forests were to be included in a new agreement on climate change, a subject under discussion in current UNFCCC negotiations. The new financial value that forests in developed countries have gained within the climate change market has still not been fully accounted for, although this may change depending on the way in which developing countries' forests are considered in climate change projects and processes.

At the global level, the *Fourth Assessment Report* of the Intergovernmental Panel on Climate Change (IPCC, 2007) indicated that global forest vegetation contains 283 Gt of carbon in biomass, 38 Gt in dead wood and 317 Gt in soils (in the top 30 cm) and litter. The total carbon content of forests ecosystems has been estimated at 638 Gt, which exceeds the amount of carbon in the atmosphere. As noted in Chapter 1 on regional trends from the Global Forest Resources Assessment 2010 (FRA 2010), forest biomass has generally increased in all regions, with Europe including the Russian Federation containing the largest amount of biomass.

The role of forest products in carbon storage is not addressed in the Kyoto Protocol. However, the contribution of harvested wood products (HWP) to the global carbon cycle and the possibility of including this in Annex B countries' GHG accounting is being debated in the UNFCCC negotiations on the second commitment period of the Kyoto Protocol. For instance, Table 41 shows estimated emissions and sequestration from the forestry value chain, based on 2006–2007 data.

Table 40. Data on afforestation and reforestation (A/R), deforestation (D) and forest management (FM) activities reported by Annex B Parties under the Kyoto Protocol for the year 2008 (in Gt CO_2 equivalent)

	A/R	D	FM	CO$_2$ balance
Australia	-16 948	49 651		32 703
Austria	-2 531	1 224		-1 307
Belgium	-399	468		69
Bulgaria	1 353	275		1 628
Canada	-738	14 643	-11 503	2 403
Czech Republic	-272	160	-6 145	-6 257
Denmark	-70	35	281	247
Estonia	-534	6 600		6 066
Finland	-1 077	2 886	-39 935	-38 126
France	-13 591	11 926	-84 620	-86 285
Germany	-2 615	16 393	-20 441	-6 663
Greece	-351	4	-2 052	-2 399
Hungary	-1 183	44	-3 885	-5 025
Iceland	-102			-102
Ireland	2 763	11		2 774
Italy	-1 736	386	-50 773	-52 122
Japan	-391	2 431	-46 105	-44 065
Latvia	-440	1 674	-23 595	-22 361
Liechtenstein	-11	4		-8
Netherlands	-547	780		233
New Zealand	-17 396	2 910		-14 486
Norway	-104	-93	-30 827	-31 023
Poland	-3 916	263	-46 865	-50 519
Portugal	-4 134	6 877	2 563	-180
Russia	-4 093	26 607	-462 469	-439 455
Slovakia		2 426	-10 324	-7 897
Slovenia	-2 456	2 385	-10 307	-7 851
Spain	-10 276	188	-39 120	-52 279
Sweden	-1 576	2 385	-18 606	-17 797
Switzerland	-35	82	-855	-808
UK	-2 696	452	-10 873	-13 116
Ukraine	-1 759	150	-47 718	-49 327

Source: http://unfccc.int/national_reports/annex_i_ghg_inventories/national_inventories_submissions/items/5270.php
Note: Belarus, Croatia, Lithuania, Luxemburg, Romania and Turkey did not report on the LULUCF sector.

Table 41: Estimated emissions and sequestration in the global forest products industry value chain, 2006–2007

Process	Emissions (million tonnes CO_2 equivalent/ year)
Direct emissions from manufacturing (Scope 1)	**297**
Fuel combustion: pulp and paper	207
Fuel combustion: wood products	26
Fuel combustion: converting	39
Methane from manufacturing waste	26
Emissions associated with electricity purchases (Scope 2)	**193**
Pulp and paper	106
Wood products	49
Converting	39
Wood production	18
Upstream emissions associated with chemicals and fossil fuels	**92**
Non-fibre inputs: pulp and paper	35
Non-fibre inputs: wood products	22
Fossil fuels: pulp and paper	31
Fossil fuels: wood products	5
Transport	**51**
Cradle-to-gate	21
Gate-to-consumer	27
Consumer-to-grave	4
Product use	**-263**
Emissions	0
Effect of additions to carbon stocks in paper products in use	-20
Effect of additions to carbon stocks in wood products in use	-243
End-of-life	**77**
Burning used products	3
Paper-derived methane	176
Effect of additions to carbon stocks in paper products in landfills	-67
Wood-derived methane	59
Effect of additions to carbon stocks in wood products in landfills	-94

Source: FAO, 2010d
Notes:
Total cradle-to-gate emissions = 622 million tonnes of CO_2 equivalent per year (not considering sequestration)
Total cradle-to-grave emissions = 890 million tonnes of CO_2 equivalent per year (not considering sequestration)
Value chain sequestration = net uptake of 424 million tonnes of CO_2 equivalent per year, based on estimates of the accumulation of carbon stocks in product pools and an assumption that globally, regeneration and regrowth are keeping carbon stocks stable in the forests the industry relies on
Net value chain emissions, cradle-to-grave = 467 million tonnes of CO_2 equivalent per year

As seen in Table 41, there is a potential to increase carbon storage in wood products. Parties to the UNFCCC are currently working on a methodology to account for carbon stored over time in harvested wood products. The role of HWPs in the carbon cycle is, however, minor when compared with other forest activities considered under the UNFCCC. The next section discusses these issues in greater detail.

Progress on forest-related climate change negotiations

UNFCCC negotiations have focused intensely on forests because an estimated 17.4 percent of global GHGs come from the forest sector, in large part from deforestation in developing countries[15] (IPCC, 2007), and because of the perception, made widespread by the Stern Review (Stern, 2006) that curbing deforestation is a highly cost-effective way of reducing GHG emissions. Efforts to provide incentives to developing countries to better realize the mitigation potential of forests have evolved from discussions on avoiding emissions from deforestation to REDD+ (Box 12). In December 2010, the Conference of Parties to the UNFCCC agreed on a framework for an instrument to incentivize REDD+ under a future agreement to the Kyoto Protocol. This mechanism could play a crucial role in combating climate change and enhancing broader sustainable development. REDD+ has drawn the attention of the highest levels of government from around the world. While the political spotlight is on forests in developing countries, the outcome of negotiations underway on LULUCF will also have a bearing on the achievement of emissions reduction commitments and forest management in industrialized countries and countries in economic transition (the so-called Annex B Parties to the Kyoto Protocol).

Two ad hoc, time-bound bodies were established under the UNFCCC to carry out negotiations on REDD+, LULUCF, CDM and adaptation up to the UNFCCC 15th COP in Copenhagen in December 2009. In 2010 the Ad hoc Working Group on Long-term Cooperative Action under the Convention (AWG-LCA) continued to address the building blocks identified in the Bali Action Plan: adaptation, mitigation, financing, technology transfer and capacity building. The Ad hoc Working Group on Further Commitments for Annex I Parties under the Kyoto Protocol (AWG-KP) is addressing emissions reduction commitments

---

[15] These emissions include those from deforestation, decay (decomposition) of aboveground biomass that remains after logging and deforestation, and CO_2 from peat fires and decay of drained peat soils.

The global importance of forests as a carbon sink and of deforestation as a source of GHG emissions have been recognized by UNFCCC since its inception. During the negotiations of the Kyoto Protocol, consideration was given to making "avoiding emissions from deforestation" eligible under the CDM, but the concept was set aside because of uncertainties associated with methodologies and data at the time. The idea resurfaced at the UNFCCC 11th COP in 2005 when a group of countries requested an item on "reducing emissions from deforestation in developing countries (RED): approaches to stimulate action" in the negotiations.

Through work by the SBSTA between COP-11 and COP-13, Parties also agreed to address emissions from forest degradation, since they were thought to be greater than those from deforestation in many countries. The concept thus was expanded to "reducing emissions from deforestation and degradation in developing countries (REDD)". At COP-13 in 2007, UNFCCC adopted a decision entitled "Policy approaches and positive incentives on issues relating to reducing emissions from deforestation and forest degradation in developing countries, and the role of conservation, sustainable management of forests and enhancement of forest carbon stocks in developing countries", which is now known as REDD+. The scope of REDD+ goes beyond deforestation and forest degradation to include the maintenance and enhancement of forest carbon stocks.

of industrialized countries and countries in economic transition, after the first commitment period of the Protocol expires in 2012. Their structure and discussion areas are shown graphically in Figure 28. These ad hoc working groups are tackling difficult, long-standing methodological and political topics, including those related to REDD+, LULUCF and CDM.

While Parties reached a considerable consensus on REDD+ in Copenhagen in December 2009, there was no formal agreement on these matters. The AWG met in June, August and October 2010. In December 2010, in Cancún, Mexico, it finally agreed on a text to forward for adoption by the UNFCCC COP. The following provides an overview of some of the topical issues discussed.[17]

REDD+

The Conference of the Parties to the UNFCCC adopted a decision on REDD+ in Cancún, Mexico. The text covers the scope, principles and safeguards for REDD+, and outlines a phased approach for implementing REDD+, moving in a step-wise fashion from pilot activities to full-fledged REDD+ implementation. The negotiating text that emerged from COP-16 contained the following activities which define the scope of REDD+:

- reducing emissions from deforestation;
- reducing emissions from forest degradation;
- sustainable management of forest;
- conservation of forest carbon stocks; and
- enhancement of forest carbon stocks.

The decision lists safeguards in order to ensure multiple benefits and avoid negative spill-over effects from REDD+ activities. These safeguards are related to:

- consistency with existing forest programmes and international agreements;
- forest governance;
- rights of indigenous peoples and members of local communities;

Figure 28: Forest issues under the UNFCCC bodies and working groups[16]

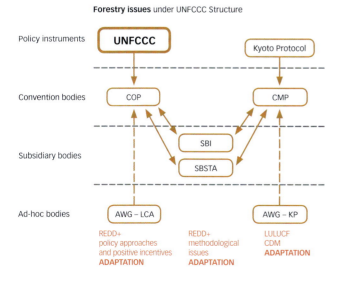

---

[16] CMP is the "Conference of Parties serving as the meeting of the parties to the Kyoto Protocol" (http://unfccc.int)
[17] The text describes the negotiations as at December 2010.

COP-13 adopted a decision (Decision 2/CP.13) based on work by SBSTA to provide some indicative methodological guidance for the implementation of demonstration projects, and encouraged Parties to mobilize resources and relevant organizations to support developing countries on their activities related to REDD.

COP-15 adopted a decision (Decision 4/CP.15) based on SBSTA's work on methodological guidance for REDD+. The COP decision requested Parties to identify drivers of deforestation and forest degradation; to identify activities that may result in reduced emissions or increased removals; to use the most adopted or encouraged IPCC Guidelines to estimate forest-related GHG emissions and removals; and to establish national forest

monitoring systems based on a combination of remote sensing and ground-based forest carbon inventory. Further work on methodological issues related to monitoring, reporting and verification (MRV) is required before a REDD+ instrument can be operationalized. SBSTA is charged with continued work on MRV for REDD+. The use of any adopted IPCC Guidance has been recommended for relevant monitoring purposes.

Both decisions encouraged Parties and other stakeholders to share information and lessons learnt by using a REDD Web Platform on the UNFCCC web site (http://unfccc.int). COP-16 in Cancún adopted a decision on REDD+ as part of the outcome of the work of the AWG-LCA.

- participatory approaches;
- conservation of natural resources and biological diversity;
- permanence of mitigation actions; and
- leakage.

The text recognizes the need for a developing country to establish several important elements: a national forest monitoring system, a national strategy or action plan and a national forest reference (emission) level.

A key issue that remains to be resolved concerns the financing modality for actions performed (market-based, fund-based or a mixture of the two). This issue will be further addressed by the UNFCCC.

SBSTA is addressing the methodological issues related to approaches to the measurement, reporting and setting of reference scenarios. Two decisions were adopted (2/CP.13 and 4/CP.15; see box 13) to provide guidance on those issues. The REDD+ decision adopted in Cancún requests SBSTA to work on certain technical and methodological aspects of REDD+, including on methodologies for monitoring, reporting and verification.

LULUCF and CDM under the Kyoto Protocol

Negotiations in the AWG-KP address the rules and modalities to account for GHG emissions and removals from LULUCF in Annex B Parties under a post-2012 mechanism. Current proposals to simplify the existing accounting rules for the first commitment period of

the Kyoto Protocol are still under discussion. Progress is being made on addressing forest management accounting provisions, including a proposal to rationalize and increase transparency in setting possible reference levels for forest management. The treatment of HWPs and natural disturbances, particularly extreme events, are also under discussion within the context of forest management, as is the voluntary versus mandatory nature of Article 3.4 additional activities, and the possible inclusion of more activities (e.g. wetland management).

AWG-KP is also considering broadening the scope of LULUCF activities that are eligible under the CDM. Currently, among LULUCF activities, only afforestation and reforestation are eligible for CDM projects. Proposals to expand the scope to include REDD, wetlands, sustainable forest management and reforestation of 'forests in exhaustion' are being debated, but Parties converge only on the need for further technical discussion before decisions can be made.

Finance for REDD+

Although the REDD+ decision adopted in Cancún does not address the financing modality, REDD+ pilot activities are being funded. REDD+ has attracted financial commitments at the highest levels, with many presidents, prime ministers and their representatives pledging to take action on REDD+ implementation. Six countries (Australia, France, Japan, Norway, the United Kingdom and the United States of America) collectively agreed to dedicate US$3.5 billion "as initial public finance towards slowing, halting and eventually reversing deforestation in developing countries". Heads of state delivered similar messages at other recent meetings, including the Oslo Climate and Forest Conference held in May 2010. At this meeting, high-level government representatives agreed to establish the REDD+ Partnership to take action to improve the effectiveness, efficiency, transparency and coordination of REDD+ initiatives and financial instruments, to facilitate knowledge transfer, capacity enhancement, mitigation actions, and technology development and transfer. Together they pledged about US$4 billion to support these related efforts. Ministers gathered in Nagoya in October 2010 for a special REDD+ Partnership meeting during CBD COP10 welcomed the achievements of the REDD+ Partnership, including the provision of transparent and comprehensive information on REDD+ finance, actions and results through the voluntary REDD+ database. They also recognized the need to take actions to narrow gaps, avoid overlaps and maximize the effective delivery of REDD+ actions and financing.

Important efforts to implement REDD+ activities are now underway. A key factor in the sustainability of REDD+ projects and activities will be the approach taken to ensure that the benefits from these projects are equitably shared by the communities implementing them. This hinges largely on the extent to which forest carbon rights can be guaranteed. The following section provides a snapshot of new and amended legislation related to forest carbon tenure, and examines the difficulties and emerging ideas around ownership of, and benefits from, forest carbon.

Forest carbon tenure: implications for sustainable REDD+ projects

In the light of the developments discussed in the previous section, countries are adopting legal instruments to regulate carbon forest rights in regulatory as well as voluntary carbon markets. This could also stimulate greater investment in REDD+ projects from public and private project developers if a stronger, more stable enabling environment guarantees minimum, appropriate forms of legal protection to contracting parties. As of 2010, over 37 developing countries and economies in transition were participating in programmes such as the United Nations Collaborative Programme on REDD (UN-REDD) or REDD readiness programmes under the World Bank's Forest Carbon Partnership Facility (FCPF) to improve their ability to implement REDD activities. Figure 29 shows some of the countries participating in the UN-REDD programme, all of which have a high potential to offset carbon emissions in forest areas.

Despite the promise of REDD+ to provide finance for forests and contribute to climate change mitigation, owning an intangible resource such as carbon poses challenges for traditional property law systems. Specifically, ownership of carbon property rights and

Figure 29: UN-REDD programme and observer countries

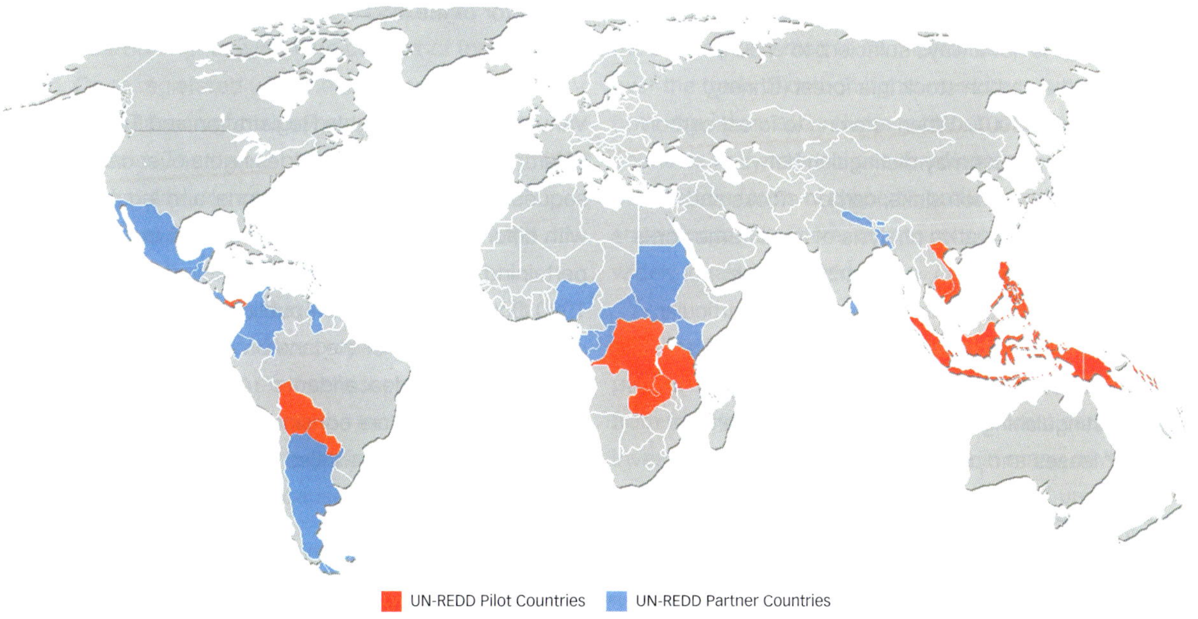

UN-REDD Pilot Countries   UN-REDD Partner Countries

Source: UN-REDD Programme

are recognized as communal property (Takacs, 2009). A related aspect would be to assess the government's capacity to implement and enforce such rights.

Community forest management agreements (Guyana) and contracts recognizing indigenous property rights as a kind of usufruct right (Brazil) are clear examples of ways in which community rights can be recognized in spite of the state's ownership over the land.

Guyana

In Guyana, the Forest Bill of 2008 (enacted on 22 January 2009), states that: "All forest produce on, or originating from, public land is the property of the State until the rights to the forest produce have been specifically disposed in accordance with this Act or any other written law" (para. no. 73).[21] However, under paragraph 11, the Guyana Forestry Commission (GFC) may, on application by any community group, enter into a legally binding community forest management agreement with the group concerned, which would authorize that group to occupy a specified area of state forest and manage it in accordance with the agreement. This option is also extended to afforestation agreements with individuals. Additionally, a forest concession agreement may be granted to carry out forest conservation operations in an area, even for commercial uses. These operations include the preservation of forests for the purpose of carbon sequestration, although there are no provisions addressing carbon sequestration rights. Some provisions may nevertheless be interpreted extensively in order to include rights derived from carbon sequestration activities under forest conservation management agreements.

Brazil

Brazil is implementing the National Plan on Climate Change (launched on 1 December 2008), which aims to reduce illegal deforestation, and established the Amazon Fund to encourage reforestation, monitoring and enforcement of forest laws. Brazil allows a wide array of entities to own land, while indigenous property rights are a type of usufruct right (or a legal right to derive profit from property) recognized by the Brazilian Constitution of 1988 (Arts. 231–232) (Box 14). While the federal government maintains expropriation rights for all subsurface oil or minerals, it is presumed (but not legally explicit) that whoever owns the rights to use the land above ground – including private parties and indigenous groups – also has rights to the carbon.

Once a group is recognized through a formal process regulated by the *Fundação Nacional do Indio* (FUNAI, part of the Ministry of Justice), its members have exclusive right to use all the goods on the land, even though the land itself continues to belong to the state. The Amazonas State Climate Change, Conservation and Sustainable Development Policy (no. 3135 of 2007) states that the property rights over forest carbon on state lands are held by the *Fundação Amazonas Sustentáve* (FAS) – a new organization created by the state for this purpose. Brazil does not have a national

---

Box 14: Brazil – an example of land rights in the Amazon

The current Brazilian Constitution was promulgated on 5 October 1988 and the latest Constitutional Amendment (64) made on 4 February 2010. The Constitution sets out that:

Art. 231: Para. no. 1: Lands traditionally occupied by indigenous peoples are those on which they live on a permanent basis, those used for their productive activities, those indispensable to the preservation of the environmental resources necessary for their well-being and for their physical and cultural reproduction, according to their uses, customs and traditions.

Para. no. 2 - The lands traditionally occupied by indigenous peoples are intended for their permanent possession and they shall have the exclusive usufruct of the riches of the soil, the rivers and the lakes existing therein.

Para. no. 4 - The lands referred to in this article are inalienable and indisposable and the rights thereto are not subject to limitation.

Art. 232: The indigenous peoples, their communities and organizations have standing under the law to defend their rights and interests, the Public Prosecution intervening in all the procedural acts.

---

[21] In Guyana, approximately 76 percent of the total land area is forested and the Guyana Forestry Commission (GFC) is responsible for the management of about 62 percent of the forest classified as State Forest Estate.

law that specifically addresses the legal ownership of carbon rights. It is nevertheless expected that the implementation of the Brazilian Climate Change Policy, which promotes the development of an organized carbon market and is overseen by the Brazilian Securities and Exchange Commission, will encourage further clarifications of the nature of carbon rights (Chiagas, 2010).

Costa Rica

The Forest Law 7575 of 1996 provides the legal basis for environmental service payments, which are clearly defined in the Forest Law as "those services provided by forest and forest plantations to protect and improve the environment". Costa Rica's legal system does not address carbon property rights explicitly. Instead, property rights in natural entities are inferred from elements of the civil code. The owner of the land also owns the trees or forest that grows on the land and the carbon sequestered. The owner can negotiate the right to sell or manage carbon and can in return reap the resulting benefits. Article 22 of the Law allows FONAFIFO (National Fund for Forestry Financing) to issue forest landowner certificates for forest conservation (CCBs) which represent payments for ecosystem services (Costenbader, 2009).

Under FONAFIFO's auspices, the government may sign a contract with individual land property owners who are responsible for managing carbon sequestration. The property owner gives the government the right to sell carbon. The government may then bundle the sequestered carbon into attractive packages for international investors. Property owners must show proof of identity, ownership and tax payment with their application, and provide a sustainable forest management plan. FONAFIFO checks eligibility requirements through databases in other government departments, thus streamlining the process. Groups of property owners can apply collectively and jointly manage their land for maximum carbon sequestration. If any pre-existing usufruct property right exists on a given parcel of land, the land cannot be included in a new contract. By signing these contracts, the government implicitly recognizes that the carbon belongs to the private owner. The government will own the right to sell the carbon and the right to define the terms under which the property owner manages carbon sequestration for the length of the contract. Private landowners are also free to negotiate their own deals with foreign investors, as the government does not maintain exclusive rights to market carbon. Foreigners are able to own land in Costa Rica and can market their own carbon. Easements are also possible but only where clear land title exists (Takacs, 2009).

Mexico

Most of the forest land in Mexico is communal land (or '*ejido*' in Spanish). The *ejido* system is a process, strengthened by the reform of the Mexican Constitution, whereby the government promotes the use of land by communities. The land is divided into communal land and 'parcelled land' owned by the community members. Therefore, in order to be effective, any forestry project has to consider local communities' needs. The national legal framework does not contemplate forest carbon rights specifically. Nevertheless, private contracts could be considered as an alternative way to regulate the interests of the parties. To stipulate a contract, the federal civil code requires only an agreement between the contracting parties and the definition of the object. Contracts could be stipulated between local land owners and buyers of carbon sequestration rights. To reduce transaction costs, potential buyers of carbon rights would presumably be encouraged to invest in projects covering an extended forest area, implying cooperation agreements among local land owners.

In this case, a contract of sale could be used. The civil code states that the object of the contract must "exist in nature", have a discernable form and have the ability to be commercialized. Carbon dioxide exists in the atmosphere and it can be quantified using an agreed technology, while the intention of the parties to conclude the agreement is expressed by the contract itself. Private contracts have the advantage that any stakeholder can take part in the agreement even if they cannot solve the technical challenge of establishing the necessary methodologies to adequately measure the stock of carbon sequestered (CEMDA, 2010).

Formal recognition of customary law: communities' rights and land

Under international law, and specifically the Indigenous and Tribal Peoples Convention of 1989, traditional land ownership is considered as a human right, with an autonomous existence rooted in indigenous peoples' customary tenure systems and norms. States have corresponding obligations to regularize and secure these traditional ownership rights.

It is now widely recognized that clear tenure rights are central to achieving social and economic development. Clarification of tenure rights is also a crucial component of forest-based approaches to combating climate change and defining related carbon rights. Today most communities seek formal legitimacy or protection to secure their customary rights. In recent decades, there has been a trend towards decentralization of national governments and devolution of natural resource management to local communities, thus encouraging tenure reforms. Nevertheless, there remains a question of enforceability and the ability of communities to exercise their rights, even when a law is in place (Angelsen *et al*., 2009).

So far, most countries have only handed over low value and degraded forests for subsistence use by local people. However, a few countries where community-based forest management has been implemented for some years, such as Bhutan, Brazil, the Gambia and the United Republic of Tanzania, have begun to allow the commercialization of NWFPs and timber. Data from FRA 2010 indicate that a large percentage of public forests in South America were transferred to community ownership between 1990 and 2005. As seen in Figure 30, South America also continued to have the largest proportion of public forests managed by communities, yet the overall percentage of community-managed forests is small when compared to other types of management on a subregional basis.

So how can local people effectively participate in, and benefit from climate change policies and REDD+ activities? Who owns the carbon sequestered in trees and forest soils when formal and secure tenure rights are not enforced? The leading approach to involving forest land managers is to establish a system of compensation financed through carbon trading or international funds that takes into account their human and customary rights.

Madagascar

The systems recognizing property rights in carbon are defined in a participatory way and recognize customary systems of ownership and management rights over ecosystem services (Suderlin, Hatcher and Liddle, 2008). For example, Law 2006-31 formalizes the legal regime for non-titled property rights of traditional users. To enforce the law, the government has adopted a formal, detailed decree specifying the operation of the new certificate titling system.

Democratic Republic of the Congo

The 2002 Forest Code has introduced a number of innovative aspects related to forest management, although it does not specifically refer to carbon rights. More recently, climate change issues have been

Figure 30: Management of public forests by subregion, 2005

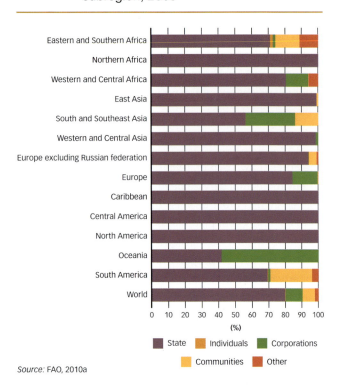

Source: FAO, 2010a

included in the 2009 Decree adopted by the Ministry of Environment, Nature Conservation and Tourism, which regulates institutional aspects of REDD implementation.

Related to this, the creation of national and provincial registers can be considered as a first step to facilitate the control of transactions of land tenure rights, which is essential for the implementation and sustainability of any REDD initiative. In addition, the existing legal framework covers forest rehabilitation measures through the implementation of reforestation and natural forest programmes (articles 77–80) that are aligned with the principles of REDD and REDD+. However, so far, forest community rights do not specifically refer to payments for environmental services such as carbon sequestration.

United Republic of Tanzania

In the United Republic of Tanzania, the Land Act of 1999 and the Village Land Act of 1999 establish that land is the property of the state and can only be leased from the government for a specific period of time and activity.

However, according to the Ministry of Lands and Human Settlements Development, land areas can be sold under a 99-year lease agreement. Under the Land Policy and Land Act, the payment of compensation by the state to the landowner extinguishes customary rights to the land, legally passing the right to lease the land to the state and its derived rights to the new land owner. The Land Act of 1999 states that "where a granted right of occupancy exists in any transferred land or a part thereof, a transferred land shall, unless the instrument of transfer provides otherwise, operate 'as a compulsory acquisition of that right of occupancy' and compensation on it shall be payable". Conditions attached by the government include: development conditions and rights, which include payment of land rent, development of the area by reforestation, protection of the boundary, and sustainable use of the land according to cross-sectoral laws associated with land management. All of these properties and crops are detailed in the title deed transfer, including the amount paid.

Brazil

A legal analysis on tribal land ownership was requested by Forest Trends (a Washington DC-based forest conservation group) on behalf of the Surui tribe in Rondônia. A new legal opinion emerging from this analysis, which was released in December 2009, states that the Surui tribe own the carbon-trading rights associated with the forests in which the tribe is located. This opinion demonstrates that there is an opportunity for indigenous groups to participate in emerging markets for carbon trading and could set a precedent in other countries as well. It also highlights that the Surui tribe needs to secure financial returns for carbon sequestered as an environmental service, and to provide transparent competitive prices for the commercialization of carbon credits, which would be in alignment with Brazil's overall national sovereign interest.

Guyana

Guyana's legal framework for forests does not contain specific provisions on forest carbon rights. However, as forest areas are traditionally occupied and used by Guyana's indigenous people, customary tenure systems are crucial in determining land ownership.[22] Between 2004 and 2007, 17 communities received titles while six communities secured extensions to their titled lands, increasing the total number of communities with legally recognized lands from 74 to 91 and the percentage of

Guyana's territory owned by Amerindian communities from approximately 7 percent to about 14 percent. Before titles were to be granted communities were requested to submit a description of the area and in-depth consultations were held.

However, several communities still remain without legally recognized lands, although many of them have requested titles. To guarantee land ownership to local communities, the Constitution of 1980 (as reformed in 1996) states that land is for social use and must go to the cultivator of the land (or 'tiller' as stated in the Constitution).

The historical stewardship role of indigenous peoples in protecting Guyana's forest on their traditional land has recently been recognized and rewarded through support for community conserved territories. Based on stable and inclusive laws such as these, Guyana has been able to attract finance from donors, most notably through its Memorandum of Understanding with Norway (Box 15).

Indonesia

The 1945 Constitution of the Republic of Indonesia recognizes the rights of *adat* communities "as customary communities". Article 28I(c) states that the "cultural identity and traditional rights of *adat* communities are respected and protected by the State as human rights".[23] In particular, article 18B(2) of the Constitution sets out that: "The State recognizes and respects customary law communities along with their traditional rights"; however, it limits these rights according to a broad notion of "societal development". These articles have been interpreted as providing the state with a broad right of control over all land in Indonesia, allowing the state to subordinate *adat* rights to the national interest.

Legislation related to carbon rights has been enacted that authorizes provincial and district governments to issue permits for the utilization of environmental services, called Izin Usaha Pemanfaatan Jasa Lingkungan (IUPJL). The IUPJLs are granted for a term of 30 years and entitle permit holders to store and absorb carbon in both production and protection forests. Ministry of Forestry Decision 36/2009 establishes procedures for granting IUPJLs (Box 16). Although there is no clear statement in the regulations to the effect that an IUPJL for carbon storage entitles the holder to all carbon

---

[22] Amerindians in Guyana number about 55 000 or 7 percent of the population. However, because 90 percent of the Guyanese population lives along the narrow coastal strip, Amerindians represent the majority population in the country's interior.

[23] Indonesian language refers to *masyarakat adat*, which is translated variously as 'customary communities', 'traditional communities', or 'indigenous peoples'. It is estimated that as many as 300 distinct adat legal systems exist throughout Indonesia.

On 9 November 2009, President Jagdeo of Guyana and Norway's Minister of the Environment and International Development, Mr Erik Solheim, signed a Memorandum of Understanding, agreeing that Norway would provide Guyana with results-based payments for forest climate services of up to US$250 million by 2015. The Governments of Norway and Guyana believe that this can provide the world with a working example of how REDD+ might operate for a High-Forest Low Deforestation (HFLD) country. The Low Carbon Development Strategy (LCDS) provides the broad framework for Guyana's response to climate change and hinges mainly on Guyana's use of its forests to mitigate global climate change. The LCDS builds on the launch in December 2008 of Guyana's Position on Avoided Deforestation, which essentially serves as the model for the Strategy's development. The key focus areas of the LCDS are investment in low-carbon economic infrastructure and in high potential low carbon sectors; expansion of access to services; new economic opportunities for indigenous and forest communities and the transformation of the village economy; improved social services and economic opportunities for the wider Guyanese population; and investment in climate change adaptation infrastructure. The third draft of the LCDS, *Transforming Guyana's Economy while Combating Climate Change*, was launched in May 2010 and identifies eight priorities that will be the initial focus of LCDS implementation 2010 and 2011. This version incorporates further feedback from national stakeholders and input based on the outcomes of UNFCCC COP-15 in Copenhagen and other international processes.

Source: Guyana's Low Carbon Development Strategy website (http://www.lcds.gov.gy/)

rights, it is generally accepted that the permit refers to carbon ownership rights. While these regulations add some clarity over carbon rights in protective and productive forests, outside these areas the situation is unclear (Dunlop, 2009). Nevertheless, communities were able to successfully influence the outcome of these developments, in large part as a result of their visibility in the international REDD+ process and the UNFCCC negotiations.

Options to integrate carbon rights in a national legal framework

As discussed in this section, one approach for allocating forest carbon ownership is to assign these rights to the owner of the forest. In cases where there are unclear land tenure property rights, as is the case in many developing countries in Africa, Latin America and Asia, the implementation of REDD programmes may be seriously limited (Rosenbaum, Schoene and Mekouar, 2004).

As noted in Angelsen *et al.* (2009), stable land tenure arrangements will assist in advancing REDD+ implementation, but other key forest governance issues (e.g. accountability, corruption and transparency) also need to be addressed. Improved information and public consultation are necessary, and funding is likely to be conditional on good governance (an approach already used by UN-REDD and FCPF, among others) to encourage devolution of greater rights to communities and land owners. International policies and guidelines can also assist in informing these processes; for instance the concept of 'free prior informed consent' should be considered when dealing with specific groups such as indigenous people.

Under an alternative approach, carbon stock is subject to a separate, alienable property right, independent of ownership of the forest, which would allow the owner to sell that right without conveying forest ownership. This may occur through the sale of a right to profit from the land or 'right of taking', governed under land ownership laws or general property rules, as in the case of CSRs created by Australian states. Carbon credits separated from land ownership would facilitate transactions on the market. Property rights registered on the land title would grant right holders with remedies against any inconsistent land uses.

Under a different scheme, CSRs may be considered as a publicly-owned asset, regardless of forest and land ownership (as in Brazil, Costa Rica, Guyana and Indonesia). Even where forests are largely privately owned, the state could manage carbon sequestration capacity as a public asset or environmental service, and distribute the benefits to the forest owners or users (as, for example, in Mexico). National governments may own the carbon under various different schemes, but in all cases there are questions about the share of benefits that need to be returned to forest owners (Costenbader, 2009). National regulatory frameworks as well as private contracts represent legal options through which to negotiate payment for environmental services transactions linked to carbon sequestration.

In 2008–2009, Indonesia established the world's first national laws relating to REDD. These laws are necessary to clarify the legal and policy framework needed to attract REDD investment. Currently three Ministry of Forestry (MoF) regulations and decisions refer directly to REDD:

- MoF Regulation 68/2008 on REDD Demonstration Activities;
- MoF Regulation 30/2009 on Procedures for REDD;
- MoF Decision 36/2009 on Procedures for the Granting of Utilization of Carbon Sequestration or Sinks in Production Forest and Protected Forest.

However, in most developing countries, national legal provisions could be strengthened and effectively enforced to guarantee benefit sharing from the international to national and subnational levels.

Governments will need to develop capacities and mechanisms to attract private investors. In order to ensure that benefits reach local land owners – in particular those lacking access to justice – processes for distributing benefits should be participatory. Provisions should also guarantee that smallholders and indigenous communities have access to public information explaining how to reduce transaction costs (Costenbader, 2009).

As discussed in the analysis of the Mexican legislation, private contracts can provide the mechanism for parties to buy and sell CSRs. In general terms, regulatory schemes for REDD should clearly determine who owns the right to the carbon sequestered in forests. However, carbon ownership may either be a separate proprietary interest, or a proprietary interest linked to forest or land ownership. There are limitations to both approaches and further development of legal frameworks at the national level is necessary to ensure sustainable implementation of REDD+ schemes.

Strengthening the role of adaptation in climate change policies

Managing forest carbon for climate change mitigation should be seen as part of a larger agenda of adapting forests, forestry and forest dependant communities to climate change. Societies have always adapted to climate variability, built dams or levees for irrigation or flood control, or developed coping mechanisms for climate extremes. However, these short-term, often mitigative approaches cannot ensure environmental sustainability in the long term. Ignoring adaptation in climate change policies will therefore undermine mitigation efforts,

especially in sectors such as forestry that rely on services from biological systems. This section examines the current treatment of forests in the adaptation dialogue, policies and actions, and identifies the challenges of integrating adaptation further into the climate change agenda.

Links to the global talks on mitigation

To date, international instruments for addressing climate change have had only a modest global impact on adaptation capacity, in part because of their understandably heavy focus on mitigation (Glück et al., 2009). The Nairobi Work Programme (2005–2010) was set up by UNFCCC to assist all Parties – and especially developing countries – to improve capacities for vulnerability and impact assessments, and adaptation actions. However, substantial funding for adaptation activities in general, and forest-related adaptation activities in particular, is still not available. This may change with the recent organization of the Adaptation Fund of the UNFCCC. There is a general sense that separating adaptation from mitigation will further weaken adaptation capacity (Aldy and Stavins, 2008), and that priority should be given to activities that can fulfil both objectives. Although this is a logical goal, mitigation and adaptation activities have different underpinnings and warrant distinct support and funding processes. The design of mitigation policies that explicitly recognize and support adaptation would offer some middle ground.

An important first step in incorporating adaptation into mitigation policies is to avoid policies that generate maladaptation. For example, although conservation of regulating services provided by forests (e.g. regulation of floods, erosion and climate) is essential for adaptation, enforced conservation measures could deprive local populations in developing countries of their provisioning services or ecosystem goods (e.g. food, fodder and livelihoods). Adaptation needs are local and policies must be designed to ensure that communities are supported in their capacity to manage local resources for adaptation purposes (Phelps, Webb and Agrawal, 2010). The maintenance of forests is essential if they are to be part of communities' adaptation responses. Policies that make non-forest land uses more financially attractive than forest-based activities or environmental services will increase deforestation pressure and reduce forest-based adaptation capacity.

Adaptation in national programmes

An analysis of recent National Communications (NCs) and National Adaptation Programmes of Action (NAPAs) by the International Union of Forest Research Organizations (IUFRO) Global Forest Expert Panel on Adaptation of Forests to Climate Change (Roberts, Parrotta and Wreford, 2009) reveals that forests are already seen as an important component of the adaptation response to climate change. Most developed and developing countries advocate the use of sustainable forest management (SFM) as an adaptation measure, and the concept is often included in national laws. However, forests generally play a minor role in adaptation policies compared with other sectors such as agriculture. In developing countries, notable exceptions are coastal afforestation in Bangladesh, forest fire prevention in Samoa and catchment reforestation in Haiti (Locatelli et al., 2008).

There is also a general recognition that adaptation of forests to climate change is necessary, with many specific actions proposed in NCs and NAPAs. In developed countries, these include measures to increase landscape connectivity, to enhance ecosystem stability and resilience, and to manage extreme disturbances (Roberts, Parrotta and Wreford, 2009). Developing countries, by contrast, generally have not included the adaptation of forests to climate change in their NAPAs (Locatelli et al., 2008).

In developing countries, forest-based policies and activities related to SFM can provide a strong foundation for adaptation while meeting REDD+ goals, but in practice their translation into national policies remains weak. Locatelli et al. (2008) identify three major challenges that need to be addressed in order to move forward on this issue. The first is the strengthening of national institutions that are responsible for the implementation and monitoring of SFM. For example, ITTO reported that, while improvements in implementation of SFM were underway, less than 5 percent of the forest domain under management in its member states clearly fulfilled the requirements of SFM (ITTO, 2006).

The second challenge for mainstreaming forest-based adaptation policies is the establishment of linkages between adaptation processes and other political processes relevant to forest management. The issues involved in the relevant processes vary according to national circumstances, but in developing countries may include land tenure, property rights, access to natural resources, and in some countries, the resettlement of communities (Box 17). Proper resolution of such related issues is a prerequisite for the effective implementation of forest-based adaptation measures.

Box 17: Resettlement affects adaptive capacity

A study of the resettlement of Adigoshu, Globel, Idris and Menakeya communities to the fringes of Kafta-Sheraro Forest Reserve in Ethiopia investigated the ways in which the increased population impacted the management objectives of the reserve. Traditional uses by the local population involve 23 forest plant species, 14 of which are harvested as livestock fodder and 10 for timber.

Key observations from the study were:
- The influx of the resettled population resulted in a rapid increase in forest resource exploitation and destruction, including increased poaching of large mammalian wildlife species.

- Escalating demand for grazing land among other needs brings with it higher risks of conflict, food shortages, habitat destruction and susceptibility to climate change impacts.
- Overall, illegal occupation, overgrazing, poaching, bush fires, and woodfuel and timber harvesting posed increasing threats to forest conservation.

These findings highlight the risks inherent in unplanned internal displacement of populations for climate change adaptation measures, and call for an integrated people and environment approach for future policy and planning to enable communities to increase forest stocks while securing livelihoods.

Source: adapted from Eniang, Mengistu and Yidego, 2008.

The final, related challenge for developed and developing countries alike is the need for coordination among institutions that are involved in the design and implementation of adaptation or development policies. Policies aimed at other land-based sectors such as agriculture and transportation may impact forests by making alternative uses of forest lands more financially attractive. Proper communication and planning among sectors is therefore necessary to enhance the effectiveness of adaptation and mitigation efforts with respect to their impact on both international objectives and the local needs of the population.

Tools for policy development

A number of approaches have been proposed for developing adaptation plans and policies. However, uncertainties in projections of future climate and the complexity of interactions between forests and climate preclude a deterministic approach to adaptation. In order to be effective, policies should be flexible and encourage experimentation. As an example, CIFOR has proposed the Adaptive Collaborative Management process for moving forward with adaptive management decisions, while taking into account both the uncertainties inherent in the adaptation process and the societal dimension of decision-making (CIFOR, 2008a). By definition, adaptive management involves trial and error, and is designed to learn from the occasional failures. As a corollary to this approach, policies that punish failures could be counterproductive in the design of adaptation measures.

In broader terms, conceptual frameworks are needed for scoping out climate change-related issues and determining adaptation objectives. The Adaptation Policy Framework (APF) of the United Nations Development Programme (UNDP) is an example of such a conceptual framework through which users can clarify their own priority issues and implement adaptation strategies, policies and measures from the local to the national levels. The APF is based on four broad principles:

- Adaptation to short-term climate variability and extreme events is used as a basis for reducing vulnerability to longer-term climate change.
- Adaptation policy and measures are assessed in the context of development.
- Adaptation occurs at different levels in society, including the local level.
- Both the strategy and the process by which adaptation is implemented are equally important.

The APF also links climate change adaptation to sustainable development and global environmental issues, and can be used to add adaptation to other types of projects. It progresses along five steps from the scoping of the project to monitoring and evaluation of actions.

One of the steps included in all adaptation frameworks is the assessment of climate change vulnerability. Over the past few years, the Tropical Forest and Climate Change Adaptation Project (TroFCCA) of CIFOR and the Center for Investigation and Teaching of Tropical Agronomy (CATIE) has been developing and applying an assessment methodology that could be used within a framework such as the APF (see Box 18). The TroFCCA framework is broad so that it can serve as a guide for discussion during its application to specific cases. It has been applied by TroFCCA to a number of communities and projects in the tropics around the world.

In short, frameworks and methodologies exist for systematically assessing and developing adaptation policies and plans for action, for doing so at local to national scales, and for linking such plans and policies with other development policies and programmes. The financial resources for adaptation are not unlimited, and efficiency will build confidence among donor and recipient communities alike, promoting further investments and adaptation measures.

Monitoring will be critical at all scales in efforts to address climate change adaptation. In forestry, remote sensing is increasingly proposed as a means of filling some of the monitoring gaps, and methods are being actively refined, especially as they relate to changes in forest cover properties (e.g. Hansen, Stehman and Potapov, 2010). Field inventories will nevertheless always be needed to assess carbon values and establish land-use change.

The way forward

It is impossible to prescribe a proper mechanism for developing forest-based adaptation policies, given the variability in local human circumstances and their interactions with forests. However, past experience highlights points around which consensus exists.

At the local level, policy-makers can benefit from the contribution of local populations to the design of adaptation measures through their intimate knowledge of the biogeography of their landscapes, and of their local social capacities. In developed and developing countries

The TroFCCA's climate change vulnerability assessment framework emphasises the role of ecosystem services for society through its three main principles: (P1) the vulnerability of ecosystem services; (P2) the vulnerability of the human system to the loss of ecosystem services; and (P3) the adaptive capacity of the system as a whole.

The first principle (P1) deals with the exposure and sensitivity of ecosystem services to climate change or variability and other threats, and with ecosystem adaptive capacity. The second principle (P2) deals with the human system (e.g. villages, communities and provinces), its dependence on ecosystem services such as clean water, and its capacity to adapt, for example, through substitutes for lost ecosystem services. The third principle (P3) considers the adaptive capacity of the system as a whole and refers to the capacity of the human systems to reduce the loss of ecosystem services through changes in practices and implementation of adaptation measures.

Source: adapted from Locatelli *et al.* (2008)

Figure A: Principles of TroFCCA's climate change vulnerability assessment framework

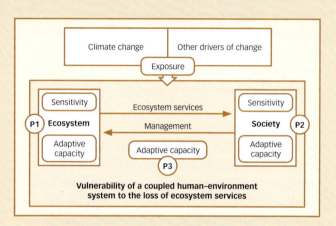

alike, local governments may be essential players in the mainstreaming of forest-based climate change adaptation into policies, laws and regulations. At the international level, adaptation to climate change must be supported distinctly from mitigation, although synergies must be sought wherever possible. For example, adaptation could be integrated across the full range of development-related assistance through measures such as mandatory climate risk assessments for projects financed with bilateral or multilateral support.

More importantly, however, there has been a notable shift in UNFCCC decisions towards recognition of adaptation as being equal in importance to mitigation, finance and technology, largely in response to three factors. The first is that impacts of climate change are being felt faster and more strongly than anticipated. The second is that containing future climate change within a 2°C limit appears increasingly difficult to achieve. Finally, and crucially, there is recognition that adaptation is no longer solely a local or national issue, but that lack of adaptation may have impacts across national boundaries. As stated by Burton (2008): "Adaptation has to be understood as a strategic and security issue that transcends national boundaries", a statement that applies to developed and developing countries alike. The local nature of forests and forest dependent communities may appear to limit the international implications of non-adaptation. However,

resilient and productive ecosystems enhance the stability of communities, which in turn decreases the pressure for internal and cross-border migration. Preparing national adaptation plans in consultation with nearby countries, increasing financial flows to adaptation at the local and national levels, and rethinking development goals and objectives through the analysis of climate change impacts on local economies and populations are measures proposed by Burton (2008) to enhance the effectiveness of adaptation.

The current draft AWG-LCA text calls for the establishment of "regional centres or platforms" to support country activities in climate change adaptation in all sectors. The forestry sector has extensive experience in regional cooperation and has well developed technical networks at regional and subregional levels. Strengthening existing institutions and networks before establishing new ones is key in order to avoid duplication of efforts, and ensure the sound use of resources and coherence with other policies.

These networks could be mobilized and supplemented, as necessary, by other regional programmes to support adaptation needs. Forestry networks or capacity support mechanisms could link with regional centres or platforms eventually established under UNFCCC, helping avoid duplication of effort.

There are strong synergies in the forestry sector between adaptation and mitigation. Support for mitigation activities, could, under many circumstances, simultaneously support adaptation efforts, and vice versa. Countries' climate change strategies should seek to capture these synergies. With the world rapidly changing around us, there is neither time nor resources to waste in the race to adapt.

Summary and conclusions

The political visibility of forests is at an all-time high. The forestry sector can capitalize on this to help attract political and financial support for activities in climate change adaptation and mitigation. It is crucial that climate change resources, including funds for REDD+, LULUCF and adaptation are used to build the foundation for SFM, which can contribute to climate change adaptation and mitigation, as well as the continued delivery of the full range of goods and ecosystem services over the long term. It will be essential to ensure that the flow of funds to developing countries is commensurate with their absorptive capacity, and building capacities and readiness activities should be a part of these efforts.

Negotiations under the UNFCCC have helped raise the profile of forests and forests' contribution to offsetting GHG emissions. Although forest management activities have a high potential to help developed countries meet their commitments under the Kyoto Protocol, there is a potentially greater role for developing countries under new activities such as REDD+. REDD+ is designed not only to enable developing countries to contribute to a reduction in emissions under future arrangements to the UNFCCC, but also to strengthen SFM at local and national levels. Consensus has formed around the concept of REDD+ and pilot activities are now underway; however, outstanding issues on adaptation, CDM, LULUCF, REDD+

methodologies and harvested wood products are still under discussion in the negotiations.

REDD+ has attracted many interest groups, leading to increasingly complex demands. Nevertheless, the economic, social and environmental sustainability of REDD and REDD+ hinges on a number of factors, including the issuance of forest carbon rights and the sharing of benefits from REDD-related activities. Different legal approaches exist to guarantee forest carbon tenure, as shown in the examples presented in this chapter. These include transferring rights directly to the forest owner, selling carbon rights but not forest rights, managing forest carbon as a public asset and issuing private contracts.

All countries are faced with the challenges of addressing vulnerabilities to and impacts of climate change on their forests and tree resources and on forest-dependent people. Adopting an adaptive management approach is one way to facilitate countries' efforts in climate change adaptation. A great deal of adaptation and mitigation can be achieved through full implementation of existing forest policies, strategies and legislation, and the application of best practices in forest management. This includes incorporating climate change into existing national forest programmes, which serve as the overarching policy framework for SFM. This is likely to require some adjustments at policy and field level, and additional investments.

Climate change clearly poses a new set of challenges for the forestry sector, but at the same time creates opportunities. International efforts over the past two decades to build a common understanding, a policy framework and a range of tools for sustainable forest management provide a sound basis for policy-makers and forest managers to address climate change effectively.

4 | The local value of forests

The theme 'Forests for People' will guide discussion and debate throughout the International Year of Forests during 2011. The theme aims to encompass the role of people in the management, conservation and sustainable development of the world's forests. A number of subjects relate to this theme including: traditional forest-related knowledge; community-based forest management (CBFM); and small and medium forest enterprises (SMFEs). This chapter explores these subjects in anticipation of debates during the Ninth Session of the UN Forum on Forests and other global activities that will be held in celebration of the International Year of Forests.

The chapter discusses the local value of forests through four interlinked sections. The first presents a brief review of some of the ways in which traditional knowledge (TK) contributes to local livelihoods and traditional forest-related practices. The second provides an update on CBFM and SMFEs, as well as the integral part played by non-wood forest products (NWFPs) in both. In contrast to the cash values of forests highlighted by the example of SMFEs that market NWFPs, the third section takes as its special focus "the non-cash values of forests". The final section provides an overview of future needs and policy recommendations to protect and strengthen the local values of forests highlighted in these three topics. Taken together, the chapter sections provide a 'thought starter' to explore the theme of local-level forest and forestry issues, and highlight the importance of recognizing the complexity of 'local value' in all approaches to development.

Traditional knowledge

Traditional knowledge is a term that combines the knowledge, innovations and practices of indigenous peoples and local communities (Box 19). It provides the basis for forest livelihoods, and contributes to traditional cultural and economic practices, subsistence use and local trade, forest management practices and the development of commercial products. Traditional forest-related knowledge falls under the larger umbrella of traditional knowledge, and includes knowledge associated with the use and management of forest species, and the broader understanding and management of forest ecosystems. This is a brief review of some of the ways in which traditional knowledge is used, first commercially and then as part of traditional management practices, and its links to biological and cultural diversity. The section concludes with an overview of current policy processes that seek to protect and respect the role of traditional knowledge.

Box 19: What is traditional knowledge?

"Traditional knowledge refers to the knowledge, innovation and practices of indigenous and local communities around the world. Developed from experience gained over the centuries and adapted to local culture and environment, traditional knowledge is transmitted orally from generation to generation. It tends to be collectively owned and takes the form of stories, songs, folklore, proverbs, cultural values, beliefs, rituals, community laws, local language, and agricultural practices, including the development of plant species and animal breeds. Traditional knowledge is mainly of a practical nature, particularly in such fields as agriculture, fisheries, health, horticulture, and forestry."

Source: The Convention on Biological Diversity Traditional Knowledge Information Portal (www.cbd.int/tk)

The use of traditional knowledge

Historically, traditional knowledge has played a central role in the development of commercial products, including those from the pharmaceutical, seed, herbal medicine, cosmetic and horticultural industries. In some industries, the role of traditional knowledge in research and development programmes has declined in recent decades, but in others it remains strong; in all sectors, products derived from traditional knowledge continue to be marketed (Laird and Wynberg, 2008; Petersen and Kuhn, 2007).

Despite the economic downturn, sales continue to grow around the world of herbal medicines, nutraceutical, functional food and beverage, personal care and cosmetic products with a traditional knowledge component (Gruenwald, 2008; Cavaliere et al., 2010). Virtually all herbal products derive from traditional knowledge, including perennial top sellers such as saw palmetto, milk thistle, gingko, goji, ginseng, devil's claw, acai, elderberry and echinacea. In 2008 in the United States of America alone, goji and echinacea generated revenues of more than US$170 million and US$120 million, respectively (Moloughney, 2009). Many top-selling products are derived from forests, and the collection and trade of raw materials continues to significantly affect forest economies.

Valuable forest tree species include yohimbe and pygeum in Africa, muira puama and pau d'arco in South America. The commercial use of these and other forest species grew directly from traditional forest-related knowledge. Indeed, 'ethnic botanicals' and 'exotic ingredients' with traditional uses are increasingly in demand in Europe and North America, driving companies to seek out herbal remedies and flavours based on traditional knowledge (Gruenwald, 2010). Long histories of traditional use also benefit products and ingredients 'new' to the market, which tend to receive more rapid regulatory approval given their proven safety over generations of use (Gruenwald, 2010).

Recent developments in science and technology provide new opportunities to research and explore applications of traditional knowledge within industries such as healthcare, agriculture and biotechnology. Traditional knowledge is increasingly consulted as part of efforts to address broader challenges such as climate change adaptation, water management, and sustainable agricultural and forest management. For example, traditional knowledge of fire management has been used to reduce greenhouse gas emissions in Western Arnhem Land, Australia (Galloway McLean, 2009). The IPCC identified traditional and local knowledge as important missing elements in its previous assessments, and these will form a focus of work for its next scientific assessment reports.

Most importantly, traditional knowledge contributes to the lives of its holders. For example, traditional medicine provides primary healthcare for much of the world's population. It is estimated that in some countries in Africa and Asia at least 80 percent of the population depend upon traditional medicine for their primary healthcare (World Health Organization, 2008). Traditional forest management, including the manipulation of forests to favour desirable species and maximize the range of products and services provided, has sustained communities in complex and often inhospitable environments for thousands of years (e.g. Gómez-Pompa, 1991; Posey and Balée, 1989; Padoch and De Jong, 1992). These indigenous silvicultural systems are usually low input yet effective, the product of hundreds of years of trial and error, and they employ a range of techniques in the same way that foresters use selective thinning, weeding and enrichment planting (Peters, 2000).

Traditional forest management has shaped the structure and composition of forests around the world, and in many cases has enhanced biodiversity beyond "that of so-called pristine conditions with no human presence" (Balée, 1994). These systems can yield important lessons for forest managers, loggers, migrant farmers, conservationists and others seeking to understand complex, biologically diverse ecosystems, and the relationships between people and their environment. FAO's National Forest Programme Facility (NFP Facility) has been working to highlight the importance of traditional knowledge and integrate it into national forest programmes (Box 20).

Traditional management of forested environments affects the composition of flora and fauna, and the biological diversity of these areas. Awareness of the link between cultural practices and biological diversity has grown over the last few decades into a widespread acceptance of the concept of 'biocultural diversity' (Box 21). This concept was the result of numerous local-level studies, as well as broader analyses that identified correlations worldwide between linguistic, ethnic and biological diversity (Maffi, 2005).

Until recently cultural and biological diversity were seen as separate disciplines and were the subjects of

enterprises play an important part in the harvesting, processing, transport and marketing of wood and non-wood products. As discussed below, the establishment of CBFM often stimulates SMFEs.

Some key drivers for community-based forest management

Many forms of CBFM exist, responding to particular political, social, economic and institutional contexts. In some countries CBFM arrangements have grown out of the need for governments to cut the costs of protecting forest resources. International and local NGOs have promoted CBFM widely in rural development projects.

The demand for more efficiency in service delivery and more accountability in the way governments manage natural resources, coupled with global trends towards economic liberalization and decentralization, have led to significant policy shifts in a number of countries. Several countries have developed enabling policy frameworks, which support community rights and participatory initiatives, and have thereby given a greater incentive for better management and protection of forest resources.

Decentralization

A number of governments have recently launched public sector reform programmes that divest central government departments, including forestry, of some authority. Forestry administrations have been decentralized, in a bid to increase efficiency and accountability in service delivery. Some governments have abandoned the more protectionist approach to forest management, and have shifted responsibility for forest use and management to lower-level local government, traditional institutions and local communities.

However, decentralization often happens on a piecemeal basis. Many times, central government retains substantial control, and imposes conditions for the local management of forest resources. There is limited devolution of power, rights and finance to local government and communities. Often the responsibility of traditional cultural institutions is poorly outlined in guiding instruments, creating a clash of mandates. All these factors stifle the realization of the full potential of CBFM.

Enabling policy frameworks

Changes in the political landscape at the country level may lead to policy and institutional reforms in forest governance systems to support decentralized forest management. However, forest tenure – so important for ensuring equity and rights for forest dependent communities – has rarely so far been fully reformed.

More frequently, a partial modification is seen. For instance in Nepal, the current basis of community forestry was formalized under the Forest Act, 1993. Forests remain formally government-owned but permanent use rights are allocated to communities, subject to agreements over management arrangements. Under the community forestry programme approximately 30 percent of total national forest has been handed over to forest user groups for management and utilization (FAO, 2011). This has produced significant gains to the local communities (Box 22).

In Liberia, the new forest law of 2006 and the law on communities' rights (currently undergoing the approval process) grant grassroots communities the possibility of owning forests and participating in their management through Community Forestry

---

Box 22: Importance of an enabling policy framework in achieving the objectives of tenure reform

One of the by-products of forest tenure reform has been the substantial increase in trees on private farm land in Nepal (in addition to improvements in community forests). In 1987, regulations that were intended to conserve trees on private land, were approved and required farmers to obtain permits to harvest and/or transport trees from their private land. These regulations had the perverse effect of acting as a disincentive for private tree planting or protection. In fact, the announcement of the regulations before they came into effect encouraged much tree cutting while it still remained acceptable. When these regulations

were removed to create a more enabling regulatory framework for community forestry, farmers responded by allowing naturally occurring tree seedlings to survive and by planting commercially desirable seedlings. Many parts of the middle hill region in Nepal are now covered by a mosaic of community forests and trees on private land. The increase in commercial timber from communal and private lands has spawned a network of private sawmills processing the timber purchased from forest user groups and private farmers.

Adapted from FAO, 2011

Development Committees (CFDC). The Committees will be mandated to negotiate with logging companies. Communities are entitled to 30 percent of the income generated by the lease of forests under license, and loggers will also have to pay US$1/m³ directly to the relevant community (Bodian, 2009).

Forest tenure studies reviewed by FAO (2011), emphasize that while security of tenure may be necessary to achieve sustainable forest management and improved livelihoods, it is not in itself sufficient. Other factors, including better governance and appropriate regulatory frameworks, are equally critical.

National poverty reduction agendas

A number of developing countries have in place national development plans and strategies with poverty reduction as the overarching objective, as part of Poverty Reduction Strategy Processes initiated by the World Bank. Some countries – including Bhutan, the Gambia, Turkey and Uganda among others – have identified forestry as one of the key drivers of socio-economic growth, and have integrated forest management into the national poverty reduction strategies. Key national forest policy and planning instruments in these countries recognize a diversity of stakeholders in the forest sector, and have moved towards a more people-centred approach and adopted CBFM as one of the major options for stimulating development in rural areas.

Emerging grassroots and global networks

In recent years, there has been an increased level of organization of local forest dependent communities into groups, associations, alliances and federations. In many countries, community forest user groups have progressively transformed into associations and forest user cooperatives. These associations have further created alliances at regional level and international federations. Their goal has been to address the powerlessness and low bargaining power which makes it difficult to use forests productively.

With facilitation of national, regional and international NGOs, and initiatives such as the Growing Forest Partnership (GFP), these associations have created stronger regional chapters and are active internationally. For example, the International Alliance for Indigenous and Tribal Peoples of Tropical Forests (IAITPTF) and the Global Alliance for Community Forests (GACF), in partnership with the International Family Forest Alliance (IFFA) have consistently demanded better community forest rights in international fora. They are also mobilizing local people's efforts to engage in commercial enterprise development and marketing, an area that will take CBFM to another level.

Impact of community-based forest management on local communities

A number of benefits from CBFM can be seen over the long term. These include improved forest conservation and management benefits, growth of community institutions and social capital, and contributions to poverty reduction.

Conservation benefits may take a long while to be realized. In the case of Nepal, CBFM took a long time to transform the rehabilitated landscapes (FAO, 2011). In the Gambia, decentralization has led to the re-establishment of customary forest resource management laws, which have enabled the protection of forest species. In the Bonga forest in Ethiopia, illegal timber-harvesting, firewood marketing and charcoal production have been contained over the years through regulated access and forest development work by the communities (Farm Africa, 2002). Studies in the United Republic of Tanzania (e.g. Kajembe, Nduwamungu and Luoga, 2005) show a remarkable increase in the density of saplings and trees following the launch of community-based management regimes. In India, studies also indicate an increase in productivity and diversity of vegetation following the introduction of CBFM (Prasad, 1999).

For CBFM to play a significant role in poverty reduction, several factors need to be favourable, including the policy context, the nature and diversity of forestry products accessible to them, community management capacity and the availability of infrastructure to support production, processing and marketing. In countries where CBFM has been developing for a long time – for instance the Gambia, India, Nepal and the United Republic of Tanzania – tangible benefits are being realized. Over time, as forests become more productive, SMFEs begin to emerge in the form of small saw mills, carpentry and joinery workshops, craft making, honey processing and herbal medicine processing. This has created employment for women and young men and allowed poor households to generate additional cash income.

Small and medium forest enterprise development

Small and medium forest enterprises consist of individual, household, and community entrepreneurs as well as associations of actors along the supply chain. For these enterprises, forests and trees are important sources of cash income and employment.

There are numerous examples of successful SMFEs producing timber and processed timber products. In the Petén, Guatemala, a multidonor funded project assisted the local community enterprise FORESCOM (Empresa Comunitaria de Servicios del Bosque) to generate a 48 percent increase in revenue after one year. The purpose of the project, which was overseen by the ITTO, was to promote the commercialization of lesser-known species in national and international markets and to achieve certification of these products. FORESCOM's revenue increased largely because of improved outreach and marketing internationally, and resulted in its products entering Hong Kong SAR, the Netherlands and the United States of America. The 11 communities working with FORESCOM were able to improve their social and economic conditions while contributing to the conservation of tropical forests in the area.

SMFEs are also important suppliers of many NWFPs such as rattan and bamboo, medicinal plants, forest insects, fruits, nuts and game meat. These products are sold in raw, semi-processed and processed forms. The provision of environmental services, such as recreation, is another area in which SMFEs are gradually becoming more

involved. In fact, SMFEs often make up 80–90 percent of enterprise numbers and more than 50 percent of forest-related jobs (MacQueen, 2008).

Sustainable SMFEs can bring positive economic, social and environmental impacts, and make a significant contribution to economic development. A number of local case studies in Latin America, Asia and Africa (see Box 23) show the major contribution of cooperatives and SMFEs to economic development.

Small-scale enterprises have certain micro-economic characteristics that are known to generate a 'multiplier effect' of increased economic benefits in rural economies, resulting in higher incomes, higher consumption and improved terms of trade (Elson, 2010). The UK Department for International Development-funded Livelihoods and Forestry Programme (LFP) in Nepal (Livelihoods and Forestry Programme, 2009) suggested this effect[24] in the country was approximately 10:1, while analyses in other locations estimate this multiplier effect to be as high as 20:1 (GEF, 2009). It is estimated, albeit roughly, that forest communities produce US$75 billion to 100 billion per year in goods and services (Elson, 2010).

Rural economic growth involving local people brings about many consequent social improvements. Additional income is commonly invested in education and health

Box 23: Importance of apiculture in Cameroon

Apiculture products include honey (*Apis mellifera*), wax and propolis, all of which are NWFPs. Apiculture products have many medicinal and cosmetic uses and are traded at the local, national and international levels, making them an important contribution for livelihoods in both rural and urban areas in Cameroon.

Despite incomplete data about the sector, it is estimated that 3.3 million litres of honey are produced in Cameroon annually, valued at around 2 000 million FCFA (about US$3.7 million). Approximately 10 percent is consumed by the beekeepers. With an estimated value of 530 million Central African CFA Francs (FCFA), about 235 tonnes of wax are produced annually,

primarily for regional export. Other apiculture products add about 1.5 million FCFA to total revenues from the sector annually. It is estimated that there were at least 20 000 beekeepers in Cameroon in 2009. More than 8 600 beekeepers were known to be members of 639 groups (Common Initiative Groups, cooperatives or NGOs) in 2008. In the northwest of the country, a major apiculture dependent region, beekeeping is an important secondary source of income, contributing from 10 percent to 70 percent of total annual income (average of 30 percent), with over 80 percent of beekeepers deriving 30–60 percent of their annual cash income from apiculture.
Source: CIFOR, 2010

---

[24] One dollar introduced into a system (e.g. a rural village) should generate much more than a dollar in economic benefits, in terms of cash and jobs created. The dollar changes hands a few times before it is eventually spent outside the community. In the case of the LFP project in Nepal, if one accounts for the money spent by the donor (an upfront cash injection into the community), and the rise in average and median incomes, the multiplier effect is at least a factor of ten. The nature of the stimulus is more important than the amount. For instance, natural resource extraction generates very few multiplier effects at source but agricultural extension or community-based forestry tends to raise skill levels, and creates more value addition, higher retention of surplus and greater multiplier effects (Elson, 2010).

Key factors for an enabling environment

National and local institutions that recognize the value of forest products including NWFPs for resource dependent people, as well as the importance of local people's roles in sustainable resource management;

National and local policies, rules and regulations that level the playing field for the development of enterprises of all sizes (such as tax incentives), and that provide additional support mechanisms such as tailored services provision and basic commercial infrastructure (roads, market infrastructure, etc.);

Access to affordable (micro) finance and promising markets through accurate information and innovative communication technologies;

Access/tenure rights should be clearly spelled out and allow for the sustainable extraction of forest products for commercial purposes.

Key factors for sustainability

Capacity development at the local level, with the facilitation of private and/or public service providers, in key areas including: formation of producer associations, business planning, marketing, basic finance principles, value adding, natural resource management planning and sustainable harvesting techniques, domestication, etc.

Added value to the products, whether through:
- linking producers, their cooperatives, and associations along the supply chain to strengthen market access and market information;
- investment into research and development by private and public sectors, to expand product uses in both raw and processed forms;
- exploration of new opportunities in labelling (fair trade, organic, etc.), certification and other niche markets.

---

services. Many rural people who develop enterprises may also eventually use surplus income to transition from agriculturalists to food purchasers, allowing more time to participate in local social and political activities. Communities that grow economically tend to be more active in political decision-making (Elson, 2010).

Widespread evidence demonstrates that private property holders, including those with communally-held property rights, can and do protect public goods if the appropriate incentive structure is in place (Elson, 2010). Rural communities are estimated to own, or administrate under license, no less than one quarter of forests in developing countries, and annually invest US$2.6 billion globally in conservation, an amount that surpasses public sector funding and all forms of international conservation expenditure combined (Scherr, White and Kaimowitz, 2003).

Creating an enabling environment for and encouraging investments in SMFEs

Enabling, maintaining and improving forest-based economic initiatives at the local-level requires a combination of several elements. An enabling environment consists of supportive policies, access to finance, tailored services and markets, and secure forest access and tenure – all crucial for the initial steps in local forest enterprise development (Box 24). Actions

to add further value will in many cases increase income, while capacity development improves the sustainability of the enterprises (Box 25).

Similar to the preconditions for community-based forest management, SMFEs require stable policy frameworks, coordination in decision-making among stakeholders, and access to land and tenure rights. However, SMFEs also require continued access to finance and markets, up-to-date technology and means by which to improve the quality of their products in order to be successful. Moreover, as SMFEs increasingly depend on the production of NWFPs as the source of their products, improved NWFP management, appropriate policies and adequate legislation are required to ensure these enterprises continue to have a sound resource base.

Non-wood forest product law and policy[25]

As noted earlier, non-wood forest products play a critical role in community forestry and SMFEs. Non-wood forest products are used as medicines, foods, spices and for a multitude of other purposes. They provide critical subsistence and trade goods for forest and other communities, and in many areas are the main source of cash to pay school fees, buy medicines, purchase equipment and supplies, and to buy food that cannot

---

[25] This section is drawn from Laird, McLain and Wynberg, 2010.

Between 1995 and 2005, various government and NGO projects in Burkina Faso targeted NWFP development. Some impact was achieved, but the sum of these initiatives was insufficient to highlight the real potential of the NWFP sector as vital to food security and rural incomes. The lack of recognition was probably the result of poor analysis of demand, and limited data on the economic value of NWFPs and SMFEs. There was also poor coordination between organizations. Moreover, the 1997 Code Forestier contained no specific clauses relating to NWFP development although it upheld the rights of indigenous communities to manage and use their traditional resources, including NWFPs.

After a workshop in 2004 hosted by the NGO TREE AID, Burkina Faso's Ministry of Environment (MECV) accepted an invitation by FAO and TREE AID to work in partnership to pilot the FAO Market Analysis and Development (MA&D) approach through a project entitled 'Promoting micro and small community-based enterprises of non-wood forest products (2005–2006)'. As a result, in 2007 the government asked FAO to support the elaboration of a national strategy on the promotion and valorization of NWFPs.

Using local solutions, policies were amended to suit conditions in the area, build capacity and develop other support mechanisms. In this case study, the most significant demonstration of national importance for this sector was the creation by the government, in 2008, of the Agence de Promotion des Produits Forestiers Non Ligneux (APFNL). The APFNL is now a national institution under the Ministry of Environment, concerned with the support, coordination and monitoring of operations and marketing of NWFPs. It pilots, implements and monitors policies and strategies to promote NWFPs in collaboration with all other actors in the field, and links the actors in the NWFP distribution chain. APFNL has attracted the interest of various international donors and NWFP development has become a priority for government to diversify rural livelihoods and generate economic growth. The recently approved 'Projet d'Amélioration de la Gestion et de l'Exploitation Durable des PFNL' (funded by the Government of Luxemburg through FAO and implemented by the APFNL) includes support for techniques to improve production and add value, and for the establishment of NWFP-specific producer organizations.

be grown. However, throughout the world NWFPs have been both overlooked and poorly regulated by governments. Inappropriate policies have not only led to overexploitation of species in the wild, but have reduced benefits for producers and generated new forms of inequity.

In part, problems with NWFP law and policy result from a narrowing of the meaning of 'forest products' over the past century to the point where it primarily only includes timber and wood fibres harvested on an industrial scale for use in the manufacture of lumber, paper, cardboard and particle board. This has occurred even in regions where NWFPs are far more valuable than so-called 'forest products'. The resulting legal and policy frameworks ignore the majority of NWFPs present in forests.

Existing NWFP legislation and policies are usually a complex and confusing mix of measures developed over time, with poor coherence or coordination. They rarely resemble an overall policy framework. Many policy instruments have been enacted as ad hoc responses to a crisis (e.g. perceived overexploitation of a species) or an overly optimistic view of potential tax revenue should informal activities be made more formal. Rarely has

regulatory activity followed from a careful and systematic assessment of the range of opportunities and threats associated with species, ecosystems and livelihoods, and a strategic approach to regulating the NWFP sector as a whole is uncommon.

This situation remains unchanged in many countries today, but in some a shift began to occur in the late 1980s as scientists, natural resource managers and policy-makers increasingly recognized the non-wood values of forests, including the socio-economic and cultural importance of NWFPs. This shift resulted from a range of factors, including a change in the focus of some conservation agencies away from a purely protectionist approach to one that also incorporates sustainable use, and views equity and social justice as integral to conservation. Originally articulated by the Brundtland Commission in 1987, this view culminated in the various agreements that emerged from the 1992 United Nations Conference on Environment and Development in Rio de Janeiro, including the legally binding CBD. Conservation and development groups experimented with NWFP-based projects as a means of supporting ecologically benign and socially just income-generating activities. The commercial use of a handful of NWFPs was promoted as a way of

In most countries, forestry laws historically focused almost exclusively on timber resources and paid limited or no attention to NWFPs. Moreover, the subsistence and commercial value of NWFPs was disregarded when timber management plans were designed and logging operations undertaken. In recent decades, however, NWFPs have been incorporated into forest laws as a response to changing international policy trends. In many cases, this resulted from the direct pressure of international agencies, such as large conservation organizations and finance institutions to diversify forest management and make it more sustainable. As a result, in the 1980s and 1990s, many countries integrated a wider range of objectives into forest policies, including forest health and biodiversity conservation, ecosystem functions and long-term sustainability, as well as broader economic values such as tourism, recreation and NWFPs.

However, initial efforts to address NWFPs in these new forest laws were poorly formulated and rarely implemented. The scope and definition of the products covered remained unclear, and few specific actions were stipulated. When actions were prescribed, they usually focused on permits, quotas (often set arbitrarily), management plans and royalties or taxes – an approach lifted directly from the timber sector, and one that proved entirely inappropriate for the diverse, complex and often less lucrative NWFP sector.

More usefully, some forest laws of this time included NWFPs in timber norms, requiring their consideration in management plans and logging operations in order to minimize negative impacts on locally valuable products. In some countries, the logging of high-value NWFP species for timber has proved their greatest threat. In Brazil in recent years, national and state governments have passed laws prohibiting the logging of high-value NWFP species, and in Bolivia, prohibitions on felling Brazil nut trees were established in 2004 as part of a decree addressing property conflicts, but the track record for implementing such policies is often poor.

In the past 10–15 years, a number of countries have begun to fine-tune well-intentioned forest policies passed in the 1990s to reflect the socio-economic, ecological and cultural realities of NWFP use. This has resulted in a number of specific improvements to the ways in which these products are regulated, including re-thinking the use of costly and complex inventories and management plans for NWFPs, and revising quota and permitting systems. There is still a long way to go, and NWFPs continue to have low priority in most forestry departments and curricula, but the trend in several countries is towards greater understanding and better-elaborated regulatory frameworks for these products.

Source: Laird, McLain and Wynberg, 2010

---

helping people live well with minimal damage to the environment.

As a result of these trends, small-scale producers and NWFPs have emerged from 'invisibility' in recent decades. Unfortunately, with a few exceptions, the NWFP policies that resulted were often opportunistic and inadequate resources were allocated for oversight and implementation. Many were tagged onto timber-centric forest laws. Regulations rarely followed from careful analysis of the complex factors involved in NWFP management, use and trade, or from consultations with producers, who are often on the political and economic margins. In many cases policy interventions also criminalized NWFP extraction, further marginalizing harvesters, and customary law and local institutions better suited to regulating many species were often undermined by efforts to establish statutory control over NWFPs.

A number of laws and policies directly address NWFPs, often to conserve or sustainably manage resources, and in some cases to improve rural livelihoods or promote broader economic growth in a region (Box 26). These

measures tend to focus on species in commercial trade, or form part of national efforts to protect endangered or indigenous species or regulate international trade under the Convention on International Trade in Endangered Species of Wild Fauna and Flora (CITES). The majority of measures directly addressing NWFPs are found in natural resource law, in particular forest laws. However, a range of other measures explicitly regulate aspects of NWFP trade and use, including those governing quality control, safety and efficacy standards, transportation, taxation and trade.

Policies and laws that indirectly impact non-wood forest products

In addition to laws that explicitly address NWFPs, there are a myriad of measures that do not mention the term and yet affect their use, management and trade as much as, or more than, those that do. The high impact of these measures is largely because forest management and livelihoods involve a complex and interconnected suite of activities, and regulating one aspect has immediate knock-on effects on others. Laws and policies with an indirect impact on NWFPs include agricultural policies, land tenure and resource rights, intellectual property, land management planning and labour law. In addition, a range of natural resource laws have a significant impact on NWFPs, including the forest laws discussed above, mining and protected area and conservation laws that discourage or forbid NWFP harvesting.

The important role of customary law

Where land tenure and resource rights are secure, customary laws are still strong, and local capacity exists to manage the resource base and deal with commercial pressures, customary laws often provide a more nuanced approach to regulation of NWFP harvest and trade than statutory laws. This is because customary laws integrate unique local cultural, ecological and economic conditions in ways that better suit this diverse and broad category of products. In cases where customary law has broken down to a significant degree, however, or outside commercial pressure has intensified well beyond the carrying capacity of traditional institutions, governments can offer important and necessary complementary levels of regulation, something often requested by local groups. But these interventions should be crafted to include local-level institutions and management systems, where these are effective (Wynberg and Laird, 2007).

Non-cash values of forests

The commercial value of forests is well recognized both in timber terms and, in a more minor way, in terms of NWFPs which are sold in great quantities all over the world. This section looks at a third, and equally vital, value for forests: the non-cash value of forests for local people. The focus here is not on religious or cultural values but on the daily support provided by forests to households living in or near forests. Researchers are informally aware of the importance of non-cash forest value (consumption value), but it is not as yet recorded in government statistics, and so remains invisible, with its value set effectively at zero.

Income in typical household budget surveys and living standards surveys, conducted according to models established originally by the World Bank or the International Labour Organization, includes:
- cash income from employment;
- cash income from sales of farm crops;
- cash income from sales of wood and non-wood forest products; and
- 'non-cash' income from household consumption of farm crops.

However, it does not factor in 'non-cash' (consumption) income from forests. This income may be literally gathered and consumed, in the case of forest fruits, nuts, vegetables, meat and medicinals, but consumption also refers to the use of wood and non-wood products in the household, such as fuelwood. As noted in Chapter 1, findings from FRA 2010 show that fuelwood data were often difficult to collect, but made up to more than 70 percent of wood removals in the Asia and the Pacific and 90 percent in Africa.

If the total annual income of a developing country rural household is calculated, factoring in not only cash income but also non-cash income, it immediately becomes apparent that this officially completely invisible income source is actually extremely important in many cases.

Table 42 shows that in Tenkodogo, a Sahelian farming village about three hours from Ouagadougou, non-cash income makes a larger contribution annually to total income than does cash income. For wealthy and average men non-cash income contributes 58 percent of total income while for the poorest category – poor women – non-cash income contributes over two-thirds of total income at 68 percent.

Forest income (cash and non-cash) averages 44 percent of total income, and it is clear for each of the wealth and gender categories that the value of the non-cash contribution of forests to household income is a great deal higher than the value of cash income from forests. The same kinds of findings are now being recorded in other parts of the world, such as Africa and Asia where 60–70 percent of inhabitants still live in rural areas.

Implications for the cash value of non-wood forest products

We have known for many years (Byron and Arnold, 1997; Angelsen and Wunder, 2003) that the *cash* contribution of forest products to household income may not be enormous. In the case of Tenkodogo, it averages 9 percent of all income. But these realities put the cash value of NWFPs into context. Cash sales of forest products are a poor indicator of the total use people are making of forests and represent only a small portion of total contributions. The recorded total value of NWFPs in 2005 was US$18.5 billion, or 15 percent of the total global value of forest product removals (FAO, 2010a). One-fifth of forest income comes from cash sales of forest products, while *four-fifths* of that income is composed of products that never enter the market.

Table 42: Forest use in the village of Tenkodogo, Burkina Faso (percent)

Category of forest user	Cash income	Non-cash income	Total	Forest income as a percentage of all income
Wealthy and average men	42	58	100	
Of which forest	**7**	**31**		**38**
Wealthy and average women	36	64	100	
Of which forest	**10**	**34**		**44**
Poor and very poor men	38	62	100	
Of which forest	**9**	**36**		**45**
Poor and very poor women	32	68	100	
Of which forest	**12**	**38**		**50**
Average contribution of cash and non-cash income to total income	37	63	100	
Average contribution of forest income to total income	9	35		44

Source: IUCN, 2009a

Not only do sales of forest products represent only a small fraction of total income from forests, they also represent a much narrower range of products than that used for consumption, as shown by the contrasting charts (Figures 31 and 32) from the Comoros.

This is particularly evident if a comparison is made of the numbers of products which enter the market, and those which are gathered for consumption, as shown above. These facts are extremely relevant to the debates that have taken place in recent years about the capacity of forests to reduce poverty (e.g. Arnold, 2001; Cavendish, 2003). As many have suggested, straightforward poverty reduction based on the kinds of cash incomes that can be generated from sales of NWFPs can be limited, even though small sums may be crucial for certain purposes.

On the other hand these smallish sums are not negligible, as the section in this chapter on SMFEs shows, in the context of the income-earning opportunities available. In Table 42, forest cash income may represent only 9 percent of total income, but it does contribute 35 percent of all non-cash income. It is therefore critical to improve assessments of the true value of both NWFPs to cash and non-cash income, as both make important contributions to poverty alleviation particularly in rural environments.

Dimensions of forest dependence

All household income in rural areas comes partly from what can be grown on farms and partly from non-farm income, which will consist of a mix of cash income earned as wages and income drawn from off-farm natural resources such as forests, rivers and the sea. The more remote the location, the smaller the cash income from wages, and the greater the dependence on farm

Figure 31: Sources of cash income for men and women in the village of Nindri, Anjouan

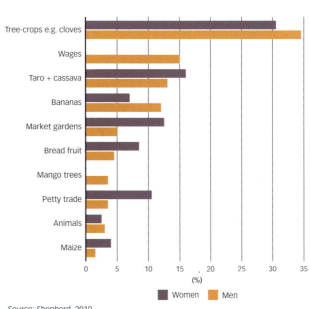

Source: Shepherd, 2010

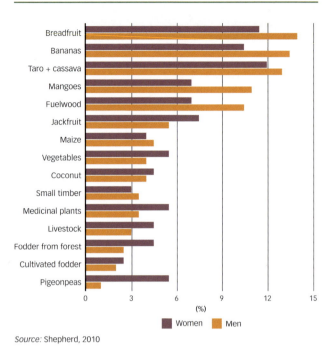

Source: Shepherd, 2010

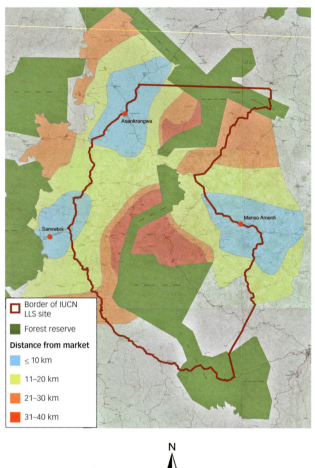

© Topographic map published by Survey of Ghana (Edition 1999)
Poverty map created by Gill Shepherd, produced by Johannes Förster

produce and off-farm natural resources. In all cases, the importance of forest co-varies with the importance of agriculture, and the two need to be understood together from the point of view of local people. There are three dimensions – spatial, gender and wealth – to the nature of forest dependence, which are discussed below.

Forest dependence in spatial terms

Forest dependence varies in predictable ways over space – increasing in remoter areas where markets are far away and only sales of very high value forest products are of interest (e.g. spices such as nutmeg) and decreasing where there are roads and markets and where sales of agricultural crops are easy to organize, and wage labouring opportunities may present themselves. Sunderlin *et al*. (2008) have shown how closely poverty levels and forests can correlate at the level of national analysis. These differences are seen over quite short distances, as well, linked to what constitutes a walkable distance to market and back. Dercon and Hoddinott (2005) have shown that those in Ethiopia within 8 km of a market centre buy and sell more, have better health and have more access to education than those further away.

In another example, the International Union for Conservation of Nature (IUCN) coded the landscape in Western Ghana (Figure 33) by time taken to get to market (a combination of distance, road quality and availability of public transport). Villages in blue

areas (Category 1) lie on an all-weather road within 10 km of a market town. Villages in a yellow area (Category 2) lie 11–20 weighted km from a market town, on mixed roads. Villages in an orange area (Category 3) lie 21–30 weighted kilometres from a market town, on mixed roads, and those in a dark red area (Category 4) lie 31–40 weighted km away, in part over poor roads or tracks. The red line is the landscape boundary; forest reserves and protected areas are indicated in dark green. Most amenities are clustered in the blue and yellow areas, while remoter orange and dark red areas are all found close to forests.

IUCN Ghana used the Forests–Poverty Toolkit to analyse the cash and non-cash income sources of the population of Pensanom village in a blue area and Kamaso village in an orange area. The results, in the case of women, are shown in Figures 34 and 35.

Women's trading, very important in Ghana, is much easier for the women of Pensanom, who can easily transport both agricultural and forest products to market to sell, than for those of Kamaso. They sell more household agricultural produce than they consume, and also earn 10 percent of all their income from other cash sources. In Kamaso, women sell less of the household's agricultural produce than is consumed and are more dependent on forests for non-cash income. They have few opportunities to earn other cash.

Forest dependence and gender

Women in many societies turn to forests both to diversify and add flavour to the range of subsistence foods they

Figure 34: Sources of income for the women of Pensanom, Wassa Amenfi West, Ghana with easy access to market

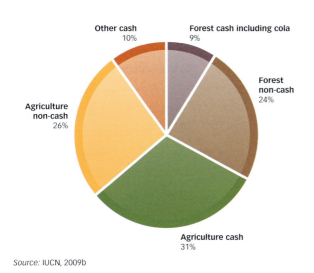

Source: IUCN, 2009b

Figure 35: Sources of income for the women of Kamaso, Wassa Amenfi West, Ghana with difficult access to market

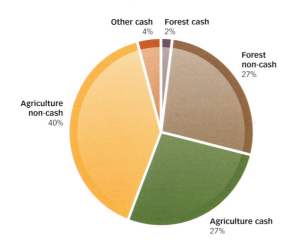

Source: IUCN, 2009b

offer their families, as well as for cash. It is normal to find that women depend on forests more than men for off-farm income, while men may depend more on wage-labouring. For instance, among the Akan in southern Ghana, while the profits from any on-farm activities go to the (male) household head, women may wish to generate income which they control themselves, to safeguard their future. Wives may choose to make remittances to their natal families, for instance, as security in case of divorce (Milton, 1998). In Benin and Cameroon, women increase their collection and sale of NWFPs right before children's school-fees are due, at times of year when ill-health is more common, and during the hungry pre-harvest period (Schreckenberg *et al.*, 2002). The pattern of income sources seen in Table 42, which is typical of many parts of Africa, shows around a third of women's total annual income from cash, a third from subsistence from the farm, and a third from forests.

Forest dependence and wealth levels

Not only women, but poorer people in general are more dependent on forests for cash and non-cash incomes. This may be because they lack land or labour resources to undertake more substantial farming activities or migrant labour. Although wealthier households may collect more forest products by volume, what is collected forms a far higher percentage of the total income of poor households (Abbott, 1997). Chronic poverty (profound, hard-to-get-out-of and intergenerationally inherited) is more common in remote forested areas than in less remote areas (Bird *et al.*, 2002).

Types of forest dependence

Types of non-cash forest dependence vary in different parts of the world, in synergy with types of agriculture. While farm production is almost always primary, the forest is relied on by the farming household both directly (through inputs to diet, for instance) and indirectly (through inputs to the sustainability of the farming enterprise more broadly).

Pastoralism, agriculture and forests

In many parts of the Africa, animals feed on forest browse for a considerable proportion of the year. The main non-cash value of forests for those with cattle is that it keeps their chief household asset alive and in good health throughout the year when there is no grass.

Forests, cattle and soil fertility on terraces

In the upland hill-farming systems of Nepal, cattle are fed in forests or on cut browse from forests, and kept on terraces, so that their manure can supply crops with nutrients. The farming system demonstrates how close the symbiosis with forests can be.

Forests, water and irrigated terraces
Forests in upper watersheds protect and support the streams, which are an essential part of irrigated rice terrace agriculture in much of South and Southeast Asia and in Madagascar.

Rotational fallowing
In almost every part of the world, before the advent of purchased fertilizer, farmers made use of forest soil fertility in shifting cultivation systems. Poor soils, where accumulating weeds and soil toxicity begin to make farming all but impossible after two or three years, drove farmers to move on around their cycle of plots. In many systems, from West Africa to Indonesia, farmers enrich the plots they temporarily abandon with desirable tree species, so that when they return in a few years' time, they will have a more valuable forest than the one they left behind. The farmed parklands of the Sudanic zone in Africa, and the slow transition into the multistorey agroforests found in Indonesia, Viet Nam and elsewhere, are both examples of this.

Forests and protein
In the rainforests of the Congo Basin, it is all but impossible to raise domestic livestock. Farming consists of the growing of carbohydrates and root vegetables, but protein, green leaves, vitamins and minerals must all come from the forest.

Challenges and emerging issues

Forestry and forests have gained new attention in international debates because of their potential role in mitigating climate change. These discussions make it urgent for governments to put in place pro-poor reforms in the forest sector to protect and enhance the livelihood benefits that forests provide to the poor. If this is to be realized, local communities will need more secure rights if they are to be involved in managing and protecting large areas of forests globally.

The sustainability of CBFM is closely linked to enabling arrangements that facilitate the generation and equitable sharing of benefits from forests. Without legal recognition of rights over forest products, however, local people have neither the interest nor the courage to protect and develop forests (Gobeze *et al*., 2009). SMFEs will also require continued investment and capacity building in order to

contribute to local livelihoods. Other aspects of local livelihoods, such as trees in areas outside forests, also need to be further integrated into policies and actions.

Long-term access rights to forest resources and equitable benefit sharing

The *Global Forest Resources Assessment 2010 – Main Report* indicates that 80 percent of the world's forests are publicly owned (FAO, 2010a) but ownership and management of forests by communities is on the rise. However, in many countries, regulatory frameworks are not clearly defined or do not provide adequate security of tenure for forest dependent communities.

The benefits accruing to communities are more minor in countries where CBFM is a relatively young concept. Here tenure issues have perhaps not yet been addressed, the low-value forests passed on to communities have not had time to show the benefits of protection, and infrastructure to valorize community forestry products is not yet in place. In the early stages, the time costs of managing forests (and the transaction costs of engaging with public forest institutions), are generally under-estimated. In these situations, it is easy for middle men and local elites to become the main beneficiaries.

The essence of cost and benefit sharing is to achieve SFM and to reduce poverty levels. Local communities expect incremental benefits from timber, woodfuel and NWFPs as an incentive and motivation to pursue sustainable forest management objectives in partnership with government. Lack of transparency about the amount of income generated and how it is to be used can be a potential source of conflict and a threat to the very existence of CBFM arrangements. Additionally, the procedure of designating forests for community use or for co-management with government forest agencies, the registration of forest management groups, the development of forest management plans and approval processes, all considerably limit the capacity of communities to get involved in forest management without external support.

The formats for community forest management plans in many countries are still based on conventional large-scale timber and production-oriented forest management. They are applied to small-scale operations without fundamental adaptation, so that high transaction costs and time delays ensue. The focus on benefits for forest dependent communities is rapidly lost in this situation (FAO, 2004). Nevertheless, countries are taking positive steps to improve collaborative forest management.

For instance, in Uganda a policy of benefit-sharing under collaborative forest management is currently being developed. The policy hinges on engaging the private sector to support forest-based enterprise development in marketing, processing, upscaling production and developing the organization of community groups.

The ability of local communities to organize, negotiate and lobby governments has proved vital in holding decision-makers accountable to key principles of good governance. There are efforts in several countries led by environmental NGOs to strengthen local communities and to lobby governments on a number of issues, including simplification of guidelines and procedures. In Ghana, for example, Community Resource Management Committees have been established by the Forestry Commission and to date over one thousand such bodies exist within forestry fringe communities across the country. Nevertheless, further work still is needed where community participation in decision-making is lacking, due to inadequate political support and economic drivers favouring small beneficiaries instead of equitable benefit sharing and income distribution (Hodgdon, 2010).

In response to the World Bank and International Monetary Fund's Poverty Reduction Strategy process, a number of countries are integrating forest management objectives (and hence CBFM) into development planning, wider landscape and catchment management approaches as cornerstones for their poverty reduction and rural development strategies. Additionally, with increasing rural populations and multiple demands on forests, local communities may find that there is now more incentive than in the past to diversify income by greater forest product commercialization. Such activities take their place, as always alongside agriculture and off-farm employment (Mirjam, Ros-Tonen and Freerk Wiersum, 2005).

Forests still take time to mature, however, and a much degraded forest will take time to yield the community income that is usually urgently needed. It is time that communities were trusted with less degraded forests in many areas or were given bridging finance to help them to restore degraded ones more rapidly.

Strengthening small and medium forest enterprises

Governments can play a critical role in strengthening SMFEs to reduce poverty. They can grant and enforce legal access to forest resources. They can simplify bureaucratic procedures for obtaining natural resource quotas and SMFE registration. Financial incentives, including tax breaks for start-up SMFEs and local or green purchasing policies are additional positive steps (Donovan et al., 2000).

Global level actors can also contribute to an enabling environment for SMFEs by providing steady demand or capital investment, as in the case of the private sector. For example, a growing number of international health and beauty companies are choosing to source products that have been produced sustainably and under certain internationally recognized standards such as 'fair trade', ensuring fair pay to NWFP harvesters and local processors. The private forest processing industry is increasingly sourcing from small and medium tree growers, particularly in places where land restrictions prohibit large-scale concessions for plantations, and is occasionally also providing capital to local growers for initial processing.

International donor agencies and organizations can provide financial and technical resources for capacity building, and collaborate with local partners to advance land tenure, policy and market reforms that are pro-poor. There are positive developments at the global level that are helping to strengthen enabling environments (see Box 27).

Investment in locally controlled forestry requires certain preconditions. Initial 'soft' investment can significantly help empower communities and local entrepreneurs as well as moderating other economic and political risks, in preparation for subsequent 'hard' investments, such as access to business knowledge and credit (Elson, 2010).

One initiative supported by 'soft' investors to tackle the multiple challenges facing SMFEs, is Forest Connect (FC). This is a collaborative effort between FAO, the International Institute for Environment and Development (IIED), the NFP Facility and the Program on Forests of the World Bank (PROFOR), with country partners. It is in the interest of SMFEs to work together in associations to reduce transaction costs, adapt to new market opportunities, and shape the policy environment in their favour. However, in many developing countries, support structures for such forest associations do not exist, or fail to reach those who need help most. Forest Connect is an international alliance with national FC hubs, dedicated to avoiding deforestation and reducing poverty by linking SMFEs to each other, to markets, to service providers and to policy processes (Box 28).

Box 27: Growing recognition of the value of forest producer organizations – the Smallholders Forest Producer Associations Development Fund

Governments are gradually recognizing that smallholder forestry producers´ active cooperation is required in policy-making for sustainable forestry management. To capitalize on this and assist governments to create an enabling environment for SMFEs, international initiatives such as the Smallholders Forest Producer Associations (SFPA) Development Fund have been created to support the establishment and functioning of forest producer organizations in developing countries.

Supported by Agricord, the Finnish Central Union of Agricultural Producers and Forest Owners (MTK), Farmers Fighting Poverty, Forest Connect, and FAO/NFP Facility, the SFPA Development Fund programme has started up activities in 2010 in Ethiopia and Viet Nam.

Source: FAO, 2010g (For more information visit: www.fao.org/forestry/enterprises/60778/en/)

As highlighted in Box 25, a critical part of Burkina Faso's success with SMFEs and the use of NWFPs was a result of the application of MA&D, a tool developed by FAO in 2000. The MA&D approach is a participatory training methodology that aims to assist people in developing forest-based income-generating enterprises while conserving natural resources. The MA&D tool sets are adapted to the specific context of each country and for many different purposes and products. It offers a preliminary planning phase, and three successive main phases: the identification of target groups and potential products; the screening of promising products and identification of markets; and the preparation of strategies and business plans, and pilot implementation. Since 2000, the FAO Forestry Department has supported projects on tree and forest product enterprises around 20 countries using the MA&D approach (FAO, 2010f).

More effective non-wood forest product law and policy[26]

With greater information, effective consultations with stakeholders and strategic approaches to policy-making, NWFP laws and policies can promote ecological sustainability, equity in trade, and improved rural livelihoods. The following suggestions aim to help governments and others working today to build more effective and equitable NWFP policy frameworks.

The extent of commercialization and the heterogeneity of NWFP resources, markets and stakeholders should be reflected in policies and laws. A 'one-size-fits-all' approach to regulating this diverse category of products is not possible. Laws need to reflect the different

types of NWFP use, including subsistence, local trade, commercial trade and recreation. Experience has also indicated that NWFP law and policy are most effective when:

- subsistence use of NWFPs is not regulated, except in clear cases of overharvesting;
- governments focus law and policy on internationally and intensively traded industrial scale NWFPs, particularly when they have limited resources;
- appropriate attention is given to the damage to NWFPs caused by forest degradation from logging, mining and clearing for commercial agriculture and other land uses;
- policies avoid criminalizing harvesting activities and further marginalizing producers;
- support and information are given to producer and harvester groups, trade associations and NGOs to strengthen stakeholder consultations;
- the negative impacts of unrelated laws are mitigated;
- there is collaboration between countries trading NWFPs;
- the burden of permits and procedures is minimized for small-scale producers; and
- governments integrate and coordinate customary and statutory law and governance systems.

NWFP policies work best when incentives and supportive legal frameworks are promoted, including government support for producer, trade and processing groups; market access and premium prices through certification; tax breaks; and outreach and education on new policies and laws. In some cases, particularly when there is sudden and high commercial demand, a more involved regulatory framework is also necessary, including permits, quotas, taxes and restrictions on trade. Governments will need to approach NWFP regulation in ways that reflect the financial, ecological and social costs and benefits of

---

[26] This section is drawn from Laird, McLain and Wynberg, 2010.

Box 28: Forest Connect – a practical networking tool

Forest Connect (FC) currently connects and strengthens small forest enterprises in Burkina Faso, China, Ethiopia, Guatemala, Guyana, Lao People's Democratic Republic, Liberia, Mali, Mozambique and Nepal. In-country FC activities start with an evaluation of the SMFE context, which informs follow-up activities leading to face-to-face networking across the value chain and up to the policy level. SMFEs are provided with information and opportunities to connect to other local producers, value chain actors and service providers (e.g. business and financial services). Each FC national hub develops and manages its own website based on its own defined priorities, to link all these stakeholders.

In the Lao People's Democratic Republic, FC works in association with FAO, the World Wide Fund For Nature (WWF), and the Netherlands Development (Organization) SNV, and is implemented by a Lao private human resource development organization. It has focused on small rattan and bamboo enterprises, and promoted collaboration among NGOs and the Lao Government. The marketing capacity of these SMFEs has been increased by making them more aware of international market requirements, and through development of bamboo and rattan production groups. National institutions have learned the importance of helping the SMFEs to gain better access to national, regional and international markets, and this in turn has stimulated both the Lao Government and the SMFEs to give more attention to the sustainable management of rattan and bamboo.

Source: Forest Connect, 2010. (For more information on Forest Connect Lao People's Democratic Republic, visit http://edclaos.com/lfc/)

---

such actions, government implementation capacity and the likelihood of compliance.

Traditional knowledge, indigenous peoples and REDD

Perhaps the most dynamic and important new development regarding forests, traditional knowledge and indigenous peoples within the United Nations, is the work within the climate change regime. In particular, indigenous peoples will have a crucial role to play in REDD and REDD+, particularly given recent decisions on REDD+ in Cancún, Mexico. Forest loss and degradation contribute 17 percent of global GHG emissions, and indigenous peoples live in all the forests being targeted by REDD activities.

Recent debates about livelihood resilience are only just beginning to factor in the enormous contribution made by forests to those livelihoods, especially in remoter areas. Yet some believe the protective effects of forests for livelihood resilience could be threatened by aspects of REDD almost before they are recognized. Although similar threats to livelihoods exist in many aspects of natural resource management (Honadle, 1999), there is a series of specific linked concerns about REDD.

There have been concerns that REDD could disadvantage people living in and around forests (on the basis, for instance, of experience with palm oil). If REDD is intended to contribute to poverty reduction or at least not to negatively impact upon use rights, then tenure clarification will be essential in many cases. At the same time, many forest authorities now see an opportunity to generate income from REDD, and this might provide a strong disincentive to decentralize control of forests to communities.

Communities could bear the costs of REDD in terms of forest use forgone. If, as we have seen, up to four-fifths of that use is invisible to governments, then there could be an underestimation of what forest dependent people might lose through REDD. Furthermore, there is a serious risk that informal forest use rights possessed by many forest peoples could be lost as forests become more valuable (Angelsen et al., 2009).

The potential contribution that a multifunctional, multiple-value forest resource might make to climate change cannot be realized unless REDD arrangements are better aligned with broader forest governance reform. REDD and carbon capture could reduce multiple functions to a single function – to the great disadvantage of local users. At the root of potential emissions reductions, and the finance mechanisms and monitoring protocols intended to deliver them, lie fundamental decisions about pro-poor forest governance which are only starting to be addressed.

Especially since the Conference of the Parties to the UNFCCC in Bali in 2007, indigenous peoples have participated actively in policy development processes and have influenced their outcomes. As a result of these efforts, references to the role of indigenous peoples and traditional knowledge can be found in UNFCCC draft texts and, notably, in the December 2010 UNFCCC decision on REDD+, which requests developing countries to ensure the full participation of indigenous people and local communities in REDD+ national strategies and action plans. These references provide a basis on which to build and ensure that indigenous peoples and local communities have an adequate role in the UNFCCC regime, their interests and rights are protected (see UNFCCC, 2010), and they can benefit from REDD+ activities. The cases mentioned in Chapter 3 provide clear examples of how this involvement has started to positively change laws and policies. More work on REDD+ is being undertaken to ensure these activities benefit local and indigenous communities.

Urban forests and local economy for jobs and income

More than half of the world's population now lives in urban areas. The proximity of urban and peri-urban forests, and other tree-based systems to these centres of population, makes them highly valuable in sustaining employment and income generation. However, urban areas are largely overlooked when examining local forests and forestry issues. Different considerations must be taken into account when assessing the productivity of urban forests, in comparison with the rural context. Three areas are particularly important in this consideration.

First, in 'core' built-up areas with high grey infrastructure (roads and buildings), urban trees and forests form line plantations and gardens, the maintenance of which provides sustainable jobs, and residues that supply raw material for local electricity generation, heating and cooking (Lohrberg, 2007). Second, the urbanizing areas around cities face major land-use changes and ingenious mosaics of trees and forest resources are needed that combine recreational, health, environmental and productive functions. Today's practices aim to increase the cost-efficiency of green infrastructure, and move towards more eco-friendly grey infrastructure, while providing employment in the construction and management of roads, parks, industrial areas and neighbourhoods that bring together small and medium enterprises and community involvement (Lohrberg, 2007). Third, a sustainable city must fit within its overall ecosystem, respecting urban watershed management and the landscape. Balanced productivity of forests and agroforestry systems around cities provides urban areas with traditional forest products, as well as water supplies and agroforestry products (Spathelf and Nutto, 2004). However, despite their value for and connectedness

to CBFM and SMFEs, these three areas are rarely considered in studies of the local 'value' of forests and forestry. Urban and peri-urban forests need special attention if they are to be measured and integrated into local ('urban') and regional ('peri-urban linking urban to rural') planning efforts.

Urban and peri-urban forestry has been defined as the art, science and technology of managing trees and forest resources in and around urban community ecosystems for the physiological, sociological, economic and aesthetic benefits that they provide (Grey and Deneke, 1986). Urban forestry has received limited attention in many poor countries as it is often perceived to be associated with beautification and recreation. Although these functions are important for all societies, they are not a top priority for cities where the restoration of the forest base and the search for productive occupations for vulnerable and poor populations are the primary concerns.

Extensive research and experience demonstrate that towns that have taken steps to invest in a green vision have subsequently enjoyed many benefits. For instance, where an efficient green infrastructure is in place, the impacts of extreme weather events (e.g. winds, floods, landslides and sand encroachment) are mitigated. Moreover, a well managed watershed produces and supplies good quality water and reduces the need for costly engineering works. The high and recurrent cost of rebuilding roads, housing and commercial infrastructure is greatly reduced, creating savings, which generate green jobs and income through multiuse management and the maintenance of woodlands and trees. Finally, farming and landscape systems that incorporate agroforestry and high-yielding plantations can supply nearby markets at competitive prices (FAO, 2009b).

Research in peri-urban areas of developing countries reveals that poor urban migrant households maintain close links with their previous rural (agricultural and forestry) areas. This connection can contribute to their subsistence and alleviate food insecurity (Iaquinta and Drescher, 2000). In the urbanized society of the Bolivian Amazon, extraction and processing of NWFPs provide livelihood options for peri-urban dwellers. Some households, especially those of poorly educated migrants from the forest hinterland, rely on NWFP-related activities for their economic survival in town (Stoian, 2005). The role of NWFPs in supporting livelihoods in different regions of developing countries, which has informally taken place for decades, was confirmed by Shackleton, Shanley and Ndoye (2007). In particular, their research illustrated the key role of NWFPs in providing an opportunity for hundreds of thousands of unemployed peri-urban and urban men and women to strengthen their livelihoods in several African countries.

In urban areas the principal sources of timber are plantations, street trees, shelterbelts or windbreaks and greenbelts, parks and gardens. In many cities timber harvesting is combined with intensive outdoor recreational activities. Systematic planting of street trees for timber production is widely practised in China, India and Malaysia (Carreiro, Song and Wu, 2008). Some cities in industrialized countries offset the costs of tree care through harvesting.

Urban trees also have the ability to maintain property values (e.g. Tyrväinen et al., 2005), create attractive settings for businesses and attract consumers to established shopping districts in more urban areas. Studies have found that urban trees improve the economic stability of retail environments by attracting consumers, setting a positive mood, and sending messages of quality (Wolf, 2004). This has been well documented through action research in Europe, including that carried out by the European Forum on Urban Forestry led by the Danish Centre for Forest, Landscape and Planning of Copenhagen University (DCFLP/KVL) and IUFRO. Production, planting, and tending trees and landscapes represent a significant economic multiplier in developed countries. Landscape services, including equipment and nursery production and retail sales in the United States of America alone in 2004 were estimated to be valued at US$147.8 billion in output, generating more than 1.9 million private sector jobs (Hall, Hodges and Haydu, 2005).

The necessary work to restore urban ecosystems, and plant and care for community trees and forests, supported by national and local governments and international donor agencies, could employ millions of people at a global scale with significant multiplier effects in local economies and around the world. Nevertheless, urban forests are still frequently an afterthought in the process of implementing comprehensive plan goals at the local and national scales. Often, there is a fundamental disconnect between the community's vision of environmental quality and the ecosystem services that are the cornerstone for achieving environmental quality and sustainable development (Schwab, 2009). Reliable data and inclusive dialogue across disciplines, sectors and institutions are necessary components of any successful planning process. Both are currently lacking in nearly all regions and nations (see Box 30). Indeed key stakeholders such as foresters, urban agriculture specialists, local authorities, emergency agencies and food security programmers do not meet to build green sustainable cities with and for citizens. However, many centres of excellence (for instance in Asia, the Chinese Academy of Forests (CAF), the Forest Resources Institute of Malaysia (FRIM), and Aravali Foundations in India) are compiling good data and instituting progressive practices to engage affected landowners and interest groups, and to develop a sustainable green vision for their communities within good governance conditions and long-term planning exercises.

Urban agriculture has already been recognized by citizens and their local authorities as a strategic way to combine a mosaic of green areas in and around cities, contributing to the stabilization of migrant societies from rural areas, establishing a natural ecosystem in the city and providing a highly competitive market in the vicinity of consumers.

Box 29: Valuation of ecological services – the example of Oakville's urban forest

Every year, trees within the town of Oakville (Ontario, Canada) provide ecological services to a value of US$2.1 million. In addition, trees save local industry US$1.1 million annually by avoiding expenditure on mechanical methods to remove the 172 tonnes (190 tons) of pollutants emitted at source. Trees save Oakville residents US$812 000 annually in reduced energy bills. This proves the concept that the urban forest functions as a 'biogenetic utility,' saving energy and preventing the accumulation of greenhouse gases.

Oakville's Urban Forest Effect (UFORE) project helped established a baseline 'performance measure' for its Corporate Strategic Plan. In combination with the Urban Forest Strategic Management Plan 2008–2027, a solid policy foundation was built in the town's official plan to help meet its Corporate Vision: "To be the most liveable town in Canada." This demonstrates the influential role that the urban forest plays, and the potential partnerships that can be attained among planning, engineering and urban forest management professionals (McNeill, 2009).

The evolution of green areas in cities and regional planning processes for these areas is well known in developed countries. However, although methodologies for assessment exist, they are not commonly used in most parts of the world, are rarely compatible among users, and are not integrated, either at national or international level. As part of the FRA 2010 process, a thematic study is being prepared on trees outside forests, which includes an analysis of methodologies and data availability. The study will provide guidance to countries when assessing urbanization, land use and land use change in and around cities in relation to forest policy and national forestry action plans (FAO, 2010e).

The existing stakeholder platforms around this discipline offer a sound basis through which to incorporate trees, agroforestry and forests in integrated land use, enabling urban and peri-urban forestry make a direct economic contribution in terms of jobs and income generation, as well as institutional savings.

Results of more comprehensive research on urban and peri-urban forests and other tree-based systems drive us toward new models of urban management and an urbanization dynamic where social inclusion, participatory processes of cultural integration, food security and well-being are adopted as core objectives.

Summary and conclusions

This chapter has shown how local forest resources are important in sustaining local livelihoods, but are often underestimated in value and underprotected in laws and policies. Local forest resources make key contributions to sustaining traditional knowledge practices, developing CBFM and SMFEs, supplying NWFPs and making 'non-cash' contributions to subsistence livelihoods. The examples in this chapter were a first attempt to shed light on these themes, all of which require further research and discussion in 2011 and beyond.

Community-based forest management builds on political goodwill and strong community institutions. It relies on long-term forest rights and tenure. When fostered in sound and appropriate enabling environments, CBFM can also help stimulate the creation of SMFEs.

It is increasingly understood in some countries and internationally that investment in SMFEs can greatly improve rural livelihood opportunities as well as strengthen natural resource management. SMFEs can be engines of development through employment, income and through these, the multiplier effect that occurs in rural economies. Yet in some countries, development of SMFEs is still lacking because of an underappreciation of their value to national economies. Governments and international organizations could create a more positive environment for SMFEs by clarifying natural resource access and tenure rules; by simplifying business registration and export procedures; and by streamlining tax and financial incentive schemes. Availability of information and support for producer networks are also important components.

Non-wood forest products have also been shown to be a large contributor to cash and non-cash contributions of livelihoods, including via SMFEs. They are often the core product of many community-based SMFEs and help provide sustainable incomes. However, the non-cash contribution of NWFPs to household income is often much greater than cash income from the forest. In addition to conducting further research on the non-cash contribution of forests, further development of effective NWFP law and policy is required to ensure NWFPs are not overexploited and are well integrated into policy frameworks.

Finally, new challenges from climate change require urgent action to explore and protect the local value of forests for livelihoods even more. This is particularly true in the case of emerging activities undertaken as part of REDD+, given recent decisions taken in Cancún in December 2010. If REDD activities are aligned with broad forest governance reform and governments encourage participation of indigenous peoples and local communities in national REDD+ strategy and action plan formation, there is hope that REDD+ activities could ensure benefits for the people that depend on forests for their livelihoods. Without such attention given to local-level issues, there is a risk of eroding traditional ways of life and threatening some of the most biologically diverse and environmentally important forests in the world.

Annex

5 | Annex

Notes on the annex tables

In all tables, the regional breakdown reflects geographical rather than economic or political groupings.

– = not available
0 = either a true zero or an insignificant value (less than half a unit)

In **Table** 1, "land area" refers to the total area of a country, excluding areas under inland water bodies. The world total corresponds to the sum of the reporting units; about 35 million hectares of land in Antarctica, some Arctic and Antarctic islands and some other minor islands are not included. Per capita gross domestic product (GDP) is expressed at purchasing power parity (PPP).

In **Table 3**, "carbon stock in living forest biomass" refers to carbon stock in above-ground and below-ground biomass.

In **Table 6**, employment is reported for the formal forestry sector only.

Table 1: Basic data on countries and areas

Country / area	Land area	Population 2008				GDP 2008	
		Total	Density	Annual growth rate	Rural	Per capita (PPP)	Annual real growth rate
	(1 000 ha)	(1 000)	(Population/ km²)	(%)	(% of total)	(US$)	(%)
Burundi	2 568	8 074	314	3.0	90	383	4.5
Cameroon	47 271	19 088	40	2.3	43	2 195	3.9
Central African Republic	62 298	4 339	7	1.9	62	741	2.2
Chad	125 920	10 914	9	2.7	73	1 337	-0.2
Republic of the Congo	34 150	3 615	11	1.8	39	3 949	5.6
Democratic Republic of the Congo	226 705	64 257	28	2.8	66	314	6.2
Equatorial Guinea	2 805	659	23	2.6	61	33 899	11.3
Gabon	25 767	1 448	6	1.8	15	14 575	2.3
Rwanda	2 467	9 721	394	2.8	82	1 027	11.2
Saint Helena, Ascension and Tristan da Cunha	39	5	13	0	60	2 500	–
Sao Tome and Principe	96	160	167	1.3	39	1 748	5.8
Total Central Africa	**530 086**	**122 280**	**23**	**2.6**	**64**	**1 235**	**5.2**
Comoros	186	850	457	2.4	72	1 170	1.0
Djibouti	2 318	849	37	1.8	13	2 138	3.9
Eritrea	10 100	4 927	49	3.1	79	642	2.0
Ethiopia	100 000	80 713	81	2.6	83	869	11.3
Kenya	56 914	38 765	68	2.7	78	1 551	1.7
Madagascar	58 154	19 111	33	2.7	71	1 054	7.3
Mauritius	203	1 280	631	0.7	58	12 356	4.5
Mayotte	38	189	504	2.7	–	4 900	–
Réunion	250	817	327	1.4	7	–	–
Seychelles	46	84	183	1.2	45	21 392	2.8
Somalia	62 734	8 926	14	2.2	64	600	2.6
Uganda	19 710	31 657	161	3.3	87	1 166	9.5
United Republic of Tanzania	88 580	42 484	48	2.9	75	1 301	7.5
Total East Africa	**399 233**	**230 652**	**58**	**2.8**	**79**	**1 181**	**6.7**
Algeria	238 174	34 373	14	1.5	35	8 036	3.0
Egypt	99 545	81 527	82	1.8	57	5 425	7.2
Libyan Arab Jamahiriya	175 954	6 294	4	2.0	23	16 208	3.8
Mauritania	103 070	3 215	3	2.4	59	2 084	3.7

Table 1 | 101

Country / area	Land area	Population 2008				GDP 2008	
		Total	Density	Annual growth rate	Rural	Per capita (PPP)	Annual real growth rate
	(1 000 ha)	(1 000)	(Population/ km²)	(%)	(% of total)	(US$)	(%)
Morocco	44 630	31 606	71	1.2	44	4 263	5.6
Sudan	237 600	41 348	17	2.3	57	2 155	8.3
Tunisia	15 536	10 169	65	1.0	34	7 956	4.5
Western Sahara	26 600	497	2	3.5	19	2 500	–
Total Northern Africa	**941 109**	**209 029**	**22**	**1.7**	**49**	**5 421**	**5.5**
Angola	124 670	18 021	14	2.7	43	5 820	13.2
Botswana	56 673	1 921	3	1.5	40	13 574	2.9
Lesotho	3 036	2 049	67	0.8	75	1 564	3.9
Malawi	9 408	14 846	158	2.8	81	805	9.7
Mozambique	78 638	22 383	28	2.4	63	838	6.8
Namibia	82 329	2 130	3	2.0	63	6 398	2.9
South Africa	121 447	49 668	41	1.0	39	10 116	3.1
Swaziland	1 720	1 168	68	1.5	75	4 927	2.4
Zambia	74 339	12 620	17	2.5	65	1 357	6.0
Zimbabwe	38 685	12 463	32	0.1	63	337	-14.5
Total Southern Africa	**590 945**	**137 269**	**23**	**1.7**	**54**	**5 158**	**4.3**
Benin	11 062	8 662	78	3.2	59	1 473	5.1
Burkina Faso	27 360	15 234	56	3.5	81	1 160	4.5
Cape Verde	403	499	124	1.4	40	3 202	2.8
Côte d'Ivoire	31 800	20 591	65	2.3	51	1 652	2.2
Gambia	1 000	1 660	166	2.7	44	1 363	5.9
Ghana	22 754	23 351	103	2.1	50	1 463	7.3
Guinea	24 572	9 833	40	2.3	66	1 056	4.7
Guinea-Bissau	2 812	1 575	56	2.2	70	537	3.3
Liberia	9 632	3 793	39	4.6	40	388	7.1
Mali	122 019	12 706	10	2.4	68	1 129	5.0
Niger	126 670	14 704	12	4.0	84	683	9.5
Nigeria	91 077	151 212	166	2.4	52	2 099	6.0
Senegal	19 253	12 211	63	2.7	58	1 793	3.3
Sierra Leone	7 162	5 560	78	2.6	62	782	5.5

Country / area	Land area	Population 2008				GDP 2008	
		Total	Density	Annual growth rate	Rural	Per capita (PPP)	Annual real growth rate
	(1 000 ha)	(1 000)	(Population/ km²)	(%)	(% of total)	(US$)	(%)
Togo	5 439	6 459	119	2.5	58	830	1.1
Total West Africa	**503 015**	**288 050**	**57**	**2.6**	**56**	**1 696**	**5.4**
Total Africa	**2 964 388**	**987 280**	**33**	**2.3**	**61**	**2 789**	**5.2**
Armenia	2 820	3 077	109	0.2	36	6 075	6.8
Azerbaijan	8 263	8 731	106	1.1	48	8 771	10.8
Georgia	6 949	4 307	62	-1.2	47	4 966	2.0
Kazakhstan	269 970	15 521	6	0.7	42	11 323	3.2
Kyrgyzstan	19 180	5 414	28	1.3	64	2 193	7.6
Tajikistan	13 996	6 836	49	1.6	74	1 907	7.9
Turkmenistan	46 993	5 044	11	1.3	51	6 625	9.8
Uzbekistan	42 540	27 191	64	1.1	63	2 658	9.0
Total Central Asia	**410 711**	**76 121**	**19**	**0.9**	**55**	**5 557**	**6.6**
China	932 749	1 344 919	144	0.6	57	5 971	9.0
Democratic People's Republic of Korea	12 041	23 819	198	0.4	37	1 800	3.7
Japan	36 450	127 293	349	-0.1	34	34 129	-0.7
Mongolia	155 356	2 641	2	1.1	43	3 557	8.9
Republic of Korea	9 692	48 152	497	0.4	19	27 658	2.2
Total East Asia	**1 146 288**	**1 546 824**	**135**	**0.5**	**53**	**8 895**	**2.3**
Bangladesh	13 017	160 000	1 229	1.4	73	1 335	6.2
Bhutan	3 839	687	18	1.6	66	4 759	13.8
India	297 319	1 181 412	397	1.4	71	2 946	6.1
Maldives	30	305	1 017	1.3	62	5 597	5.2
Nepal	14 335	28 810	201	1.8	83	1 104	5.3
Pakistan	77 088	176 952	230	2.2	64	2 538	2.0
Sri Lanka	6 271	20 061	320	0.9	85	4 564	6.0
Total South Asia	**411 899**	**1 568 227**	**381**	**1.5**	**70**	**2 724**	**5.7**
Brunei Darussalam	527	392	74	1.8	25	50 665	-1.9
Cambodia	17 652	14 562	82	1.7	79	1 951	6.7
Indonesia	181 157	227 345	125	1.2	49	3 994	6.1

Table 1 | 103

Country / area	Land area	Population 2008				GDP 2008	
		Total	Density	Annual growth rate	Rural	Per capita (PPP)	Annual real growth rate
	(1 000 ha)	(1 000)	(Population/ km²)	(%)	(% of total)	(US$)	(%)
Lao People's Democratic Republic	23 080	6 205	27	1.9	69	2 124	7.5
Malaysia	32 855	27 014	82	1.7	30	14 215	4.6
Myanmar	65 352	49 563	76	0.9	67	1 110	3.6
Philippines	29 817	90 348	303	1.8	35	3 513	3.8
Singapore	70	4 615	6 593	2.9	0	49 321	1.1
Thailand	51 089	67 386	132	0.6	67	8 086	2.5
Timor-Leste	1 487	1 098	74	3.2	73	802	13.2
Viet Nam	31 007	87 096	281	1.1	72	2 787	6.2
Total Southeast Asia	**434 093**	**575 624**	**133**	**1.2**	**53**	**4 764**	**4.1**
Afghanistan	65 223	27 208	42	3.5	76	1 103	2.3
Bahrain	76	776	1 021	2.1	12	34 899	6.3
Cyprus	924	862	93	0.9	30	26 919	3.6
Iran (Islamic Republic of)	162 855	73 312	45	1.2	32	11 666	5.6
Iraq	43 737	30 096	69	2.1	34	3 477	9.5
Israel	2 164	7 051	326	1.7	8	27 905	4.0
Jordan	8 824	6 136	70	3.3	22	5 474	7.9
Kuwait	1 782	2 919	164	2.4	2	39 941	6.4
Lebanon	1 023	4 194	410	0.8	13	11 777	8.5
Occupied Palestinian Territory	602	4 147	689	3.2	28	2 900	2.0
Oman	30 950	2 785	9	2.2	28	24 799	12.3
Qatar	1 159	1 281	111	12.6	4	84 350	15.8
Saudi Arabia	214 969	25 201	12	2.1	18	23 991	4.4
Syrian Arab Republic	18 364	21 227	116	3.5	46	4 583	5.2
Turkey	76 963	73 914	96	1.2	31	13 417	0.9
United Arab Emirates	8 360	4 485	54	2.8	22	37 442	5.1
Yemen	52 797	22 917	43	2.9	69	2 416	3.9
Total Western Asia	**690 772**	**308 511**	**45**	**2.0**	**37**	**11 483**	**4.2**
Total Asia	**3 093 763**	**4 075 307**	**132**	**1.1**	**59**	**6 070**	**3.0**
Albania	2 740	3 143	115	0.4	53	7 293	6.0
Andorra	47	84	179	1.2	11	42 500	3.6

Country / area	Land area	Population 2008				GDP 2008	
		Total	Density	Annual growth rate	Rural	Per capita (PPP)	Annual real growth rate
	(1 000 ha)	(1 000)	(Population/ km²)	(%)	(% of total)	(US$)	(%)
Austria	8 245	8 337	101	0.4	33	37 912	1.8
Belarus	20 290	9 679	48	-0.5	27	12 278	10
Belgium	3 028	10 590	350	0.6	3	35 238	1.1
Bosnia and Herzegovina	5 120	3 773	74	-0.1	53	8 095	5.4
Bulgaria	10 861	7 593	70	-0.6	29	11 792	6.0
Croatia	5 596	4 423	79	-0.1	43	17 663	2.4
Czech Republic	7 725	10 319	134	0.5	27	24 643	2.5
Denmark	4 243	5 458	129	0.2	13	36 845	-1.1
Estonia	4 239	1 341	32	-0.1	31	20 651	-3.6
Faroe Islands	140	50	36	2.0	58	31 000	–
Finland	30 390	5 304	17	0.4	37	36 195	0.9
France	54 766	62 036	113	0.5	23	33 058	0.4
Germany	34 863	82 264	236	-0.1	26	35 374	1.3
Gibraltar	1	31	3 100	0	0	38 200	–
Greece	12 890	11 137	86	0.2	39	29 356	2.9
Guernsey	8	66	846	0.2	69	44 600	–
Holy See	0	1	1 877	0	0	–	–
Hungary	8 961	10 012	112	-0.2	33	19 789	0.6
Iceland	10 025	315	3	2.3	8	36 902	0.3
Ireland	6 889	4 437	64	1.9	39	41 850	-3.0
Isle of Man	57	80	140	0	49	35 000	–
Italy	29 414	59 604	203	0.5	32	31 283	
Jersey	12	92	767	0.2	69	57 000	–
Latvia	6 220	2 259	36	-0.4	32	16 357	-4.6
Liechtenstein	16	36	225	2.9	86	118 000	1.8
Lithuania	6 268	3 321	53		33	17 753	3.0
Luxembourg	259	481	186	1.3	18	78 922	-0.9
Malta	32	407	1 272	0.2	6	23 971	2.1
Monaco	0	33	16 483	0	0	30 000	10
Montenegro	1 345	622	46	0.2	40	13 385	8.1
Netherlands	3 376	16 528	490	0.4	18	40 961	2.1
Norway	30 547	4 767	16	1.0	23	58 714	2.1

Table 1 | 105

Country / area	Land area	Population 2008				GDP 2008	
		Total	Density	Annual growth rate	Rural	Per capita (PPP)	Annual real growth rate
	(1 000 ha)	(1 000)	(Population/ km²)	(%)	(% of total)	(US$)	(%)
Poland	30 422	38 104	125	-0.1	39	17 275	4.9
Portugal	9 147	10 677	117	0.3	41	23 254	0
Republic of Moldova	3 289	3 633	110	-0.9	58	2 979	7.2
Romania	22 990	21 361	93	-0.4	46	13 449	9.4
Russian Federation	1 637 687	141 394	9	-0.4	27	15 923	5.6
San Marino	6	31	517	0	7	41 900	1.9
Serbia	8 836	9 839	111	0.1	48	10 554	1.2
Slovakia	4 810	5 400	112	0.1	44	22 138	6.2
Slovenia	2 014	2 015	100	0.2	52	27 866	3.5
Spain	49 911	44 486	89	1.0	23	31 674	1.2
Svalbard and Jan Mayen Islands	6 100	2	0	0	–	–	–
Sweden	41 034	9 205	22	0.5	16	36 961	-0.2
Switzerland	4 000	7 541	189	0.4	27	42 415	1.8
The former Yugoslav Republic of Macedonia	2 523	2 041	81	0	33	9 337	5.0
Ukraine	57 933	45 992	79	-0.6	32	7 277	2.1
United Kingdom	24 193	61 461	254	0.5	10	35 468	0.7
Total Europe	**2 213 507**	**731 805**	**33**	**0.1**	**28**	**25 585**	**1.1**
Anguilla	9	15	167	7.1	0	8 800	15.3
Antigua and Barbuda	44	87	198	1.2	69	20 970	2.5
Aruba	18	105	583	1.0	53	21 800	-1.6
Bahamas	1 001	338	34	1.2	16	30 700	1.0
Barbados	43	255	593	0	60	18 977	0.2
Bermuda	5	65	1 300	0	0	69 900	4.4
British Virgin Islands	15	23	153	0	61	38 500	2.5
Cayman Islands	24	56	233	1.8	0	43 800	3.2
Cuba	10 644	11 205	105	0	24	9 500	4.3
Dominica	75	67	89	0	25	8 706	4.3
Dominican Republic	4 832	9 953	206	1.4	31	8 125	5.3
Grenada	34	104	306	1.0	69	8 882	2.1
Guadeloupe	169	464	275	0.4	2	–	–

Country / area	Land area	Population 2008				GDP 2008	
		Total	Density	Annual growth rate	Rural	Per capita (PPP)	Annual real growth rate
	(1 000 ha)	(1 000)	(Population/ km²)	(%)	(% of total)	(US$)	(%)
Haiti	2 756	9 876	358	1.6	53	1 124	1.3
Jamaica	1 083	2 708	250	0.4	47	7 716	-1.3
Martinique	106	403	380	0.2	2	–	–
Montserrat	10	6	60	0	83	3 400	11.8
Netherlands Antilles	80	195	244	1.6	7	16 000	2.2
Puerto Rico	887	3 965	447	0.4	2	17 800	0.2
Saint Barthélemy	2	7	333	–	–	–	–
Saint Kitts and Nevis	26	51	196	2.0	69	16 467	8.2
Saint Lucia	61	170	279	0.6	72	9 836	0.5
Saint Martin (French part)	5	30	600	–	–	–	–
Saint Vincent and the Grenadines	39	109	279	0	53	8 998	-1.1
Trinidad and Tobago	513	1 333	260	0.4	87	25 173	3.5
Turks and Caicos Islands	95	33	35	3.1	9	11 500	12.9
United States Virgin Islands	35	110	314	0	6	14 500	–
Total Caribbean	**22 611**	**41 733**	**185**	**0.8**	**34**	**8 648**	**3.4**
Belize	2 281	301	13	2.0	48	6 743	3.8
Costa Rica	5 106	4 519	89	1.3	37	11 232	2.6
El Salvador	2 072	6 134	296	0.4	39	6 799	2.5
Guatemala	10 716	13 686	128	2.5	52	4 760	4.0
Honduras	11 189	7 319	65	2.0	52	3 932	4.0
Nicaragua	12 034	5 667	47	1.3	43	2 689	3.5
Panama	7 434	3 399	46	1.7	27	12 498	9.2
Total Central America	**50 832**	**41 025**	**81**	**1.7**	**45**	**6 000**	**4.3**
Canada	909 351	33 259	4	1.0	20	39 078	0.4
Greenland	41 045	57	0	0	16	20 000	0.3
Mexico	194 395	108 555	56	1.0	23	14 570	1.8
Saint Pierre and Miquelon	23	6	26	0	17	7 000	–
United States of America	914 742	311 666	34	1.0	18	46 350	0.4
Total North America	**2 059 556**	**453 543**	**22**	**1.0**	**19**	**38 206**	**0.5**
Total North and Central America	**2 132 999**	**536 301**	**25**	**1.0**	**23**	**33 443**	**0.5**

Table 1 | 107

Country / area	Land area	Population 2008				GDP 2008	
		Total	Density	Annual growth rate	Rural	Per capita (PPP)	Annual real growth rate
	(1 000 ha)	(1 000)	(Population/ km²)	(%)	(% of total)	(US$)	(%)
American Samoa	20	66	330	1.5	8	8 000	–
Australia	768 230	21 074	3	1.1	11	38 784	3.7
Cook Islands	24	20	83	0	25	9 100	2.9
Fiji	1 827	844	46	0.6	48	4 358	0.2
French Polynesia	366	266	73	1.5	49	18 000	2.6
Guam	54	176	326	1.7	7	15 000	–
Kiribati	81	97	120	2.1	56	2 426	3.0
Marshall Islands	18	61	339	3.4	30	2 500	1.5
Micronesia (Federated States of)	70	110	157	0	78	3 091	-2.9
Nauru	2	10	500	0	0	5 000	-12.1
New Caledonia	1 828	246	13	1.2	35	15 000	0.6
New Zealand	26 331	4 230	16	0.9	14	27 260	-1.1
Niue	26	2	8	0	50	5 800	–
Norfolk Island	4	2	50	0	–	–	–
Northern Mariana Islands	46	85	185	1.2	9	12 500	–
Palau	46	20	43	0	20	8 100	
Papua New Guinea	45 286	6 577	15	2.4	88	2 180	6.6
Pitcairn	5	0	1	0	100	–	–
Samoa	283	179	63	0	77	4 555	-3.4
Solomon Islands	2 799	511	18	2.6	82	2 613	6.9
Tokelau	1	1	100	0	100	1 000	–
Tonga	72	104	144	1.0	75	3 837	0.8
Tuvalu	3	10	333	0	50	1 600	2.0
Vanuatu	1 219	234	19	2.6	75	3 935	6.6
Wallis and Futuna Islands	14	15	107	0	100	3 800	–
Total Oceania	**848 655**	**34 940**	**4**	**1.3**	**30**	**27 706**	**3.2**
Argentina	273 669	39 883	15	1.0	8	14 303	6.8
Bolivia (Plurinational state of)	108 330	9 694	9	1.8	34	4 277	6.1
Brazil	845 942	191 972	23	1.0	14	10 304	5.1
Chile	74 353	16 804	23	1.0	12	14 436	3.2
Colombia	110 950	45 012	41	1.5	26	8 797	2.5

Country / area	Land area	Population 2008				GDP 2008	
		Total	Density	Annual growth rate	Rural	Per capita (PPP)	Annual real growth rate
	(1 000 ha)	(1 000)	(Population/ km²)	(%)	(% of total)	(US$)	(%)
Ecuador	24 836	13 481	54	1.0	34	8 014	6.5
Falkland Islands (Malvinas)†	1 217	3	0	0	0	35 400	–
French Guiana	8 220	220	3	2.8	24	–	–
Guyana	19 685	763	4	-0.1	72	3 064	3.0
Paraguay	39 730	6 238	16	1.8	40	4 704	5.8
Peru	128 000	28 837	23	1.2	29	8 509	9.8
Suriname	15 600	515	3	1.0	25	7 401	5.1
Uruguay	17 502	3 349	19	0.3	8	12 744	8.9
Venezuela (Bolivarian Republic of)	88 205	28 121	32	1.7	7	12 818	4.8
Total South America	**1 756 239**	**384 892**	**22**	**1.2**	**17**	**10 446**	**5.4**
TOTAL WORLD	**13 009 550**	**6 750 525**	**52**	**1.2**	**50**	**10 384**	**1.7**

† A dispute exists between the governments of Argentina and the United Kingdom of Great Britain and Northern Ireland concerning sovereignty over the Falkland Islands (Malvinas).

Source: FAOSTAT (ResourceSTAT and PopSTAT), World Bank (World Development Indicators), IMF (World Economic Outlook database), UNSD (National Accounts Main Aggregates Database) and CIA (World Factbook), last accessed 16 September 2010.

Table 1 | 109

Table 2: Forest area and area change

Country / area	Extent of forest 2010			Annual change rate			
	Forest area	% of land area	Area per 1 000 people	1990–2000		2000–2010	
	(1 000 ha)	(%)	(ha)	(1 000 ha)	(%)	(1 000 ha)	(%)
Burundi	172	7	21	-9	-3.7	-3	-1.4
Cameroon	19 916	42	1 043	-220	-0.9	-220	-1.0
Central African Republic	22 605	36	5 210	-30	-0.1	-30	-0.1
Chad	11 525	9	1 056	-79	-0.6	-79	-0.7
Republic of the Congo	22 411	66	6 199	-17	-0.1	-15	-0.1
Democratic Republic of the Congo	154 135	68	2 399	-311	-0.2	-311	-0.2
Equatorial Guinea	1 626	58	2 467	-12	-0.6	-12	-0.7
Gabon	22 000	85	15 193	0	0	0	0
Rwanda	435	18	45	3	0.8	9	2.4
Saint Helena, Ascension and Tristan da Cunha	2	6	400	0	0	0	0
Sao Tome and Principe	27	28	169	0	0	0	0
Total Central Africa	**254 854**	**48**	**2 084**	**-676**	**-0.3**	**-660**	**-0.3**
Comoros	3	2	4	0	-4.0	-1	-9.3
Djibouti	6	0	7	0	0	0	0
Eritrea	1 532	15	311	-5	-0.3	-4	-0.3
Ethiopia	12 296	11	152	-141	-1.0	-141	-1.1
Kenya	3 467	6	89	-13	-0.3	-12	-0.3
Madagascar	12 553	22	657	-57	-0.4	-57	-0.4
Mauritius	35	17	27	0	0	0	-1.0
Mayotte	14	37	73	0	-1.2	0	-1.3
Réunion	88	35	108	0	0	0	0.1
Seychelles	41	88	485	0	0	0	0
Somalia	6 747	11	756	-77	-1.0	-77	-1.1
Uganda	2 988	15	94	-88	-2.0	-88	-2.6
United Republic of Tanzania	33 428	38	787	-403	-1.0	-403	-1.1
Total East Africa	**73 197**	**18**	**317**	**-784**	**-0.9**	**-783**	**-1.0**
Algeria	1 492	1	43	-9	-0.5	-9	-0.6
Egypt	70	0	1	2	3.0	1	1.7

Country / area	Extent of forest 2010			Annual change rate			
	Forest area	% of land area	Area per 1 000 people	1990–2000		2000–2010	
	(1 000 ha)	(%)	(ha)	(1 000 ha)	(%)	(1 000 ha)	(%)
Libyan Arab Jamahiriya	217	0	34	0	0	0	0
Mauritania	242	0	75	-10	-2.7	-8	-2.7
Morocco	5 131	11	162	-3	-0.1	11	0.2
Sudan	69 949	29	1 692	-589	-0.8	-54	-0.1
Tunisia	1 006	6	99	19	2.7	17	1.9
Western Sahara	707	3	1 423	0	0	0	0
Total Northern Africa	**78 814**	**8**	**377**	**-590**	**-0.7**	**-41**	**-0.1**
Angola	58 480	47	3 245	-125	-0.2	-125	-0.2
Botswana	11 351	20	5 909	-118	-0.9	-118	-1.0
Lesotho	44	1	21	0	0.5	0	0.5
Malawi	3 237	34	218	-33	-0.9	-33	-1.0
Mozambique	39 022	50	1 743	-219	-0.5	-217	-0.5
Namibia	7 290	9	3 423	-73	-0.9	-74	-1.0
South Africa	9 241	8	186	0	0	0	0
Swaziland	563	33	482	5	0.9	5	0.8
Zambia	49 468	67	3 920	-167	-0.3	-167	-0.3
Zimbabwe	15 624	40	1 254	-327	-1.6	-327	-1.9
Total Southern Africa	**194 320**	**33**	**1 416**	**-1 057**	**-0.5**	**-1 056**	**-0.5**
Benin	4 561	41	527	-70	-1.3	-50	-1.0
Burkina Faso	5 649	21	371	-60	-0.9	-60	-1.0
Cape Verde	85	21	171	2	3.6	0	0.4
Côte d'Ivoire	10 403	33	505	11	0.1	8	0.1
Gambia	480	48	289	2	0.4	2	0.4
Ghana	4 940	22	212	-135	-2.0	-115	-2.1
Guinea	6 544	27	666	-36	-0.5	-36	-0.5
Guinea-Bissau	2 022	72	1 284	-10	-0.4	-10	-0.5
Liberia	4 329	45	1 141	-30	-0.6	-30	-0.7
Mali	12 490	10	983	-79	-0.6	-79	-0.6
Niger	1 204	1	82	-62	-3.7	-12	-1.0
Nigeria	9 041	10	60	-410	-2.7	-410	-3.7

Table 2 | 111

Country / area	Extent of forest 2010			Annual change rate			
	Forest area	% of land area	Area per 1 000 people	1990–2000		2000–2010	
	(1 000 ha)	(%)	(ha)	(1 000 ha)	(%)	(1 000 ha)	(%)
Albania	776	28	247	-2	-0.3	1	0.1
Andorra	16	36	190	0	0	0	0
Austria	3 887	47	466	6	0.2	5	0.1
Belarus	8 630	42	892	49	0.6	36	0.4
Belgium	678	22	64	-1	-0.2	1	0.2
Bosnia and Herzegovina	2 185	43	579	-3	-0.1	0	0
Bulgaria	3 927	36	517	5	0.1	55	1.5
Croatia	1 920	34	434	4	0.2	4	0.2
Czech Republic	2 657	34	257	1	0	2	0.1
Denmark	544	13	100	4	0.9	6	1.1
Estonia	2 217	52	1 653	15	0.7	-3	-0.1
Faroe Islands	0	0	2	0	0	0	0
Finland	22 157	73	4 177	57	0.3	-30	-0.1
France	15 954	29	257	82	0.5	60	0.4
Germany	11 076	32	135	34	0.3	0	0
Gibraltar	0	0	0	0	–	0	–
Greece	3 903	30	350	30	0.9	30	0.8
Guernsey	0	3	3	0	0	0	0
Holy See	0	0	0	0	–	0	–
Hungary	2 029	23	203	11	0.6	12	0.6
Iceland	30	0	95	1	7.8	1	5.0
Ireland	739	11	167	17	3.2	10	1.5
Isle of Man	3	6	43	0	0	0	0
Italy	9 149	31	153	78	1.0	78	0.9
Jersey	1	5	7	0	0	0	0
Latvia	3 354	54	1 485	7	0.2	11	0.3
Liechtenstein	7	43	192	0	0.6	0	0
Lithuania	2 160	34	650	8	0.4	14	0.7
Luxembourg	87	33	180	0	0.1	0	0
Malta	0	1	1	0	0	0	0
Monaco	0	0	0	0	–	0	–
Montenegro	543	40	873	0	0	0	0

Country / area	Extent of forest 2010			Annual change rate			
	Forest area	% of land area	Area per 1 000 people	1990–2000		2000–2010	
	(1 000 ha)	(%)	(ha)	(1 000 ha)	(%)	(1 000 ha)	(%)
Netherlands	365	11	22	2	0.4	1	0.1
Norway	10 065	33	2 111	17	0.2	76	0.8
Poland	9 337	30	245	18	0.2	28	0.3
Portugal	3 456	38	324	9	0.3	4	0.1
Republic of Moldova	386	12	106	1	0.2	6	1.8
Romania	6 573	29	308	-1	0	21	0.3
Russian Federation	809 090	49	5 722	32	0	-18	0
San Marino	0	0	0	0	–	0	–
Serbia	2 713	31	276	15	0.6	25	1.0
Slovakia	1 933	40	358	0	0	1	0.1
Slovenia	1 253	62	622	5	0.4	2	0.2
Spain	18 173	36	409	317	2.1	119	0.7
Svalbard and Jan Mayen Islands	0	0	0	0	–	0	–
Sweden	28 203	69	3 064	11	0	81	0.3
Switzerland	1 240	31	164	4	0.4	5	0.4
The former Yugoslav Republic of Macedonia	998	39	489	5	0.5	4	0.4
Ukraine	9 705	17	211	24	0.3	20	0.2
United Kingdom	2 881	12	47	18	0.7	9	0.3
Total Europe	**1 005 001**	**45**	**1 373**	**877**	**0.1**	**676**	**0.1**
Anguilla	6	60	367	0	0	0	0
Antigua and Barbuda	10	22	113	0	-0.3	0	-0.2
Aruba	0	2	4	0	0	0	0
Bahamas	515	51	1 524	0	0	0	0
Barbados	8	19	33	0	0	0	0
Bermuda	1	20	15	0	0	0	0
British Virgin Islands	4	24	158	0	-0.1	0	-0.1
Cayman Islands	13	50	227	0	0	0	0
Cuba	2 870	26	256	38	1.7	44	1.7
Dominica	45	60	667	0	-0.5	0	-0.6

Table 2 | 115

Country / area	Extent of forest 2010			Annual change rate			
	Forest area	% of land area	Area per 1 000 people	1990–2000		2000–2010	
	(1 000 ha)	(%)	(ha)	(1 000 ha)	(%)	(1 000 ha)	(%)
Dominican Republic	1 972	41	198	0	0	0	0
Grenada	17	50	163	0	0	0	0
Guadeloupe	64	39	137	0	-0.3	0	-0.3
Haiti	101	4	10	-1	-0.6	-1	-0.8
Jamaica	337	31	124	0	-0.1	0	-0.1
Martinique	49	46	120	0	0	0	0
Montserrat	3	24	417	0	-3.3	0	0
Netherlands Antilles	1	1	6	0	0	0	0
Puerto Rico	552	62	139	18	4.9	9	1.8
Saint Barthélemy	0	0	0	0*	–	0	–
Saint Kitts and Nevis	11	42	216	0	0	0	0
Saint Lucia	47	77	276	0	0.6	0	0.1
Saint Martin (French part)	1	19	33	0	0	0	0
Saint Vincent and the Grenadines	27	68	245	0	0.3	0	0.3
Trinidad and Tobago	226	44	170	-1	-0.3	-1	-0.3
Turks and Caicos Islands	34	80	1 042	0	0	0	0
United States Virgin Islands	20	58	184	0	-0.7	0	-0.8
Total Caribbean	**6 933**	**30**	**166**	**53**	**0.9**	**50**	**0.7**
Belize	1 393	61	4 628	-10	-0.6	-10	-0.7
Costa Rica	2 605	51	576	-19	-0.8	23	0.9
El Salvador	287	14	47	-5	-1.3	-5	-1.4
Guatemala	3 657	34	267	-54	-1.2	-55	-1.4
Honduras	5 192	46	709	-174	-2.4	-120	-2.1
Nicaragua	3 114	26	549	-70	-1.7	-70	-2.0
Panama	3 251	44	956	-42	-1.2	-12	-0.4
Total Central America	**19 499**	**38**	**475**	**-374**	**-1.6**	**-248**	**-1.2**
Canada	310 134	34	9 325	0	0	0	0
Greenland	0	0	4	0	0	0	0
Mexico	64 802	33	597	-354	-0.5	-195	-0.3

Country / area	Extent of forest 2010			Annual change rate			
	Forest area	% of land area	Area per 1 000 people	1990–2000		2000–2010	
	(1 000 ha)	(%)	(ha)	(1 000 ha)	(%)	(1 000 ha)	(%)
Saint Pierre and Miquelon	3	13	483	0	-0.6	0	-1.0
United States of America	304 022	33	975	386	0.1	383	0.1
Total North America	**678 961**	**33**	**1 497**	**32**	**0**	**188**	**0**
Total North and Central America	**705 393**	**33**	**1 315**	**-289**	**0**	**-10**	**0**
American Samoa	18	89	268	0	-0.2	0	-0.2
Australia	149 300	19	7 085	42	0	-562	-0.4
Cook Islands	16	65	775	0	0.4	0	0
Fiji	1 014	56	1 202	3	0.3	3	0.3
French Polynesia	155	42	583	5*	6.7	5	4.0
Guam	26	47	147	0	0	0	0
Kiribati	12	15	125	0	0	0	0
Marshall Islands	13	70	207	0	0	0	0
Micronesia (Federated States of)	64	92	583	0	0	0	0
Nauru	0	0	0	0	–	0	–
New Caledonia	839	46	3 411	0	0	0	0
New Zealand	8 269	31	1 955	55	0.7	0	0
Niue	19	72	9 300	0	-0.5	0	-0.5
Norfolk Island	0	12	230	0	0	0	0
Northern Mariana Islands	30	66	357	0	-0.5	0	-0.5
Palau	40	88	2 015	0	0.4	0	0.2
Papua New Guinea	28 726	63	4 368	-139	-0.4	-141	-0.5
Pitcairn	4	83	74 468	0	0	0	0
Samoa	171	60	955	4	2.8	0	0
Solomon Islands	2 213	79	4 331	-6	-0.2	-6	-0.2
Tokelau	0	0	0	0	–	0	–
Tonga	9	13	87	0	0	0	0
Tuvalu	1	33	100	0	0	0	0
Vanuatu	440	36	1 880	0	0	0	0
Wallis and Futuna Islands	6	42	391	0	0	0	0.1
Total Oceania	**191 384**	**23**	**5 478**	**-36**	**0**	**-700**	**-0.4**

Table 2 | 117

| Country / area | Extent of forest 2010 | | | Annual change rate | | | |
| | Forest area | % of land area | Area per 1 000 people | 1990–2000 | | 2000–2010 | |
	(1 000 ha)	(%)	(ha)	(1 000 ha)	(%)	(1 000 ha)	(%)
Argentina	29 400	11	737	-293	-0.9	-246	-0.8
Bolivia (Plurinational state of)	57 196	53	5 900	-270	-0.4	-290	-0.5
Brazil	519 522	62	2 706	-2 890	-0.5	-2 642	-0.5
Chile	16 231	22	966	57	0.4	40	0.2
Colombia	60 499	55	1 344	-101	-0.2	-101	-0.2
Ecuador	9 865	36	732	-198	-1.5	-198	-1.8
Falkland Islands (Malvinas)†	0	0	0	0	–	0	–
French Guiana	8 082	98	36 736	-7	-0.1	-4	0
Guyana	15 205	77	19 928	0	0	0	0
Paraguay	17 582	44	2 819	-179	-0.9	-179	-1.0
Peru	67 992	53	2 358	-94	-0.1	-122	-0.2
Suriname	14 758	95	28 656	0	0	-2	0
Uruguay	1 744	10	521	49	4.4	33	2.1
Venezuela (Bolivarian Republic of)	46 275	52	1 646	-288	-0.6	-288	-0.6
Total South America	**864 351**	**49**	**2 246**	**-4 213**	**-0.5**	**-3 997**	**-0.5**
TOTAL WORLD	**4 033 060**	**31**	**597**	**-8 323**	**-0.2**	**-5 211**	**-0.1**

† A dispute exists between the governments of Argentina and the United Kingdom of Great Britain and Northern Ireland concerning sovereignty over the Falkland Islands (Malvinas).

* FAO estimates based on information provided by these two countries for 2000 and 2005.

Source: FAO, 2010a.

Table 3: Carbon stock and stock change in living forest biomass

Country / area	Carbon stock in living forest biomass					Annual change rate	
	(million tonnes)				(tonnes/ha)	(1 000 tonnes)	
	1990	2000	2005	2010	2010	1990–2000	2000–2010
Burundi	25	19	18	17	96	-1	0
Cameroon	3 292	2 993	2 844	2 696	135	-30	-30
Central African Republic	2 936	2 898	2 879	2 861	127	-4	-4
Chad	722	677	655	635	55	-5	-4
Republic of the Congo	3 487	3 461	3 448	3 438	153	-3	-2
Democratic Republic of the Congo	20 433	20 036	19 838	19 639	127	-40	-40
Equatorial Guinea	232	217	210	203	125	-1	-1
Gabon	2 710	2 710	2 710	2 710	123	0	0
Rwanda	35	18	35	39	91	-2	2
Saint Helena, Ascension and Tristan da Cunha	–	–	–	–	–	–	–
Sao Tome and Principe	4	4	4	4	141	0	0
Total Central Africa							
Comoros	2	1	1	0	117	0	0
Djibouti	0	0	0	0	41	0	0
Eritrea	–	–	–	–	–	–	–
Ethiopia	289	254	236	219	18	-4	-4
Kenya	525	503	489	476	137	-2	-3
Madagascar	1 778	1 691	1 663	1 626	130	-9	-7
Mauritius	3	3	2	2	65	0	0
Mayotte	–	–	–	–	–	–	–
Réunion	6	6	6	6	68	0	0
Seychelles	4	4	4	4	88	0	0
Somalia	482	439	415	394	58	-4	-5
Uganda	171	140	124	109	36	-3	-3
United Republic of Tanzania	2 505	2 262	2 139	2 019	60	-24	-24
Total East Africa							
Algeria	78	74	72	70	47	0	0
Egypt	4	6	7	7	99	0	0
Libyan Arab Jamahiriya	6	6	6	6	28	0	0

Table 3 | 119

Country / area	Carbon stock in living forest biomass (million tonnes)				(tonnes/ha)	Annual change rate (1 000 tonnes)	
	1990	2000	2005	2010	2010	1990–2000	2000–2010
Mauritania	13	10	8	7	30	0	0
Morocco	190	212	224	223	43	2	1
Sudan	1 521	1 403	1 398	1 393	20	-12	-1
Tunisia	6	8	8	9	9	0	0
Western Sahara	33	33	33	33	46	0	0
Total Northern Africa							
Angola	4 573	4 479	4 432	4 385	75	-9	-9
Botswana	680	663	655	646	57	-2	-2
Lesotho	2	2	2	2	53	0	0
Malawi	173	159	151	144	44	-1	-2
Mozambique	1 878	1 782	1 733	1 692	43	-10	-9
Namibia	253	232	221	210	29	-2	-2
South Africa	807	807	807	807	87	0	0
Swaziland	23	22	22	22	39	0	0
Zambia	2 579	2 497	2 457	2 416	49	-8	-8
Zimbabwe	697	594	543	492	31	-10	-10
Total Southern Africa							
Benin	332	291	277	263	58	-4	-3
Burkina Faso	355	323	308	292	52	-3	-3
Cape Verde	3	5	5	5	58	0	0
Côte d'Ivoire	1 811	1 832	1 847	1 842	177	2	1
Gambia	29	30	31	32	66	0	0
Ghana	564	465	423	381	77	-10	-8
Guinea	687	653	636	619	95	-3	-3
Guinea-Bissau	106	101	98	96	47	-1	-1
Liberia	666	625	605	585	135	-4	-4
Mali	317	300	291	282	23	-2	-2
Niger	60	41	38	37	31	-2	0
Nigeria	2 016	1 550	1 317	1 085	120	-47	-47
Senegal	377	357	348	340	40	-2	-2

Country / area	Carbon stock in living forest biomass					Annual change rate	
	(million tonnes)				(tonnes/ha)	(1 000 tonnes)	
	1990	2000	2005	2010	2010	1990–2000	2000–2010
Sierra Leone	247	232	224	216	79	-2	-2
Togo	–	–	–	–	–	–	–
Total West Africa							
Total Africa							
Armenia	17	15	14	13	48	0	0
Azerbaijan	54	54	54	54	58	0	0
Georgia	192	203	207	212	77	1	1
Kazakhstan	137	137	137	137	41	0	0
Kyrgyzstan	27	34	37	56	59	1	2
Tajikistan	3	3	3	3	7	0	0
Turkmenistan	11	11	12	12	3	0	0
Uzbekistan	8	14	18	19	6	1	1
Total Central Asia							
China	4 414	5 295	5 802	6 203	30	88	91
Democratic People's Republic of Korea	239	207	190	171	30	-3	-4
Japan	1 159	1 381	1 526	–	–	22	–
Mongolia	671	626	605	583	53	-5	-4
Republic of Korea	109	181	224	268	43	7	9
Total East Asia							
Bangladesh	84	82	82	80	55	0	0
Bhutan	296	313	324	336	103	2	2
India	2 223	2 377	2 615	2 800	41	15	42
Maldives	–	–	–	–	–	–	–
Nepal	602	520	485	485	133	-8	-4
Pakistan	330	271	243	213	126	-6	-6
Sri Lanka	90	74	66	61	33	-2	-1
Total South Asia							
Brunei Darussalam	81	76	74	72	188	0	0
Cambodia	609	537	495	464	46	-7	-7

Table 3 | 121

Country / area	Carbon stock in living forest biomass				(tonnes/ha)	Annual change rate	
	(million tonnes)					(1 000 tonnes)	
	1990	2000	2005	2010	2010	1990–2000	2000–2010
Indonesia	16 335	15 182	14 299	13 017	138	-115	-217
Lao People's Democratic Republic	1 186	1 133	1 106	1 074	68	-5	-6
Malaysia	2 822	3 558	3 362	3 212	157	74	-35
Myanmar	2 040	1 814	1 734	1 654	52	-23	-16
Philippines	641	655	660	663	87	1	1
Singapore	–	–	–	–	–	–	–
Thailand	908	881	877	880	46	-3	0
Timor-Leste	–	–	–	–	–	–	–
Viet Nam	778	927	960	992	72	15	7
Total Southeast Asia							
Afghanistan	38	38	38	38	28	0	0
Bahrain	–	–	–	–	–	–	–
Cyprus	3	3	3	3	18	0	0
Iran (Islamic Republic of)	249	249	254	258	23	0	1
Iraq	–	–	–	–	–	–	–
Israel	5	5	5	5	31	0	0
Jordan	2	2	2	2	24	0	0
Kuwait	–	–	–	–	–	–	–
Lebanon	–	–	2	2	13	–	–
Occupied Palestinian Territory	–	–	–	–	–	–	–
Oman	–	–	–	–	–	–	–
Qatar	0	0	0	0	–	0	0
Saudi Arabia	6	6	6	6	6	0	0
Syrian Arab Republic	–	–	–	–	–	–	–
Turkey	686	743	782	822	73	6	8
United Arab Emirates	12	15	16	16	50	0	0
Yemen	5	5	5	5	9	0	0
Total Western Asia							
Total Asia							
Albania	49	49	48	49	63	0	0
Andorra	–	–	–	–	–	–	–

Country / area	Carbon stock in living forest biomass					Annual change rate	
	(million tonnes)				(tonnes/ha)	(1 000 tonnes)	
	1990	2000	2005	2010	2010	1990–2000	2000–2010
Austria	339	375	399	393	101	4	2
Belarus	386	482	540	611	71	10	13
Belgium	50	61	63	64	95	1	0
Bosnia and Herzegovina	96	118	118	118	54	2	0
Bulgaria	127	161	182	202	51	3	4
Croatia	190	221	237	253	132	3	3
Czech Republic	287	322	339	356	134	4	3
Denmark	22	26	36	37	68	0	1
Estonia	–	168	167	165	74	–	0
Faroe Islands	–	–	–	–	–	–	–
Finland	721	802	832	832	38	8	3
France	965	1 049	1 165	1 208	76	8	16
Germany	981	1 193	1 283	1 405	127	21	21
Gibraltar	0	0	0	0	–	0	0
Greece	67	73	76	79	20	1	1
Guernsey	–	–	–	–	–	–	–
Holy See	0	0	0	0	–	0	0
Hungary	117	130	136	142	70	1	1
Iceland	0	0	0	0	9	0	0
Ireland	16	18	20	23	31	0	0
Isle of Man	–	–	–	–	–	–	–
Italy	375	467	512	558	61	9	9
Jersey	–	–	–	–	–	–	–
Latvia	193	234	244	272	81	4	4
Liechtenstein	0	1	1	1	74	0	0
Lithuania	134	146	151	153	71	1	1
Luxembourg	7	9	9	9	108	0	0
Malta	0	0	0	0	173	0	0
Monaco	0	0	0	0	–	0	0
Montenegro	33	33	33	33	61	0	0
Netherlands	21	24	26	28	76	0	0
Norway	280	323	360	395	39	4	7
Poland	691	807	887	968	104	12	16

Table 3 | 123

| Country / area | Carbon stock in living forest biomass | | | | | Annual change rate | |
| | (million tonnes) | | | | (tonnes/ha) | (1 000 tonnes) | |
	1990	2000	2005	2010	2010	1990–2000	2000–2010
Portugal	–	–	102	102	30	–	–
Republic of Moldova	22	26	28	29	75	0	0
Romania	600	599	601	618	94	0	2
Russian Federation	32 504	32 157	32 210	32 500	40	-35	34
San Marino	0	0	0	0	–	0	0
Serbia	122	138	147	240	88	2	10
Slovakia	163	190	202	211	109	3	2
Slovenia	116	141	159	178	142	2	4
Spain	289	396	400	422	23	11	3
Svalbard and Jan Mayen Islands	0	0	0	0	–	0	0
Sweden	1 178	1 183	1 219	1 255	45	0	7
Switzerland	126	136	139	143	115	1	1
The former Yugoslav Republic of Macedonia	60	62	60	60	61	0	0
Ukraine	499	662	712	761	78	16	10
United Kingdom	120	119	128	136	47	0	2
Total Europe							
Anguilla	–	–	–	–	–	–	–
Antigua and Barbuda	–	–	–	–	–	–	–
Aruba	–	–	–	–	–	–	–
Bahamas	–	–	–	–	–	–	–
Barbados	–	–	–	–	–	–	–
Bermuda	–	–	–	–	–	–	–
British Virgin Islands	–	–	–	–	–	–	–
Cayman Islands	–	–	–	–	–	–	–
Cuba	113	180	212	226	79	7	5
Dominica	–	–	–	–	–	–	–
Dominican Republic	114	114	114	114	58	0	0
Grenada	1	1	1	1	63	0	0
Guadeloupe	13	13	13	12	195	0	0
Haiti	6	6	6	5	54	0	0
Jamaica	48	48	48	48	141	0	0

| Country / area | Carbon stock in living forest biomass | | | | | Annual change rate | |
| | (million tonnes) | | | | (tonnes/ha) | (1 000 tonnes) | |
	1990	2000	2005	2010	2010	1990–2000	2000–2010
Martinique	–	8	8	8	173	–	0
Montserrat	–	–	–	–	–	–	–
Netherlands Antilles	–	–	–	–	–	–	–
Puerto Rico	14	23	26	28	51	1	0
Saint Barthélemy	0	0	0	0	–	0	0
Saint Kitts and Nevis	–	–	–	–	–	–	–
Saint Lucia	–	–	–	–	–	–	–
Saint Martin (French part)	–	–	–	–	–	–	–
Saint Vincent and the Grenadines	–	–	–	–	–	–	–
Trinidad and Tobago	21	20	20	19	85	0	0
Turks and Caicos Islands	–	–	–	–	–	–	–
United States Virgin Islands	1	1	1	1	27	0	0
Total Caribbean							
Belize	195	184	178	171	123	-1	-1
Costa Rica	233	217	227	238	91	-2	2
El Salvador	–	–	–	–	–	–	–
Guatemala	365	324	303	281	77	-4	-4
Honduras	517	407	368	330	64	-11	-8
Nicaragua	506	428	389	349	112	-8	-8
Panama	429	381	374	367	113	-5	-1
Total Central America							
Canada	14 284	14 317	14 021	13 908	45	3	-41
Greenland	–	–	–	–	–	–	–
Mexico	2 186	2 111	2 076	2 043	32	-8	-7
Saint Pierre and Miquelon	–	–	–	–	–	–	–
United States of America	16 951	17 998	18 631	19 308	64	105	131
Total North America							
Total North and Central America							
American Samoa	2	2	2	2	110	0	0
Australia	6 724	6 702	6 641	–	–	-2	–

Table 3 | 125

Country / area	Carbon stock in living forest biomass					Annual change rate	
	(million tonnes)				(tonnes/ha)	(1 000 tonnes)	
	1990	2000	2005	2010	2010	1990–2000	2000–2010
Cook Islands	–	–	–	–	–	–	–
Fiji	–	–	–	–	–	–	–
French Polynesia	–	–	–	21	132	–	–
Guam	2	2	2	2	69	0	0
Kiribati	–	–	–	–	–	–	–
Marshall Islands	2	2	2	2	183	0	0
Micronesia (Federated States of)	20	20	20	20	318	0	0
Nauru	0	0	0	0	–	0	0
New Caledonia	60	60	60	60	72	0	0
New Zealand	–	–	1 263	1 292	156	–	–
Niue	–	–	–	–	–	–	–
Norfolk Island	–	–	–	–	–	–	–
Northern Mariana Islands	3	3	3	3	100	0	0
Palau	10	10	11	11	264	0	0
Papua New Guinea	2 537	2 423	2 365	2 306	80	-11	-12
Pitcairn	–	–	–	–	–	–	–
Samoa	–	–	–	–	–	–	–
Solomon Islands	191	186	184	182	82	0	0
Tokelau	0	0	0	0	–	0	0
Tonga	1	1	1	1	114	0	0
Tuvalu	–	–	–	–	–	–	–
Vanuatu	–	–	–	–	–	–	–
Wallis and Futuna Islands	–	–	–	–	–	–	–
Total Oceania							
Argentina	3 414	3 236	3 143	3 062	104	-18	-17
Bolivia (Plurinational state of)	4 877	4 666	4 561	4 442	78	-21	-22
Brazil	68 119	65 304	63 679	62 607	121	-282	-270
Chile	1 294	1 328	1 338	1 349	83	3	2
Colombia	7 032	6 918	6 862	6 805	112	-11	-11
Ecuador	–	–	–	–	–	–	–
Falkland Islands (Malvinas)[†]	0	0	0	0	–	0	0
French Guiana	1 672	1 657	1 654	1 651	204	-2	-1

| Country / area | Carbon stock in living forest biomass | | | | | Annual change rate | |
| | (million tonnes) | | | | (tonnes/ha) | (1 000 tonnes) | |
	1990	2000	2005	2010	2010	1990–2000	2000–2010
Guyana	1 629	1 629	1 629	1 629	107	0	0
Paraguay	–	–	–	–	–	–	–
Peru	8 831	8 713	8 654	8 560	126	-12	-15
Suriname	3 168	3 168	3 168	3 165	214	0	0
Uruguay	–	–	–	–	–	–	–
Venezuela (Bolivarian Republic of)	–	–	–	–	–	–	–
Total South America							
TOTAL WORLD							

† A dispute exists between the governments of Argentina and the United Kingdom of Great Britain and Northern Ireland concerning sovereignty over the Falkland Islands (Malvinas).
Source: FAO, 2010a.

Table 3 | 127

Table 4: Production, trade and consumption of woodfuel, roundwood and sawnwood, 2008

Country / area	Woodfuel (1 000 m³)				Industrial roundwood (1 000 m³)				Sawnwood (1 000 m³)			
	Production	Imports	Exports	Consumption	Production	Imports	Exports	Consumption	Production	Imports	Exports	Consumption
Burundi	8 965	0	0	8 965	333	0	3	330	83	0	0	83
Cameroon	9 733	0	0	9 733	2 616	0	157	2 459	773	0	258	515
Central African Republic	6 017	0	0	6 017	841	0	57	784	95	0	11	84
Chad	6 830	0	0	6 830	761	1	0	762	2	0	0	2
Republic of the Congo	1 295	0	0	1 295	2 431	1	251	2 180	268	0	40	228
Democratic Republic of the Congo	74 315	0	0	74 315	4 452	5	156	4 301	15	17	29	3
Equatorial Guinea	189	0	0	189	419	0	82	337	4	0	1	3
Gabon	534	0	0	534	3 400	0	2 178	1 222	230	0	62	169
Rwanda	9 591	0	0	9 591	495	6	0	501	79	9	0	87
Saint Helena, Ascension and Tristan da Cunha	0	0	0	0	0	0	0	0	0	0	0	0
Sao Tome and Principe	0	0	0	0	9	0	0	9	5	0	1	5
Total Central Africa	**117 469**	**0**	**0**	**117 469**	**15 757**	**14**	**2 884**	**12 886**	**1 555**	**26**	**402**	**1 179**
Comoros	0	0	0	0	9	0	0	9	0	1	0	1
Djibouti	0	0	0	0	0	3	0	3	0	1	0	1
Eritrea	2 565	0	0	2 565	2	1	0	3	0	1	0	1
Ethiopia	98 489	0	0	98 490	2 928	3	0	2 931	18	14	12	20
Kenya	21 141	0	0	21 141	1 246	11	2	1 256	142	14	0	155
Madagascar	11 910	0	0	11 910	277	16	16	277	92	1	35	58
Mauritius	7	0	0	7	9	3	0	11	3	25	0	28
Mayotte	–	–	–	–	–	–	–	–	–	–	–	–
Réunion	31	0	0	31	5	1	2	3	2	85	0	87
Seychelles	0	0	0	0	0	0	0	0	0	0	0	0
Somalia	11 807	0	0	11 807	110	1	0	111	14	11	0	25
Uganda	38 468	0	0	38 468	3 489	1	19	3 471	117	4	1	121
United Republic of Tanzania	22 352	0	0	22 352	2 314	0	6	2 308	24	4	22	6
Total East Africa	**206 769**	**0**	**0**	**206 769**	**10 389**	**41**	**46**	**10 384**	**412**	**162**	**71**	**503**

Country / area	Woodfuel (1 000 m³)				Industrial roundwood (1 000 m³)				Sawnwood (1 000 m³)			
	Production	Imports	Exports	Consumption	Production	Imports	Exports	Consumption	Production	Imports	Exports	Consumption
Algeria	7 968	0	0	7 968	103	35	1	136	13	802	0	815
Egypt	17 283	0	0	17 283	268	116	0	384	2	1 911	0	1 913
Libyan Arab Jamahiriya	926	0	0	926	116	8	0	124	31	202	0	232
Mauritania	1 747	0	0	1 747	3	0	0	3	14	2	0	16
Morocco	339	0	0	339	577	407	3	981	83	723	92	714
Sudan	18 326	0	0	18 326	2 173	1	2	2 172	51	91	0	142
Tunisia	2 170	0	0	2 170	218	18	1	235	20	278	0	298
Western Sahara	–	–	–	–	–	–	–	–	–	–	–	–
Total Northern Africa	**48 759**	**0**	**0**	**48 760**	**3 458**	**585**	**7**	**4 035**	**214**	**4 010**	**93**	**4 131**
Angola	3 828	4	0	3 832	1 096	2	6	1 092	5	3	0	8
Botswana	674	0	0	674	105	0	0	105	0	15	0	15
Lesotho	2 076	0	0	2 076	0	0	0	0	0	0	0	0
Malawi	5 293	0	2	5 291	520	0	9	511	45	0	45	0
Mozambique	16 724	1	0	16 724	1 304	10	14	1 300	57	13	47	23
Namibia	–	–	–	–	–	–	–	–	–	–	–	–
South Africa	19 560	0	0	19 561	19 867	60	273	19 654	2 056	488	55	2 488
Swaziland	1 028	0	0	1 028	330	0	0	330	102	0	0	102
Zambia	8 840	0	0	8 840	1 325	4	5	1 324	157	5	25	137
Zimbabwe	8 543	0	0	8 543	771	2	3	770	565	1	54	512
Total Southern Africa	**66 567**	**5**	**2**	**66 570**	**25 318**	**79**	**311**	**25 086**	**2 986**	**526**	**227**	**3 285**
Benin	6 184	0	0	6 184	427	0	51	377	84	0	4	80
Burkina Faso	12 418	0	0	12 418	1 171	2	3	1 170	5	4	0	9
Cape Verde	2	0	0	2	0	4	0	3	0	17	0	17
Côte d'Ivoire	8 835	0	2	8 833	1 469	11	59	1 422	456	0	279	177
Gambia	675	0	0	675	113	0	0	113	1	1	0	2
Ghana	35 363	0	0	35 363	1 392	3	1	1 393	513	0	192	322
Guinea	11 846	0	0	11 846	651	0	18	633	30	0	25	6
Guinea-Bissau	422	0	0	422	170	0	2	168	16	1	0	16
Liberia	6 503	0	0	6 503	420	0	1	419	80	0	0	80

Table 4 | 129

Country / area	Woodfuel (1 000 m³)				Industrial roundwood (1 000 m³)				Sawnwood (1 000 m³)			
	Production	Imports	Exports	Consumption	Production	Imports	Exports	Consumption	Production	Imports	Exports	Consumption
Mali	5 203	0	0	5 203	413	0	0	413	13	22	1	34
Niger	9 432	0	0	9 432	411	1	0	411	4	8	0	12
Nigeria	62 389	0	2	62 387	9 418	1	40	9 379	2 000	2	8	1 994
Senegal	5 366	0	0	5 366	794	13	0	807	23	81	2	103
Sierra Leone	5 509	0	0	5 509	124	0	2	122	5	0	1	4
Togo	5 927	0	0	5 927	166	1	23	144	15	0	1	14
Total West Africa	**176 073**	**1**	**4**	**176 069**	**17 138**	**36**	**201**	**16 974**	**3 245**	**138**	**514**	**2 869**
Total Africa	**615 636**	**7**	**7**	**615 636**	**72 059**	**754**	**3 449**	**69 365**	**8 412**	**4 862**	**1 307**	**11 967**
Armenia	40	0	0	40	2	1	0	3	0	47	0	47
Azerbaijan	3	1	0	4	3	3	0	7	2	747	1	748
Georgia	733	0	0	733	105	17	1	121	70	2	51	21
Kazakhstan	50	0	0	50	198	98	0	296	111	758	0	869
Kyrgyzstan	18	0	0	18	9	4	0	13	60	107	2	165
Tajikistan	90	0	0	90	0	0	0	0	0	109	0	109
Turkmenistan	10	0	0	10	0	0	0	0	0	24	0	24
Uzbekistan	22	0	0	22	8	134	4	138	10	0	0	10
Total Central Asia	**966**	**1**	**0**	**967**	**326**	**257**	**5**	**577**	**252**	**1 794**	**54**	**1 992**
China	196 031	14	2	196 043	95 819	38 044	687	133 176	29 311	8 719	911	37 119
Democratic People's Republic of Korea	5 911	0	0	5 911	1 500	73	92	1 481	280	1	1	280
Japan	96	1	0	97	17 709	6 766	49	24 426	10 884	6 522	43	17 363
Mongolia	634	0	0	634	40	4	1	43	300	1	0	301
Republic of Korea	2 475	0	0	2 475	2 702	4 896	0	7 598	4 366	564	8	4 922
Total East Asia	**205 147**	**15**	**2**	**205 160**	**117 770**	**49 783**	**830**	**166 724**	**45 141**	**15 807**	**963**	**59 985**
Bangladesh	27 433	0	0	27 433	282	28	1	310	388	1	0	389
Bhutan	4 723	0	0	4 723	257	0	3	254	27	23	0	50
India	307 782	13	1	307 794	23 192	1 768	14	24 946	14 789	48	40	14 797
Maldives	0	0	0	0	0	0	0	0	0	0	0	0

Country / area	Woodfuel (1 000 m³)				Industrial roundwood (1 000 m³)				Sawnwood (1 000 m³)			
	Production	Imports	Exports	Consumption	Production	Imports	Exports	Consumption	Production	Imports	Exports	Consumption
Nepal	12 586	0	0	12 586	1 260	0	2	1 258	630	2	0	631
Pakistan	29 660	0	0	29 660	2 990	283	0	3 273	1 381	129	0	1 510
Sri Lanka	5 357	0	0	5 357	694	0	3	691	61	23	2	82
Total South Asia	**387 540**	**14**	**1**	**387 553**	**28 675**	**2 080**	**23**	**30 732**	**17 276**	**226**	**43**	**17 459**
Brunei Darussalam	12	0	0	12	112	0	0	112	51	1	0	52
Cambodia	8 735	0	0	8 735	118	1	0	119	10	0	6	5
Indonesia	65 034	0	1	65 033	35 551	120	685	34 986	4 330	318	73	4 575
Lao People's Democratic Republic	5 945	0	0	5 944	194	0	44	150	130	0	84	46
Malaysia	2 908	0	11	2 897	22 744	217	4 811	18 150	4 486	203	2 514	2 174
Myanmar	16 789	0	0	16 789	4 262	0	1 476	2 786	1 610	0	315	1 295
Philippines	12 581	0	0	12 581	3 025	78	7	3 095	358	134	215	278
Singapore	0	1	0	1	0	21	2	19	25	224	195	54
Thailand	19 503	0	0	19 503	8 700	159	0	8 859	2 868	387	384	2 871
Timor-Leste	0	0	0	0	0	0	1	0	0	0	0	0
Viet Nam	22 000	0	0	22 000	5 850	203	8	6 045	5 000	563	129	5 433
Total Southeast Asia	**153 506**	**2**	**12**	**153 496**	**80 555**	**800**	**7 034**	**74 321**	**18 868**	**1 830**	**3 914**	**16 784**
Afghanistan	1 564	0	0	1 564	1 760	0	2	1 758	400	130	1	529
Bahrain	6	0	0	6	0	2	1	2	0	15	0	15
Cyprus	7	0	0	7	13	0	0	13	10	116	1	125
Iran (Islamic Republic of)	67	1	0	68	819	107	0	926	50	909	14	945
Iraq	60	0	0	60	59	2	0	61	12	52	0	64
Israel	2	0	0	2	25	140	0	164	0	454	0	454
Jordan	286	0	0	285	4	5	2	7	0	279	4	275
Kuwait	0	0	0	0	0	1	0	1	0	123	0	123
Lebanon	80	0	0	80	7	38	1	45	9	289	39	259
Occupied Palestinian Territory	–	–	–	–	–	–	–	–	–	–	–	–

Table 4 | 131

Country / area	Woodfuel (1 000 m³)				Industrial roundwood (1 000 m³)				Sawnwood (1 000 m³)			
	Production	Imports	Exports	Consumption	Production	Imports	Exports	Consumption	Production	Imports	Exports	Consumption
Oman	0	0	0	0	0	57	0	57	0	90	0	90
Qatar	5	1	0	5	0	3	2	0	0	63	0	63
Saudi Arabia	0	4	0	4	0	25	0	25	0	1 426	0	1 426
Syrian Arab Republic	26	0	9	18	40	15	3	52	9	280	4	285
Turkey	4 958	110	0	5 068	14 462	1 239	5	15 696	6 175	667	28	6 814
United Arab Emirates	0	1	0	0	0	648	19	630	0	610	109	501
Yemen	410	0	0	410	0	10	0	10	0	160	0	160
Total Western Asia	**7 469**	**118**	**10**	**7 577**	**17 189**	**2 292**	**35**	**19 447**	**6 665**	**5 663**	**200**	**12 128**
Total Asia	**754 627**	**150**	**25**	**754 753**	**244 515**	**55 212**	**7 926**	**291 801**	**88 202**	**25 319**	**5 174**	**108 347**
Albania	350	0	56	294	80	1	0	80	8	24	21	10
Andorra	0	2	0	2	0	0	0	0	0	10	0	10
Austria	5 024	267	39	5 252	16 772	7 550	974	23 348	10 835	1 638	7 196	5 277
Belarus	1 345	1	75	1 271	7 411	76	1 443	6 044	2 458	116	1 197	1 377
Belgium	700	42	7	735	4 000	3 251	1 026	6 225	1 400	2 612	1 948	2 064
Bosnia and Herzegovina	1 440	0	434	1 006	2 571	154	122	2 603	998	39	910	127
Bulgaria	2 692	5	74	2 623	3 379	723	339	3 764	816	122	151	787
Croatia	763	3	241	525	3 706	17	487	3 236	721	424	536	609
Czech Republic	1 880	29	100	1 809	14 307	751	1 906	13 152	4 636	554	1 960	3 230
Denmark	1 106	276	30	1 352	1 680	336	1 142	874	300	4 622	444	4 477
Estonia	1 152	6	87	1 071	3 708	562	1 469	2 802	1 120	540	566	1 094
Faroe Islands	0	0	0	0	0	1	0	1	0	4	0	4
Finland	4 705	242	7	4 940	45 965	13 371	710	58 626	9 881	468	5 992	4 357
France	29 176	35	452	28 759	28 366	2 346	3 505	27 207	9 690	3 992	1 077	12 606
Germany	8 561	473	144	8 890	46 806	5 758	7 040	45 524	23 060	6 303	12 928	16 435
Gibraltar	0	0	0	0	0	0	0	0	0	1	0	1
Greece	795	320	5	1 110	948	588	7	1 529	108	928	14	1 023
Guernsey	–	–	–	–	–	–	–	–	–	–	–	–
Holy See	–	–	–	–	–	–	–	–	–	–	–	–
Hungary	2 561	84	166	2 479	2 822	207	661	2 367	207	374	151	430
Iceland	0	0	0	0	0	1	0	1	0	86	1	85

Country / area	Woodfuel (1 000 m³)				Industrial roundwood (1 000 m³)				Sawnwood (1 000 m³)			
	Production	Imports	Exports	Consumption	Production	Imports	Exports	Consumption	Production	Imports	Exports	Consumption
Ireland	52	5	5	53	2 180	326	258	2 248	697	412	389	720
Isle of Man	–	–	–	–	–	–	–	–	–	–	–	–
Italy	5 673	782	1	6 455	2 994	3 478	33	6 438	1 384	6 733	243	7 874
Jersey	–	–	–	–	–	–	–	–	–	–	–	–
Latvia	598	2	471	129	8 207	566	3 193	5 581	2 545	232	1 544	1 232
Liechtenstein	13	0	0	13	12	0	8	4	10	0	0	10
Lithuania	1 382	80	63	1 399	4 213	155	1 171	3 197	1 109	300	429	980
Luxembourg	21	5	0	26	332	462	545	249	202	219	89	332
Malta	0	0	0	0	0	0	0	0	0	21	0	21
Monaco	–	–	–	–	–	–	–	–	–	–	–	–
Montenegro	265	0	30	235	192	1	44	149	62	2	49	15
Netherlands	290	9	41	258	827	353	489	691	243	3 101	423	2 921
Norway	2 253	138	2	2 389	8 071	1 808	897	8 981	2 228	936	416	2 747
Poland	3 804	3	67	3 740	30 470	1 868	369	31 969	3 786	918	481	4 222
Portugal	600	0	2	598	10 266	521	1 345	9 442	1 010	203	294	919
Republic of Moldova	309	2	0	311	43	39	3	79	34	143	4	174
Romania	4 150	3	47	4 106	9 517	212	210	9 519	3 794	49	1 910	1 933
Russian Federation	44 700	0	275	44 425	136 700	286	36 784	100 202	21 618	23	15 258	6 383
San Marino	–	–	–	–	–	–	–	–	–	–	–	–
Serbia	1 571	1	3	1 569	1 615	95	45	1 665	672	496	155	1 013
Slovakia	555	58	97	515	8 714	750	2 192	7 272	2 842	143	442	2 543
Slovenia	928	123	318	733	2 062	163	477	1 747	500	795	1 240	55
Spain	2 600	18	153	2 465	14 427	2 860	1 014	16 273	3 142	2 446	240	5 347
Svalbard and Jan Mayen Islands	–	–	–	–	–	–	–	–	–	–	–	–
Sweden	5 900	142	104	5 938	64 900	6 781	2 349	69 332	17 601	381	12 006	5 976
Switzerland	1 195	8	24	1 179	3 755	341	1 155	2 941	1 540	450	446	1 544
The former Yugoslav Republic of Macedonia	516	0	3	513	193	1	3	191	14	181	17	178
Ukraine	9 520	0	814	8 706	7 364	133	2 582	4 916	2 467	12	1 475	1 004
United Kingdom	558	16	106	468	7 867	491	727	7 631	2 815	5 886	222	8 479
Total Europe	**149 702**	**3 183**	**4 543**	**148 341**	**507 442**	**57 383**	**76 723**	**488 103**	**136 552**	**46 939**	**72 866**	**110 625**

Table 4 | 133

Country / area	Woodfuel (1 000 m³)				Industrial roundwood (1 000 m³)				Sawnwood (1 000 m³)			
	Production	Imports	Exports	Consumption	Production	Imports	Exports	Consumption	Production	Imports	Exports	Consumption
Anguilla	–	–	–	–	–	–	–	–	–	–	–	–
Antigua and Barbuda	0	0	0	0	0	0	0	0	0	11	0	11
Aruba	2	0	0	2	0	1	0	1	0	16	0	16
Bahamas	33	0	0	33	17	80	0	97	1	2	2	2
Barbados	5	0	0	5	6	2	0	8	0	11	0	11
Bermuda	–	–	–	–	–	–	–	–	–	–	–	–
British Virgin Islands	1	0	0	1	0	0	0	0	0	4	0	4
Cayman Islands	0	0	0	0	0	2	0	2	0	14	0	14
Cuba	1 273	0	0	1 273	761	0	0	761	182	0	0	182
Dominica	8	0	0	8	0	1	0	1	0	4	0	4
Dominican Republic	895	0	0	895	10	30	0	39	39	289	0	328
Grenada	0	0	0	0	0	0	0	0	0	10	0	10
Guadeloupe	32	0	0	32	0	5	0	5	1	46	0	47
Haiti	2 024	0	0	2 024	239	1	0	240	14	24	0	38
Jamaica	552	0	0	552	277	3	0	280	66	102	0	168
Martinique	24	0	0	24	2	3	0	5	1	29	0	30
Montserrat	0	0	0	0	0	0	0	0	0	4	0	4
Netherlands Antilles	3	0	0	3	0	23	0	23	0	8	0	8
Puerto Rico	–	–	–	–	–	–	–	–	–	–	–	–
Saint Barthélemy	–	–	–	–	–	–	–	–	–	–	–	–
Saint Kitts and Nevis	0	0	0	0	0	1	0	1	0	5	0	5
Saint Lucia	10	0	0	10	0	7	0	7	0	10	0	10
Saint Martin (French part)	–	–	–	–	–	–	–	–	–	–	–	–
Saint Vincent and the Grenadines	8	0	0	8	0	6	0	6	0	6	0	6
Trinidad and Tobago	33	0	0	33	47	5	1	52	30	26	0	56
Turks and Caicos Islands	1	0	0	1	0	0	0	0	0	4	0	4
United States Virgin Islands	0	0	0	0	0	0	0	0	0	0	0	0
Total Caribbean	**4 904**	**1**	**0**	**4 905**	**1 359**	**170**	**1**	**1 529**	**334**	**624**	**2**	**956**

Country / area	Woodfuel (1 000 m³)				Industrial roundwood (1 000 m³)				Sawnwood (1 000 m³)			
	Production	Imports	Exports	Consumption	Production	Imports	Exports	Consumption	Production	Imports	Exports	Consumption
Belize	674	0	0	674	41	4	2	42	35	7	1	40
Costa Rica	3 398	0	0	3 398	1 198	21	144	1 074	1 227	39	7	1 259
El Salvador	4 217	0	0	4 217	682	0	28	654	16	31	0	47
Guatemala	17 319	0	0	17 319	454	6	16	445	366	25	40	350
Honduras	8 617	0	1	8 616	662	5	68	600	349	47	125	271
Nicaragua	6 033	1	0	6 033	93	3	0	95	54	1	3	52
Panama	1 158	0	0	1 158	151	6	80	77	9	7	16	0
Total Central America	**41 415**	**1**	**1**	**41 414**	**3 281**	**45**	**338**	**2 988**	**2 057**	**157**	**194**	**2 020**
Canada	2 715	131	113	2 733	132 232	4 608	2 839	134 001	41 548	1 754	24 219	19 083
Greenland	0	0	0	0	0	1	0	1	0	7	0	7
Mexico	38 676	2	7	38 671	6 425	174	9	6 590	2 814	3 468	64	6 218
Saint Pierre and Miquelon	0	0	0	0	0	0	0	0	0	2	0	2
United States of America	43 614	122	220	43 515	336 895	1 430	10 200	328 125	72 869	22 136	3 703	91 303
Total North America	**85 005**	**255**	**340**	**84 920**	**475 552**	**6 213**	**13 048**	**468 717**	**117 231**	**27 367**	**27 986**	**116 612**
Total North and Central America	**131 324**	**256**	**341**	**131 239**	**480 192**	**6 428**	**13 387**	**473 233**	**119 622**	**28 148**	**28 182**	**119 588**
American Samoa	0	0	0	0	0	0	0	0	0	1	0	1
Australia	7 774	0	0	7 774	27 083	2	1 065	26 020	5 064	575	377	5 262
Cook Islands	0	0	0	0	5	0	1	4	0	4	0	4
Fiji	107	0	0	107	472	0	11	461	90	2	12	80
French Polynesia	4	0	0	4	0	3	0	3	0	22	0	22
Guam	–	–	–	–	–	–	–	–	–	–	–	–
Kiribati	3	0	0	3	0	0	0	0	0	2	0	2
Marshall Islands	0	0	0	0	0	0	0	0	0	6	0	6
Micronesia (Federated States of)	2	0	0	3	0	0	0	0	0	7	0	7
Nauru	0	0	0	0	0	0	0	0	0	0	0	0
New Caledonia	0	0	0	0	5	3	1	7	3	13	1	15
New Zealand	–	–	–	–	20 214	6	6 684	13 536	4 341	42	1 794	2 589
Niue	0	0	0	0	0	0	0	0	0	0	0	0

Table 4 | 135

Country / area	Wood-based panels (1 000 m³)				Pulp for paper (1 000 tonnes)				Paper and paperboard (1 000 tonnes)			
	Production	Imports	Exports	Consumption	Production	Imports	Exports	Consumption	Production	Imports	Exports	Consumption
Algeria	48	76	0	123	2	19	0	21	45	286	4	327
Egypt	56	276	1	331	120	183	0	303	460	918	54	1 324
Libyan Arab Jamahiriya	0	52	0	52	0	4	0	4	6	38	0	44
Mauritania	2	1	0	3	0	0	0	0	1	3	0	4
Morocco	35	96	19	111	151	22	88	85	129	289	7	411
Sudan	2	9	0	11	0	1	1	0	3	34	1	36
Tunisia	104	65	6	162	10	137	8	139	106	193	25	274
Western Sahara	–	–	–	–	–	–	–	–	–	–	–	–
Total Northern Africa	**247**	**575**	**27**	**795**	**283**	**365**	**96**	**552**	**749**	**1 762**	**92**	**2 420**
Angola	11	28	0	39	15	1	1	15	0	25	5	20
Botswana	0	0	0	0	0	0	0	0	0	10	0	10
Lesotho	–	–	–	–	–	–	–	–	–	–	–	–
Malawi	18	3	16	4	0	0	0	0	0	19	1	18
Mozambique	3	6	2	8	0	1	0	1	0	18	0	18
Namibia	–	–	–	–	–	–	–	–	–	–	–	–
South Africa	973	130	42	1 061	1 939	85	195	1 828	3 033	544	974	2 604
Swaziland	8	0	0	8	142	0	140	2	0	0	0	0
Zambia	18	4	3	19	0	0	0	0	4	32	0	36
Zimbabwe	80	4	4	80	49	2	0	51	144	16	11	149
Total Southern Africa	**1 111**	**174**	**67**	**1 218**	**2 145**	**88**	**336**	**1 897**	**3 181**	**665**	**991**	**2 855**
Benin	0	5	0	5	0	0	0	0	0	9	0	9
Burkina Faso	0	4	0	4	0	0	0	0	0	3	0	3
Cape Verde	0	5	0	5	0	0	0	0	0	1	0	1
Côte d'Ivoire	395	3	114	283	0	3	2	1	0	101	4	98
Gambia	0	4	1	3	0	0	0	0	0	1	1	0
Ghana	453	1	208	246	0	0	0	0	0	65	0	65
Guinea	42	6	4	43	0	0	0	0	0	3	0	3
Guinea-Bissau	0	0	0	0	0	0	0	0	0	0	0	0
Liberia	0	2	0	2	0	0	0	0	0	1	0	1
Mali	0	4	0	4	0	0	0	0	0	8	0	8

Country / area	Wood-based panels (1 000 m³)				Pulp for paper (1 000 tonnes)				Paper and paperboard (1 000 tonnes)			
	Production	Imports	Exports	Consumption	Production	Imports	Exports	Consumption	Production	Imports	Exports	Consumption
Niger	0	6	0	6	0	2	0	2	0	3	0	2
Nigeria	95	68	3	161	23	35	1	57	19	357	1	375
Senegal	0	10	0	10	0	1	0	1	0	47	3	44
Sierra Leone	0	5	0	4	0	2	1	1	0	2	1	1
Togo	1	4	4	0	0	0	0	0	0	9	1	8
Total West Africa	**986**	**126**	**336**	**775**	**23**	**43**	**3**	**63**	**19**	**610**	**12**	**617**
Total Africa	**2 962**	**1 019**	**574**	**3 407**	**2 632**	**515**	**437**	**2 710**	**4 285**	**3 604**	**1 153**	**6 737**
Armenia	6	189	0	196	0	0	0	0	6	4	0	10
Azerbaijan	0	266	0	266	0	0	0	0	3	56	0	60
Georgia	5	92	3	94	0	0	0	0	2	28	0	29
Kazakhstan	4	647	0	651	0	3	0	3	238	180	10	408
Kyrgyzstan	0	34	0	34	0	0	0	0	0	17	0	17
Tajikistan	0	0	0	0	0	0	0	0	0	1	0	1
Turkmenistan	0	3	1	2	0	0	0	0	0	1	0	1
Uzbekistan	3	457	3	458	9	2	3	9	2	37	6	33
Total Central Asia	**19**	**1 689**	**8**	**1 700**	**9**	**6**	**3**	**13**	**251**	**324**	**16**	**560**
China	79 947	3 359	10 977	72 329	20 506	9 761	99	30 168	83 685	5 388	4 850	84 223
Democratic People's Republic of Korea	0	8	0	8	106	38	0	144	80	14	2	92
Japan	4 609	4 656	42	9 223	10 706	1 916	176	12 447	28 360	1 544	1 624	28 280
Mongolia	2	8	0	10	0	0	0	0	0	14	0	14
Republic of Korea	3 689	1 825	37	5 478	536	2 482	0	3 018	10 642	804	2 675	8 771
Total East Asia	**88 247**	**9 856**	**11 056**	**87 046**	**31 854**	**14 197**	**275**	**45 776**	**122 767**	**7 765**	**9 152**	**121 380**
Bangladesh	9	19	3	25	65	52	0	117	58	140	0	198
Bhutan	43	0	15	28	0	1	0	0	10	1	1	10
India	2 592	126	65	2 653	4 048	432	21	4 459	7 600	1 734	373	8 961
Maldives	0	4	0	4	0	0	0	0	0	1	0	1
Nepal	30	2	2	30	15	0	1	14	13	19	2	30

Table 5 | 139

Country / area	Wood-based panels (1 000 m³)				Pulp for paper (1 000 tonnes)				Paper and paperboard (1 000 tonnes)			
	Production	Imports	Exports	Consumption	Production	Imports	Exports	Consumption	Production	Imports	Exports	Consumption
Pakistan	547	288	0	835	411	92	0	503	1 079	443	2	1 520
Sri Lanka	161	53	150	64	21	1	0	22	25	308	2	331
Total South Asia	**3 383**	**492**	**235**	**3 640**	**4 560**	**578**	**22**	**5 115**	**8 785**	**2 647**	**380**	**11 051**
Brunei Darussalam	0	2	0	2	0	0	0	0	0	6	1	5
Cambodia	7	4	2	9	0	0	0	0	0	44	0	44
Indonesia	4 332	656	3 329	1 659	5 282	813	2 622	3 473	7 777	401	3 574	4 603
Lao People's Democratic Republic	24	4	10	19	0	4	0	4	0	8	0	8
Malaysia	13 054	785	6 266	7 573	124	220	10	334	1 105	2 016	308	2 812
Myanmar	148	4	79	73	40	1	0	41	45	34	0	79
Philippines	341	208	76	474	212	77	23	267	1 097	421	132	1 386
Singapore	355	314	147	522	0	12	1	11	87	699	163	623
Thailand	3 788	186	2 556	1 417	935	398	125	1 208	4 108	756	1 026	3 838
Timor-Leste	0	0	0	0	0	0	0	0	0	0	0	0
Viet Nam	564	488	33	1 018	626	132	0	758	1 324	648	24	1 948
Total Southeast Asia	**22 613**	**2 651**	**12 498**	**12 766**	**7 218**	**1 657**	**2 780**	**6 095**	**15 543**	**5 032**	**5 228**	**15 347**
Afghanistan	1	20	1	21	0	0	0	0	0	4	0	4
Bahrain	0	30	0	30	0	4	0	4	15	38	0	53
Cyprus	2	148	0	150	0	1	0	1	0	75	0	75
Iran (Islamic Republic of)	797	574	7	1 364	495	75	0	570	370	571	4	936
Iraq	5	36	0	41	11	1	0	12	33	12	0	45
Israel	181	289	13	456	15	139	17	137	396	518	20	894
Jordan	0	143	7	136	8	92	2	99	54	190	45	199
Kuwait	0	76	0	75	0	12	1	12	56	160	11	206
Lebanon	46	294	2	338	0	42	0	42	103	204	13	294
Occupied Palestinian Territory	–	–	–	–	–	–	–	–	–	–	–	–
Oman	0	107	0	106	0	1	0	1	0	78	4	74
Qatar	0	129	0	129	0	3	0	3	0	47	14	33

Country / area	Wood-based panels (1 000 m³)				Pulp for paper (1 000 tonnes)				Paper and paperboard (1 000 tonnes)			
	Production	Imports	Exports	Consumption	Production	Imports	Exports	Consumption	Production	Imports	Exports	Consumption
Saudi Arabia	0	1 274	20	1 254	0	68	0	68	279	1 704	47	1 935
Syrian Arab Republic	27	103	0	129	0	41	0	41	75	233	3	304
Turkey	5 614	933	781	5 766	118	591	1	709	4 442	2 212	288	6 366
United Arab Emirates	0	788	209	579	0	47	1	46	81	657	69	668
Yemen	0	167	0	167	0	0	0	0	1	84	0	85
Total Western Asia	**6 674**	**5 109**	**1 041**	**10 741**	**647**	**1 118**	**21**	**1 743**	**5 905**	**6 787**	**521**	**12 172**
Total Asia	**120 935**	**19 796**	**24 838**	**115 893**	**44 289**	**17 556**	**3 102**	**58 743**	**153 251**	**22 555**	**15 296**	**160 510**
Albania	11	112	0	123	0	4	0	4	0	18	1	17
Andorra	0	2	0	2	0	0	0	0	0	2	0	2
Austria	3 713	725	3 079	1 359	1 715	674	272	2 117	5 153	1 284	4 278	2 158
Belarus	895	190	359	726	66	26	0	92	285	141	86	340
Belgium	2 295	1 740	2 404	1 631	920	737	1 337	320	2 006	4 134	3 390	2 750
Bosnia and Herzegovina	29	229	15	243	33	0	0	33	160	12	0	172
Bulgaria	845	807	447	1 205	137	11	68	81	326	278	104	500
Croatia	181	344	145	380	96	0	45	51	535	266	124	677
Czech Republic	1 681	688	1 164	1 205	702	178	351	529	932	1 389	813	1 508
Denmark	446	2 421	231	2 636	5	75	18	62	418	1 205	253	1 370
Estonia	422	176	285	313	200	0	125	75	68	149	97	120
Faroe Islands	0	1	0	1	0	0	0	0	0	2	0	1
Finland	1 715	411	1 287	839	12 087	396	2 226	10 257	13 549	497	11 852	2 195
France	6 168	2 271	3 065	5 373	2 220	1 972	624	3 568	9 420	6 144	4 932	10 632
Germany	14 674	5 284	8 783	11 175	2 909	4 887	1 002	6 794	22 842	11 139	13 254	20 727
Gibraltar	0	0	0	0	0	0	0	0	0	0	0	0
Greece	918	367	71	1 214	0	80	1	79	409	701	119	991
Guernsey	–	–	–	–	–	–	–	–	–	–	–	–
Holy See	–	–	–	–	–	–	–	–	–	–	–	–
Hungary	779	345	396	728	20	107	1	126	424	853	262	1 015
Iceland	0	17	0	17	0	0	0	0	0	33	0	32
Ireland	778	263	614	427	0	2	0	2	45	529	77	497

Table 5 | 141

Country / area	Wood-based panels (1 000 m³)				Pulp for paper (1 000 tonnes)				Paper and paperboard (1 000 tonnes)			
	Production	Imports	Exports	Consumption	Production	Imports	Exports	Consumption	Production	Imports	Exports	Consumption
Isle of Man	–	–	–	–	–	–	–	–	–	–	–	–
Italy	5 136	2 570	997	6 709	664	3 210	45	3 828	9 467	5 048	3 389	11 125
Jersey	–	–	–	–	–	–	–	–	–	–	–	–
Latvia	664	121	599	186	0	0	0	0	52	141	39	153
Liechtenstein	2	0	0	2	1	0	0	1	0	0	0	0
Lithuania	617	487	208	896	0	21	0	21	123	184	95	212
Luxembourg	409	32	275	166	0	0	0	0	31	168	40	159
Malta	0	33	0	32	0	0	0	0	0	32	2	30
Monaco	–	–	–	–	–	–	–	–	–	–	–	–
Montenegro	0	11	11	0	0	0	0	0	0	7	0	6
Netherlands	33	1 894	411	1 516	142	1 333	600	875	2 977	3 413	2 374	4 016
Norway	498	342	217	623	2 099	44	490	1 653	1 900	484	1 643	741
Poland	8 124	1 887	2 275	7 735	1 151	648	33	1 766	3 044	2 843	1 496	4 391
Portugal	1 347	597	984	960	2 022	139	945	1 216	1 669	778	1 284	1 163
Republic of Moldova	0	0	0	0	0	0	0	0	98	55	6	147
Romania	1 917	1 794	862	2 849	42	27	4	65	422	356	102	676
Russian Federation	10 665	1 594	2 220	10 039	7 003	80	1 875	5 208	7 700	1 478	2 634	6 544
San Marino	–	–	–	–	–	–	–	–	–	–	–	–
Serbia	179	397	56	520	20	15	1	34	268	456	84	640
Slovakia	952	680	652	980	693	157	130	720	921	444	598	767
Slovenia	517	259	535	241	73	230	67	236	672	274	605	341
Spain	3 853	1 333	2 234	2 952	2 878	981	894	2 965	6 605	3 997	2 860	7 741
Svalbard and Jan Mayen Islands	–	–	–	–	–	–	–	–	–	–	–	–
Sweden	875	1 099	331	1 644	12 060	450	3 412	9 098	12 557	985	10 580	2 962
Switzerland	977	588	761	804	142	520	22	640	1 698	973	823	1 848
The former Yugoslav Republic of Macedonia	0	112	5	107	0	1	0	1	23	99	10	112
Ukraine	2 029	676	491	2 214	0	113	0	113	937	839	198	1 578
United Kingdom	3 140	3 390	520	6 010	277	1 216	9	1 483	4 983	7 297	898	11 382
Total Europe	**77 484**	**36 291**	**36 992**	**76 783**	**50 377**	**18 336**	**14 598**	**54 114**	**112 719**	**59 126**	**69 405**	**102 440**

Country / area	Wood-based panels (1 000 m³)				Pulp for paper (1 000 tonnes)				Paper and paperboard (1 000 tonnes)			
	Production	Imports	Exports	Consumption	Production	Imports	Exports	Consumption	Production	Imports	Exports	Consumption
Anguilla	–	–	–	–	–	–	–	–	–	–	–	–
Antigua and Barbuda	0	4	0	4	0	0	0	0	0	0	0	0
Aruba	0	6	0	6	0	0	0	0	0	1	0	1
Bahamas	0	19	0	19	0	0	0	0	0	8	1	8
Barbados	0	14	0	14	0	0	0	0	2	13	1	14
Bermuda	–	–	–	–	–	–	–	–	–	–	–	–
British Virgin Islands	0	1	0	1	0	0	0	0	0	0	0	0
Cayman Islands	0	5	0	5	0	0	0	0	0	1	0	1
Cuba	149	31	0	180	1	3	0	4	34	71	0	105
Dominica	0	2	1	2	0	0	0	0	0	1	0	0
Dominican Republic	0	76	0	76	0	1	0	1	130	228	1	357
Grenada	0	4	0	4	0	0	0	0	0	0	0	0
Guadeloupe	0	23	0	23	0	0	0	0	0	6	0	6
Haiti	0	10	0	10	0	0	0	0	0	18	0	18
Jamaica	0	48	0	48	0	0	0	0	0	29	0	29
Martinique	0	7	0	7	0	0	0	0	0	5	0	5
Montserrat	0	0	0	0	0	0	0	0	0	0	0	0
Netherlands Antilles	0	11	0	10	0	0	0	0	0	8	1	7
Puerto Rico	–	–	–	–	–	–	–	–	–	–	–	–
Saint Barthélemy	–	–	–	–	–	–	–	–	–	–	–	–
Saint Kitts and Nevis	0	1	0	1	0	0	0	0	0	0	0	0
Saint Lucia	0	7	0	7	0	0	0	0	0	10	0	10
Saint Martin (French part)	–	–	–	–	–	–	–	–	–	–	–	–
Saint Vincent and the Grenadines	0	2	0	2	0	0	0	0	0	4	0	4
Trinidad and Tobago	2	62	0	64	0	4	0	4	0	138	1	137
Turks and Caicos Islands	0	1	0	1	0	0	0	0	0	0	0	0
United States Virgin Islands	–	–	–	–	–	–	–	–	–	–	–	–
Total Caribbean	**151**	**335**	**1**	**485**	**1**	**9**	**0**	**10**	**166**	**542**	**6**	**703**

Table 5 | 143

Country / area	Wood-based panels (1 000 m³)				Pulp for paper (1 000 tonnes)				Paper and paperboard (1 000 tonnes)			
	Production	Imports	Exports	Consumption	Production	Imports	Exports	Consumption	Production	Imports	Exports	Consumption
Belize	0	8	1	7	0	2	0	2	0	6	0	6
Costa Rica	69	43	21	91	10	36	0	46	20	566	28	558
El Salvador	0	18	0	17	0	3	1	2	56	182	11	227
Guatemala	57	32	10	79	0	4	1	3	31	350	17	364
Honduras	10	30	4	35	7	0	0	7	95	140	2	233
Nicaragua	8	8	0	16	0	0	0	0	0	42	3	39
Panama	9	22	0	31	0	2	0	2	0	110	28	83
Total Central America	**153**	**160**	**36**	**277**	**17**	**47**	**1**	**62**	**202**	**1 396**	**90**	**1 508**
Canada	12 220	3 689	6 153	9 756	20 405	337	9 343	11 399	15 789	2 914	12 289	6 414
Greenland	0	5	0	5	0	0	0	0	0	1	0	1
Mexico	398	1 079	52	1 425	345	1 264	20	1 589	5 141	3 956	445	8 652
Saint Pierre and Miquelon	0	1	0	0	0	0	0	0	0	0	0	0
United States of America	35 576	9 195	2 498	42 274	52 244	5 601	6 828	51 017	80 178	13 411	11 707	81 882
Total North America	**48 194**	**13 969**	**8 703**	**53 461**	**72 994**	**7 202**	**16 191**	**64 005**	**101 108**	**20 282**	**24 442**	**96 949**
Total North and Central America	**48 499**	**14 464**	**8 741**	**54 222**	**73 012**	**7 258**	**16 193**	**64 077**	**101 476**	**22 220**	**24 537**	**99 160**
American Samoa	0	0	0	0	0	0	0	0	0	0	0	0
Australia	1 662	545	427	1 780	1 195	348	10	1 533	2 541	1 490	684	3 347
Cook Islands	0	2	0	2	0	0	0	0	0	0	0	0
Fiji	20	5	2	24	0	1	0	1	0	21	1	20
French Polynesia	0	6	0	6	0	0	0	0	0	8	0	8
Guam	–	–	–	–	–	–	–	–	–	–	–	–
Kiribati	0	0	0	0	0	0	0	0	0	0	0	0
Marshall Islands	0	3	0	3	0	0	0	0	0	0	0	0
Micronesia (Federated States of)	0	1	0	1	0	0	0	0	0	0	0	0
Nauru	0	0	0	0	0	0	0	0	0	0	0	0
New Caledonia	0	6	2	4	0	2	0	2	0	12	7	5

Country / area	Wood-based panels (1 000 m³)				Pulp for paper (1 000 tonnes)				Paper and paperboard (1 000 tonnes)			
	Production	Imports	Exports	Consumption	Production	Imports	Exports	Consumption	Production	Imports	Exports	Consumption
New Zealand	1 939	73	900	1 112	1 546	32	791	787	871	472	600	743
Niue	0	0	0	0	0	0	0	0	0	0	0	0
Norfolk Island	0	0	0	0	0	0	0	0	0	0	0	0
Northern Mariana Islands	0	0	0	0	0	0	0	0	0	0	0	0
Palau	0	1	0	1	0	0	0	0	0	0	0	0
Papua New Guinea	94	2	10	86	0	0	0	0	0	17	0	17
Pitcairn	0	0	0	0	0	0	0	0	0	0	0	0
Samoa	0	2	0	2	0	0	0	0	0	1	0	1
Solomon Islands	0	1	0	1	0	0	0	0	0	0	0	0
Tokelau	0	0	0	0	0	0	0	0	0	0	0	0
Tonga	0	1	0	1	0	0	0	0	0	0	0	0
Tuvalu	0	0	0	0	0	0	0	0	0	0	0	0
Vanuatu	0	1	0	1	0	1	0	1	0	0	0	0
Wallis and Futuna Islands	0	0	0	0	0	0	0	0	0	0	0	0
Total Oceania	**3 715**	**649**	**1 342**	**3 022**	**2 741**	**384**	**801**	**2 324**	**3 412**	**2 023**	**1 292**	**4 143**
Argentina	1 444	190	428	1 206	999	193	178	1 014	1 755	1 641	152	3 244
Bolivia (Plurinational state of)	41	11	17	34	0	0	0	0	0	87	0	87
Brazil	8 611	163	2 757	6 017	12 697	330	7 057	5 971	8 977	1 268	2 592	7 654
Chile	2 657	179	2 193	643	4 981	13	4 061	933	1 391	523	586	1 328
Colombia	290	174	27	437	360	183	1	542	1 025	525	200	1 351
Ecuador	997	41	206	832	2	24	0	26	100	212	47	265
Falkland Islands (Malvinas)[†]	0	0	0	0	0	0	0	0	0	0	0	0
French Guiana	0	3	0	3	0	0	0	0	0	0	0	0
Guyana	39	4	25	18	0	0	0	0	0	6	0	5
Paraguay	161	9	18	152	0	0	0	0	13	97	5	105
Peru	96	143	25	215	17	100	0	117	132	447	15	564
Suriname	1	10	2	9	0	0	0	0	0	8	0	8
Uruguay	176	55	137	94	967	9	603	373	90	83	37	136

Table 5 | 145

Country / area	Wood-based panels (1 000 m³)				Pulp for paper (1 000 tonnes)				Paper and paperboard (1 000 tonnes)			
	Production	Imports	Exports	Consumption	Production	Imports	Exports	Consumption	Production	Imports	Exports	Consumption
Venezuela (Bolivarian Republic of)	680	56	22	714	73	186	2	257	610	371	1	980
Total South America	15 193	1 038	5 856	10 375	20 096	1 038	11 902	9 233	14 093	5 268	3 635	15 726
TOTAL WORLD	268 788	73 257	78 342	263 702	193 146	45 087	47 032	191 201	389 237	114 797	115 319	388 715

† A dispute exists between the governments of Argentina and the United Kingdom of Great Britain and Northern Ireland concerning sovereignty over the Falkland Islands (Malvinas).

Source: FAOSTAT (ForesSTAT), last accessed 16 September 2010.

Table 6: Forestry sector's contribution to employment and gross domestic product, 2006

Country / area	Employment					Gross value added				
	Roundwood production	Wood processing	Pulp and paper	Total for the forestry sector		Roundwood production	Wood processing	Pulp and paper	Total for the forestry sector	
	(1 000 FTE)	(1 000 FTE)	(1 000 FTE)	(1 000 FTE)	(% of total labour force)	(US$ million)	(US$ million)	(US$ million)	(US$ million)	(% contribution to GDP)
Burundi	0	2	0	2	0	10	5	0	15	1.8
Cameroon	12	8	1	20	0.3	236	74	13	324	1.9
Central African Republic	2	2	0	4	0.2	133	10	1	144	11.1
Chad	1	0	–	1	0	122	0	–	122	1.9
Republic of the Congo	4	3	0	7	0.5	45	27	–	72	1.1
Democratic Republic of the Congo	6	0	–	6	0	185	2	–	186	2.3
Equatorial Guinea	1	0	–	1	0.5	86	2	–	87	0.9
Gabon	8	4	0	12	1.9	171	118	0	290	3.0
Rwanda	1	1	–	1	0	30	1	–	31	1.3
Saint Helena, Ascension and Tristan da Cunha	–	–	–	–	–	–	–	–	–	–
Sao Tome and Principe	–	–	–	–	–	–	–	–	–	–
Total Central Africa	**35**	**19**	**1**	**55**	**0.1**	**1 017**	**239**	**15**	**1 271**	**2.0**
Comoros	–	–	–	–	–	18	–	–	18	4.4
Djibouti	–	–	–	–	–	0	–	–	0	0.1
Eritrea	0	0	0	0	0	0	0	0	1	0.1
Ethiopia	1	2	2	5	0	630	4	9	643	5.2
Kenya	1	10	8	19	0.1	242	20	106	368	1.7
Madagascar	2	41	1	44	0.4	148	8	0	157	3.1
Mauritius	1	1	1	2	0.4	7	4	12	23	0.4
Mayotte	–	–	–	–	–	–	–	–	–	–
Réunion	0	0	0	0	0.1	2	8	8	18	0.1
Seychelles	–	–	–	–	–	0	–	–	0	0.1
Somalia	0	1	–	1	0	15	1	–	15	0.6
Uganda	2	1	1	4	0	354	16	9	379	4.0
United Republic of Tanzania	3	6	6	15	0.1	205	1	22	228	1.9
Total East Africa	**11**	**61**	**19**	**90**	**0.1**	**1 623**	**62**	**166**	**1 851**	**2.1**

Table 6 | 147

Country / area	Employment					Gross value added				
	Roundwood production	Wood processing	Pulp and paper	Total for the forestry sector		Roundwood production	Wood processing	Pulp and paper	Total for the forestry sector	
	(1 000 FTE)	(1 000 FTE)	(1 000 FTE)	(1 000 FTE)	(% of total labour force)	(US$ million)	(US$ million)	(US$ million)	(US$ million)	(% contribution to GDP)
Algeria	0	11	2	13	0.1	37	118	66	220	0.2
Egypt	1	3	18	21	0.1	131	7	157	296	0.3
Libyan Arab Jamahiriya	0	1	0	2	0.1	57	4	2	62	0.1
Mauritania	0	0	0	0	0	1	0	–	1	0.1
Morocco	13	8	5	26	0.2	343	80	126	549	0.9
Sudan	1	2	1	4	0	57	15	36	107	0.3
Tunisia	4	9	4	16	0.4	106	147	149	402	1.4
Western Sahara	–	–	–	–	–	–	–	–	–	–
Total Northern Africa	**19**	**34**	**30**	**83**	**0.1**	**731**	**372**	**535**	**1 638**	**0.4**
Angola	2	1	0	3	0	260	2	1	262	0.6
Botswana	0	0	0	1	0.1	25	1	5	30	0.4
Lesotho	1	0	–	1	0.1	67	–	–	67	5.0
Malawi	1	1	0	2	0	40	2	8	50	2.6
Mozambique	12	3	0	15	0.1	221	2	2	224	3.1
Namibia	0	0	0	0	0.1	–	6	0	6	0.1
South Africa	45	37	34	116	0.5	920	948	1 677	3 545	1.6
Swaziland	1	2	3	6	1.5	11	10	60	80	5.2
Zambia	1	1	2	5	0.1	547	61	21	629	5.9
Zimbabwe	1	6	7	13	0.2	49	14	12	74	5.3
Total Southern Africa	**63**	**51**	**47**	**161**	**0.3**	**2 139**	**1 044**	**1 785**	**4 969**	**1.6**
Benin	1	0	–	1	0	103	5	0	108	2.6
Burkina Faso	2	2	0	4	0.1	88	0	–	88	1.5
Cape Verde	0	1	–	1	0.5	20	0	–	20	2.0
Côte d'Ivoire	19	8	1	28	0.4	672	96	33	801	5.0
Gambia	0	1	–	1	0.1	1	0	–	1	0.2
Ghana	12	30	1	43	0.4	542	202	10	754	7.2
Guinea	9	1	–	10	0.2	39	6	–	45	1.7

Country / area	Employment					Gross value added				
	Roundwood production	Wood processing	Pulp and paper	Total for the forestry sector		Roundwood production	Wood processing	Pulp and paper	Total for the forestry sector	
	(1 000 FTE)	(1 000 FTE)	(1 000 FTE)	(1 000 FTE)	(% of total labour force)	(US$ million)	(US$ million)	(US$ million)	(US$ million)	(% contribution to GDP)
Guinea-Bissau	1	0	–	1	0.1	18	2	–	20	6.3
Liberia	1	1	–	2	0.1	113	9	–	121	17.7
Mali	1	0	–	1	0	102	0	–	102	1.9
Niger	1	0	–	1	0	98	0	7	105	3.3
Nigeria	24	3	18	45	0.1	1 506	32	282	1 819	1.4
Senegal	1	0	1	2	0	65	3	9	77	0.9
Sierra Leone	0	0	0	1	0	84	0	0	85	4.8
Togo	1	0	–	1	0	31	2	–	33	1.6
Total West Africa	**73**	**46**	**20**	**140**	**0.1**	**3 480**	**357**	**342**	**4179**	**2.2**
Total Africa	**202**	**211**	**117**	**530**	**0.1**	**8 991**	**2 075**	**2 843**	**13 908**	**1.3**
Armenia	2	1	0	3	0.2	4	1	2	7	0.1
Azerbaijan	2	2	0	4	0.1	2	3	1	6	0
Georgia	6	3	0	9	0.3	11	4	1	16	0.2
Kazakhstan	10	1	3	14	0.2	29	13	17	59	0.1
Kyrgyzstan	3	1	1	5	0.2	2	1	1	4	0.2
Tajikistan	2	0	0	3	0.1	0	0	0	1	0
Turkmenistan	2	0	–	2	0.1	0	0	–	0	0
Uzbekistan	6	1	0	7	0.1	2	9	2	14	0.1
Total Central Asia	**34**	**8**	**5**	**47**	**0.1**	**51**	**32**	**24**	**107**	**0.1**
China	1 172	937	1 409	3 518	0.4	13 687	8 834	18 687	41 208	1.3
Democratic People's Republic of Korea	19	4	4	26	0.2	220	33	46	299	2.5
Japan	32	150	211	393	0.6	892	9 590	22 422	32 904	0.7
Mongolia	1	1	0	1	0.1	2	3	1	7	0.2
Republic of Korea	12	25	63	99	0.4	1 498	1 099	5 877	8 473	1.1
Total East Asia	**1 235**	**1 115**	**1 686**	**4037**	**0.4**	**16 298**	**19 559**	**47 033**	**82 890**	**1.0**

Table 6 | 149

Country / area	Employment					Gross value added				
	Roundwood production	Wood processing	Pulp and paper	Total for the forestry sector		Roundwood production	Wood processing	Pulp and paper	Total for the forestry sector	
	(1 000 FTE)	(1 000 FTE)	(1 000 FTE)	(1 000 FTE)	(% of total labour force)	(US$ million)	(US$ million)	(US$ million)	(US$ million)	(% contribution to GDP)
Bangladesh	1	11	24	36	0	997	76	45	1 118	1.7
Bhutan	1	2	–	3	0.2	49	12	–	61	6.9
India	246	55	180	481	0.1	5 927	132	1 092	7 151	0.9
Maldives	–	0	–	0	0	–	–	–	–	–
Nepal	12	4	3	19	0.1	318	5	8	330	4.3
Pakistan	30	5	22	58	0.1	288	9	213	510	0.4
Sri Lanka	17	4	3	23	0.3	199	17	31	247	1.0
Total South Asia	**308**	**80**	**231**	**619**	**0.1**	**7 777**	**251**	**1 388**	**9 416**	**0.9**
Brunei Darussalam	1	0	–	2	0.9	3	6	–	9	0.1
Cambodia	0	1	0	1	0	139	5	29	173	2.8
Indonesia	69	148	104	321	0.3	3 283	3 896	2 386	9 564	2.5
Lao People's Democratic Republic	1	2	0	3	0.1	103	1	0	104	3.0
Malaysia	88	126	35	248	2.3	2 423	1 514	661	4 598	3.0
Myanmar	24	21	3	48	0.2	35	1	1	38	0.3
Philippines	8	20	21	49	0.1	94	157	308	560	0.5
Singapore	0	2	4	6	0.3	–	38	181	218	0.2
Thailand	8	62	67	137	0.4	149	333	1 211	1 693	0.8
Timor-Leste	–	–	–	–	–	1	–	–	1	0.4
Viet Nam	22	120	70	212	0.5	674	370	328	1 372	2.4
Total Southeast Asia	**221**	**502**	**304**	**1027**	**0.4**	**6 904**	**6 322**	**5 105**	**18 331**	**1.7**
Afghanistan	–	–	–	–	–	4	2	–	5	0.1
Bahrain	–	0	0	0	0.1	–	1	6	6	0
Cyprus	1	2	1	3	0.8	3	91	30	123	0.8
Iran (Islamic Republic of)	7	8	22	36	0.1	270	86	355	711	0.3
Iraq	–	0	6	6	0.1	–	12	26	39	0.1
Israel	1	5	8	14	0.5	–	121	312	433	0.3

Country / area	Employment					Gross value added				
	Roundwood production	Wood processing	Pulp and paper	Total for the forestry sector		Roundwood production	Wood processing	Pulp and paper	Total for the forestry sector	
	(1 000 FTE)	(1 000 FTE)	(1 000 FTE)	(1 000 FTE)	(% of total labour force)	(US$ million)	(US$ million)	(US$ million)	(US$ million)	(% contribution to GDP)
Jordan	0	4	4	8	0.3	–	16	70	86	0.7
Kuwait	–	1	1	2	0.2	–	26	56	82	0.1
Lebanon	–	3	6	10	0.7	1	63	189	253	1.1
Occupied Palestinian Territory	–	1	0	2	0.7	–	12	9	21	0.6
Oman	–	1	1	2	0.2	–	20	15	35	0.1
Qatar	–	5	0	5	1.5	–	73	16	89	0.2
Saudi Arabia	1	21	13	35	0.4	–	–	279	279	0.1
Syrian Arab Republic	1	16	2	19	0.3	4	87	31	122	0.4
Turkey	33	89	45	167	0.5	1 342	609	834	2 786	0.7
United Arab Emirates	–	1	4	5	0.4	–	–	81	81	0
Yemen	–	3	2	5	0.1	–	31	22	54	0.3
Total Western Asia	44	160	115	318	0.3	1 624	1 250	2 331	5 205	0.3
Total Asia	**1 843**	**1 866**	**2 341**	**6 049**	**0.3**	**32 655**	**27 414**	**55 881**	**115 950**	**0.9**
Albania	2	1	0	2	0.1	6	4	3	13	0.2
Andorra	–	0	0	0	1.0	–	–	–	–	–
Austria	7	36	17	61	1.5	1 494	2 661	2 013	6 168	2.1
Belarus	33	46	23	103	1.9	180	399	97	677	2.1
Belgium	2	14	14	31	0.7	191	1 114	1 424	2 729	0.8
Bosnia and Herzegovina	7	5	2	14	0.7	129	85	17	232	2.5
Bulgaria	15	23	11	49	1.2	59	97	77	232	0.9
Croatia	9	12	5	26	1.2	115	186	161	462	1.3
Czech Republic	35	83	20	138	2.5	832	1 225	596	2 654	2.1
Denmark	4	15	7	25	0.9	201	1 002	602	1 805	0.8
Estonia	7	19	2	28	3.6	148	345	43	536	3.7
Faroe Islands	–	–	–	–	–	–	–	–	–	–
Finland	23	32	35	90	3.6	3 329	1 918	5 082	10 329	5.7
France	31	87	74	191	0.7	5 107	4 147	5 653	14 907	0.7
Germany	44	165	134	342	0.8	2 259	9 315	12 324	23 898	0.9

Table 6 | 151

Country / area	Employment					Gross value added				
	Roundwood production	Wood processing	Pulp and paper	Total for the forestry sector		Roundwood production	Wood processing	Pulp and paper	Total for the forestry sector	
	(1 000 FTE)	(1 000 FTE)	(1 000 FTE)	(1 000 FTE)	(% of total labour force)	(US$ million)	(US$ million)	(US$ million)	(US$ million)	(% contribution to GDP)
Saint Kitts and Nevis	–	–	–	–	–	0	–	–	0	0
Saint Lucia	–	–	–	–	–	0	–	4	4	0.5
Saint Martin (French part)	–	–	–	–	–	–	–	–	–	–
Saint Vincent and the Grenadines	–	–	0	0	0.2	2	–	–	2	0.5
Trinidad and Tobago	1	2	2	5	0.8	16	10	42	68	0.4
Turks and Caicos Islands	–	–	–	–	–	–	–	–	–	–
United States Virgin Islands	–	0	0	0	0.1	–	–	–	–	–
Total Caribbean	**14**	**29**	**9**	**52**	**0.3**	**57**	**165**	**215**	**436**	**0.2**
Belize	1	2	0	3	2.6	7	11	1	19	1.7
Costa Rica	1	7	5	13	0.7	12	42	118	171	0.8
El Salvador	4	5	4	13	0.4	121	2	70	193	1.1
Guatemala	7	1	2	10	0.2	483	51	52	587	2.0
Honduras	3	15	2	20	0.7	73	49	27	149	1.8
Nicaragua	3	1	–	4	0.2	40	45	7	92	1.9
Panama	1	1	2	3	0.2	26	6	36	67	0.4
Total Central America	**20**	**32**	**13**	**65**	**0.4**	**762**	**206**	**311**	**1 279**	**1.3**
Canada	63	128	84	275	1.6	7 229	13 488	11 284	32 000	2.7
Greenland	–	–	–	–	–	–	–	–	–	–
Mexico	84	85	125	293	0.6	1 720	1 855	3 477	7 052	0.9
Saint Pierre and Miquelon	0	–	–	0	0	–	–	–	–	–
United States of America	85	565	459	1 109	0.7	18 528	37 400	52 500	108 428	0.8
Total North America	**232**	**778**	**667**	**1 677**	**0.8**	**27 477**	**52 743**	**67 261**	**147 480**	**1.0**
Total North and Central America	**266**	**839**	**690**	**1 794**	**0.7**	**28 296**	**53 114**	**67 786**	**149 196**	**1.0**

Country / area	Employment					Gross value added				
	Roundwood production	Wood processing	Pulp and paper	Total for the forestry sector		Roundwood production	Wood processing	Pulp and paper	Total for the forestry sector	
	(1 000 FTE)	(1 000 FTE)	(1 000 FTE)	(1 000 FTE)	(% of total labour force)	(US$ million)	(US$ million)	(US$ million)	(US$ million)	(% contribution to GDP)
American Samoa	–	–	–	–	–	–	–	–	–	–
Australia	11	42	21	74	0.7	695	2 806	2 061	5 562	0.8
Cook Islands	–	–	–	–	–	–	–	–	–	–
Fiji	0	2	1	3	0.6	29	52	11	92	3.4
French Polynesia	0	0	0	0	0.3	–	–	–	–	–
Guam	0	–	–	0	0	–	–	–	–	–
Kiribati	–	–	–	–	–	0	–	–	0	0
Marshall Islands	–	–	–	–	–	–	–	–	–	–
Micronesia (Federated States of)	–	–	–	–	–	–	–	–	–	–
Nauru	–	–	–	–	–	–	–	–	–	–
New Caledonia	0	0	0	0	0.1	1	1	–	2	0
New Zealand	7	16	5	28	1.4	691	897	584	2 172	2.1
Niue	–	–	–	–	–	–	–	–	–	–
Norfolk Island	–	–	–	–	–	–	–	–	–	–
Northern Mariana Islands	–	–	–	–	–	–	–	–	–	–
Palau	–	–	–	–	–	–	–	–	–	–
Papua New Guinea	8	4	–	12	0.4	316	84	–	400	6.7
Pitcairn	–	–	–	–	–	–	–	–	–	–
Samoa	0	0	–	1	0.8	6	8	–	14	3.2
Solomon Islands	8	0	–	8	3.0	53	4	–	57	16.7
Tokelau	–	–	–	–	–	–	–	–	–	–
Tonga	0	0	0	0	0.3	1	0	0	1	0.5
Tuvalu	–	–	–	–	–	–	–	–	–	–
Vanuatu	0	1	–	1	1.4	3	10	–	13	3.5
Wallis and Futuna Islands	–	–	–	–	–	–	–	–	–	–
Total Oceania	**36**	**65**	**27**	**128**	**0.8**	**1 794**	**3 862**	**2 657**	**8 313**	**1.0**

Table 6 | 155

Country / area	Employment					Gross value added				
	Roundwood production	Wood processing	Pulp and paper	Total for the forestry sector		Roundwood production	Wood processing	Pulp and paper	Total for the forestry sector	
	(1 000 FTE)	(1 000 FTE)	(1 000 FTE)	(1 000 FTE)	(% of total labour force)	(US$ million)	(US$ million)	(US$ million)	(US$ million)	(% contribution to GDP)
Argentina	54	32	30	116	0.7	311	156	1 098	1 564	0.8
Bolivia (Plurinational state of)	4	3	2	9	0.2	92	111	38	241	2.7
Brazil	306	503	201	1 010	1.2	18 198	3 953	6 055	28 206	2.8
Chile	44	27	15	86	1.2	448	1 008	2 153	3 609	2.6
Colombia	3	4	18	25	0.1	140	166	503	810	0.7
Ecuador	13	4	7	24	0.4	277	427	190	893	2.3
Falkland Islands (Malvinas)[†]	–	–	–	–	–	–	–	–	–	–
French Guiana	0	0	–	0	0.3	2	2	–	4	0.1
Guyana	3	5	–	8	1.9	18	13	–	31	4.1
Paraguay	3	2	1	5	0.2	163	81	56	301	3.6
Peru	19	6	6	31	0.3	278	204	458	940	1.1
Suriname	1	3	0	4	2.2	6	9	–	15	0.9
Uruguay	4	3	2	8	0.8	163	35	40	239	1.2
Venezuela (Bolivarian Republic of)	8	25	33	66	0.5	540	629	484	1 653	1.0
Total South America	**463**	**616**	**314**	**1 393**	**0.8**	**20 638**	**6 793**	**11 074**	**38 506**	**2.1**
TOTAL WORLD	**3 876**	**5 459**	**4 374**	**13 709**	**0.4**	**117 508**	**149 811**	**200 589**	**467 908**	**1.0**

† A dispute exists between the governments of Argentina and the United Kingdom of Great Britain and Northern Ireland concerning sovereignty over the Falkland Islands (Malvinas).

Source: FAO, 2008.

6 | References

Abbott, P. 1997. *The supply and demand dynamics of miombo: a household perspective*. Aberdeen, UK, Aberdeen University (PhD dissertation).

Alcorn, A. 2003. *Embodied energy and CO_2 coefficients for NZ building materials*. Centre for Building Performance Research Report. Wellington, New Zealand, Victoria University of Wellington (also available at www.victoria.ac.nz/cbpr/documents/pdfs/ee-co2_report_2003.pdf).

Aldy, J.E. & Stavins, R.N. 2008. *Designing the post-Kyoto climate regime: lessons from the Harvard project on international climate agreements. An interim progress report for the 14th Conference of the Parties, Framework Convention on Climate Change, Poznan, Poland, December 2008*. Cambridge, USA, Harvard Project on International Climate Agreements (also available at http://belfercenter.ksg.harvard.edu/files/Interim%20Report%20081203%20Akiko%20v6.pdf).

Anbumozhi, V. 2007. *Eco-industrial clusters in urban-rural fringe areas: a strategic approach for integrated environmental and economic planning*. Kobe, Japan, Institute for Global Environmental Strategies – Kansai Research Centre (also available at http://enviroscope.iges.or.jp/modules/envirolib/upload/973/attach/973_eco-industrial-clusters.pdf).

Angelsen, A. & Wunder, S. 2003. *Exploring the forest—poverty link: key concepts, issues and research implications*. Center for International Forestry Research (CIFOR) Occasional Paper 40. Bogor, Indonesia, CIFOR (also available at www.cifor.cgiar.org/publications/pdf_files/OccPapers/OP-40.pdf).

Angelsen, A., Brockhaus, M., Kanninen, M., Sills, E. Sunderlin, W. & Wertz-Kanounnikoff, S., eds. 2009. *Realising REDD+: national strategy and policy options*. Bogor, Indonesia, Center for International Forestry Research (CIFOR) (also available at www.cifor.cgiar.org/publications/pdf_files/Books/BAngelsen0902.pdf).

Arnold, J.E.M. 2001. *Forests and people: 25 years of community forestry*. Rome, Italy, FAO.

Australian Property Institute. 2007. *Policy paper: conceiving property rights in carbon*. NSW & Queensland Divisions – Australian Property Institute, 26 July 2007.

Balée, W. 1994. *Footprints of the forest: Ka'apor ethnobotany – the historical ecology of plant utilization by an Amazonian people*. New York, USA, Columbia University Press.

Bird, K., Hulme, D., Moore, K. & Shepherd, A. 2002. *Chronic poverty and remote rural areas*. Chronic Poverty Research Centre Working Paper No. 13. Manchester, UK, University of Manchester (also available at www.chronicpoverty.org/uploads/publication_files/WP13_Bird_et_al.pdf).

Bodian, M.L. 2009. *Comparative study of forest resources management, decentralization processes in the ECOWAS space*. Accra, Ghana, FAO.

Burton, I.E. 2008. *Beyond borders: the need for strategic global adaptation*. IIED Sustainable Development Opinion December 2008. London, UK, International Institute for Environment and Development (also available at www.iied.org/pubs/pdfs/17046IIED.pdf).

Byron, R.N. & Arnold, J.E.M. 1997. *What futures for the people of the tropical forests?* Center for International Forestry Research (CIFOR) Working Paper 19. Bogor, Indonesia, CIFOR (also available at www.cifor.cgiar.org/ntfpcd/pdf/OWP5.pdf).

Canby, C. 2006. Investing in natural tropical forest industries. *ITTO Tropical Forest Update*, 16(2): 4–8. Yokohama, Japan, International Tropical Timber Organization (also available at www.itto.int/en/tfu/id=15910000).

Carreiro, M. M., Song, Y.C. and Wu, J. 2008. Ecology, planning and management of urban forests. International perspectives. New York, USA, Spring Editions.

Cavaliere, C., Rea, P., Lynch, M.E. & Blumenthal, M. 2010. Herbal supplement sales rise in all channels in 2009. *Herbalgram,* 86: 62–65. Austin, USA, American Botanical Council (also available at http://cms.herbalgram.org/herbalgram/issue86/article3530.html?Issue=86).

Cavendish, W. 2003. *How do forests support, insure and improve the livelihoods of the rural poor? A research note.* Background paper written for CIFOR's Poverty-Environment Network (PEN). Bogor, Indonesia, Center for International Forestry Research (available at http://www.cifor.cgiar.org/pen/_ref/home/index.htm).

CBD. 1997. Traditional knowledge and biological diversity: note by the Executive Secretary. Workshop on traditional knowledge and biological diversity, Madrid, Spain, 24–28 November 1997. UNEP/CBD/TKBD/1/2.

CEMDA. 2010. *Tesis privada sobre contratos privados para la compraventa de CO$_2$.* Condesa, Mexico, Centro Mexicano de Derecho Ambiental.

CEPF. 2008. *European forest owner organisations – forest owner cooperation: main figures, aims and goals.* Brussels, Belgium, Confederation of European Forest Owners (also available at www.unece.org/timber/docs/tc-sessions/tc-66/pd-docs/CEPF_report.pdf).

Chiagas, T. 2010. *Forest carbon rights in Brazil: case study.* REDDnet. UK, Overseas Development Institute (also available at http://redd-net.org/resource-library/redd-net-case-studies-carbon-rights).

Christensen Fund. 2010. *Vision statement.* San Francisco, USA (available at www.christensenfund.org).

Christy, L.C., Di Leva, C.E. & Lindsay, J.M. 2007. *Forest law and sustainable development. Addressing contemporary challenges through legal reform.* Washington, DC, USA, World Bank.

CIFOR. 2008a. *Adaptive collaborative management can help us cope with climate change.* CIFOR Infobrief No.13. Bogor, Indonesia, Center for International Forestry Research (also available at www.cifor.cgiar.org/publications/pdf_files/Infobrief/013-infobrief.pdf).

CIFOR. 2008b. *CIFOR's strategy, 2008–2018 – making a difference for forests and people.* Bogor, Indonesia, Center for International Forestry Research (also available at www.cifor.cgiar.org/publications/pdf_files/Books/CIFORStrategy0801.pdf).

CIFOR. 2010. *Apiculture products in Cameroon – fact sheet.* Bogor, Indonesia, Center for International Forestry Research.

Costenbader, J. 2009. *Legal frameworks for REDD. Design and implementation at the national level.* IUCN Environmental Policy and Law Paper No. 77. Gland, Switzerland, International Union for Conservation of Nature (also available at http://data.iucn.org/dbtw-wpd/edocs/EPLP-077.pdf).

Cushion, E., Whiteman, A. & Dieterle, G. 2010. *Bioenergy development: issues and impacts for poverty and natural resource management.* Washington, DC, USA, World Bank (also available at www.globalbioenergy.org/uploads/media/1001_WB_-_Bioenergy_development_SIT.pdf).

DAFF. 2009. *Forest industries development fund.* Canberra, Australia, Australian Government, Department of Agriculture, Forestry and Fisheries (also available at www.daff.gov.au/fidf).

Dercon, S. & Hoddinott, J. 2005. *Livelihoods, growth, and links to market towns in 15 Ethiopian villages.* Food Consumption and Nutrition Division Discussion Paper 194. Washington, DC, USA, International Food Policy Research Institute (also available at www.ifpri.org/sites/default/files/publications/fcnbr194.pdf).

Donovan, J., Stoian, D., Grouwels, S., Macqueen, D., van Leeuwen, A., Boetekees, G. & Nicholson, K. 2000. *Towards an enabling environment for small and medium forest enterprise development.* Policy Brief. Rome, Italy, FAO (also available at www.fao.org/forestry/15444-1-0.pdf).

Dunlop, J. 2009. *REDD, tenure and local communities: a study from Aceh, Indonesia.* Rome, Italy, International Development Law Organization.

EC. 2002. *Perception of the wood-based industries – qualitative study of the image of wood-based industries amongst the public in the Member States of the European Union*. Brussels, Belgium, European Commission Directorate–General for Enterprise (also available at http://ec.europa.eu/enterprise/sectors/wood-paper-printing/files/perceptionstudy_en.pdf).

EIA. 2010. *Online energy statistics*. Washington, DC, USA, U.S. Energy Information Administration (available at www.eia.doe.gov).

EIU. 2010. *Economist Intelligence Unit country data (economic projections)* (available at www.eiu.com).

Elson, D. 2010. *Investing in locally controlled forestry: reviewing the issues from a financial investment perspective*. Background paper for The Forests Dialogue's initiative on investing in locally controlled forestry conference, London, UK, 24–25 May 2010.

Eniang, E.A., Mengistu, G.F. & Yidego, T. 2008. Climate change, resettled communities, forest resources conservation and livelihood options around Kafta-Sheraro Forest Reserve, Tigray Region, Ethiopia. *In* Swedish University of Agricultural Sciences/FAO/International Union of Forest Research Organizations. *Book of abstracts and preliminary programme: international conference on adaptation of forests and forest management to changing climate with emphasis on forest health: a review of science, policies, and practices*, p. 68. SLU/FAO/IUFRO. 328pp. (available at www.fao.org/docrep/010/k2985e/k2985e00.htm).

European Cluster Observatory. 2010. *European cluster organization directory – Q1 2010*. Stockholm, Sweden, European Cluster Observatory (available at www.clusterobservatory.eu).

EUROSTAT. 2010. *Online statistical databases of the European Commission's Directorate General for Statistics (EUROSTAT)* (available at http://ec.europa.eu/eurostat).

FAO. 2002. *Conference proceedings: towards equitable partnerships between corporate and smallholder partners*. Bogor, Indonesia, 21–23 May 2002 (also available at www.fao.org/docrep/005/y4803e/y4803e00.htm).

FAO. 2004. *Simpler forest management plans for participatory forestry*. FONP Working Paper 4. Rome, Italy (also available at www.fao.org/docrep/008/j4817e/j4817e00.htm).

FAO. 2008. Contribution of the forestry sector to national economies, 1990–2006. Forest Finance Working Paper FSFM/ACC/08. Rome, Italy.

FAO. 2009a. *State of the world's forests 2009*. Rome, Italy (also available at www.fao.org/docrep/011/i0350e/i0350e00.HTM).

FAO. 2009b. *Stratégie de développement et plan d'action pour la promotion de la foresterie urbaine et périurbaine de la ville de Bangui*. Urban and Peri-urban Forestry Working Paper 3, edited by Fabio Salbitano. Rome, Italy.

FAO. 2010a. *Global forest resources assessment, 2010 – Main report*. FAO Forestry Paper 163. Rome, Italy. (Also available at www.fao.org/forestry/fra/fra2010/en/).

FAO. 2010b. *FAOSTAT – FAO's online statistical database*. Rome, Italy (available at http://faostat.fao.org).

FAO. 2010c. *Report of the 51st Advisory Committee on Paper and Wood Products*. Rome, Italy.

FAO. 2010d. *Impact of the global forest industry on atmospheric greenhouse gases*. FAO Forestry Paper 159. Rome, Italy.

FAO. 2010e. *Thematic study on trees outside forest for the Forest Resource Assessment 2010*. Summary of the inception workshop, Rome, Italy, 9–10 June 2010.

FAO. 2010f. *Market analysis & development*. FAO website (available at www.fao.org/forestry/enterprises/25492/en/).

FAO. 2010g. *Smallholder forest producer associations in developing countries (SFPA development fund)*. Rome, Italy. FAO website (available at www.fao.org/forestry/enterprises/60778/en/).

FAO. 2011. *Reforming forest tenure: issues, principles and process*. FAO Forestry Paper. Rome, Italy (in press).

Farm Africa. 2002. *Articulating rights and responsibilities in co-management of forests: the case of Chilimo and Bonga state forests*. Addis Ababa, Ethiopia, Farm Africa/SPOS Sahel.

Five Winds International. 2008. *Inventory of sustainable packaging initiatives and proposed approach to develop sustainable packaging guidelines*. Canadian Council of Ministers of the Environment (also available at www.ccme.ca/assets/pdf/pn_1405_sp_inventory_e.pdf).

Forest Connect. 2010. *Reducing poverty by connecting small forest enterprises* (available at http://forestconnect.ning.com).

Galloway McLean, K. 2009. *Advance guard: climate change impacts, adaptation, mitigation and indigenous peoples – a compendium of case studies*. Darwin, Australia, United Nations University – Traditional Knowledge Initiative.

GEF. 2009. *Timberland investment & emerging markets: a fresh review & outlook: September 2009*. Washington, DC, USA, Global Environment Fund.

Glück, P., Rayner, J., Berghäll, O., Braatz, S., Robledo C. & Wreford, A. 2009. Governance and policies for adaptation. *In* R. Seppälä, A. Buck and P. Katila, eds. *Adaptation of forests and people to climate change – a global assessment report*. pp. 187–210. IUFRO World Series Volume 22. Helsinki, Finland, International Union of Forest Research Organizations. 224 pp. (also available at www.iufro.org/download/file/4485/4496/Full_Report.pdf).

Gobeze, T., Bekele, M., Lemenih M. & Kassa H. 2009. Participatory forestry management and its impacts on livelihoods and forest status: the case of Bonga forest in Ethiopia. *International Forestry Review*, 11(3): 346–358.

Gómez-Pompa, A. 1991. Learning from traditional ecological knowledge: insights from Mayan silviculture. *In* A. Gómez-Pompa, T.C. Whitmore & M. Hadley, eds. *Rain forest regeneration and management*. pp. 335–342. Paris, France, UNESCO and The Parthenon Publishing Group Limited.

Grey, G.W. & Deneke, F.J. 1986. *Urban forestry*. New York, USA, Wiley.

Gruenwald, J. 2008. The global herbs and botanicals market. *Nutraceuticals World July/August 2008* (also available at www.nutraceuticalsworld.com/contents/view/13953).

Gruenwald, J. 2010. Eurotrends: ethnic botanicals – a growing trend. *Nutraceuticals World January/February 2010* (also available at www.nutraceuticalsworld.com/contents/view/17426).

Hall, C.R., Hodges, A.W. & Haydu, J.J. 2005. *Economic impacts of the green industry in the United States*. Knoxville, USA, University of Tennessee Press.

Hammond, G. & Jones, C. 2008. *Inventory of carbon and energy (ICE): version 1.6a*. Sustainable Energy Research Team, University of Bath, UK.

Hansen, M.C., Stehman, S.V. & Potapov, P.V. 2010. Quantification of global gross forest cover loss. *Proc. Nat. Acad. Sci. Early Edition*, doi/10.1073/pnas.0912668107.

Hepburn, S. 2008. Carbon rights as new property: the benefits of statutory verification. *Sydney Law Review*.

Hodgdon, B.D. 2010. Community forestry in Laos. *Journal of Sustainable Forestry*, 29 (1): 50–78.

Holt, L., O'Sullivan, and Weaver, S.A. 2007. *Land and forestry law in Vanuatu: carbon rights and existing law*. Vanuatu Carbon Credits Project. Wellington, New Zealand, School of Geography, Environment and Earth Sciences, Victoria University of Wellington.

Honadle, G. 1999. *How context matters: linking environmental policy to people and place*. Connecticut, USA, Kumarian Press.

IEA. 2010. *Online energy statistics*. Paris, France, International Energy Agency (available at www.iea.org).

IIASA. 2007. *Study of the effects of globalization on the economic viability of EU forestry*. Laxenburg, Austria, International Institute for Applied Systems Analysis (also available at http://ec.europa.eu/agriculture/analysis/external/viability_forestry/full_text.pdf).

IPCC. 2007. *Fourth assessment report, climate change 2007. Synthesis report: summary for policymakers*. Geneva, Switzerland, IPCC. (also available at www.ipcc.ch/pdf/assessment-report/ar4/syr/ar4_syr_spm.pdf).

ITTO. 2006. *Status of tropical forest management 2005*. ITTO Technical Series No. 24. Yokohama, Japan, International Tropical Timber Organization.

IUCN. 2009a. *Applying the forests-poverty toolkit in the village of Tenkodogo, Sablogo Forest*. International Union for Conservation of Nature. Ouagadougou, Burkina Faso.

IUCN. 2009b. The forests–poverty toolkit. Available for download at the following link: www.iucn.org/about/work/ programmes/forest/fp_our_work/fp_our_work_initiatives/ fp_our_work_ll/fp_livelihoods_landscapes_our_work/fp_ livelihoods_landscapes_our_work_added/fp_livelihoods_ landscapes_our_work_toolkits.cfm

Kajembe, G.C., Nduwamungu, N. & Luoga, E.J. 2005. *The impact of community-based forest management and joint forest management on the forest resource base and local people's livelihoods: case studies from Tanzania.* Commons Southern Africa Occasional Paper 8. Harare, Zimbabwe, Centre for Applied Social Studies, University of Zimbabwe/Cape Town, South Africa, Programme for Land and Agrarian Studies, University of Western Cape.

Laird, S.A. & Wynberg, R. 2008. *Access and benefit-sharing in practice: trends in partnerships across sectors.* CBD Technical Series No. 38. Montreal, Canada, Secretariat of the Convention on Biological Diversity (CBD) (also available at www.cbd.int/doc/publications/ cbd-ts-38-en.pdf).

Laird, S.A., McLain, R.J. & Wynberg, R.P. 2010. *Wild product governance: finding policies that work for non-timber forest products.* London, UK, Earthscan.

Iaquinta, D.L. & Drescher, A.W. 2000. *Defining peri-urban: understanding rural-urban linkages and their connection to institutional contexts.* Paper presented at the Tenth World Congress, IRSA, Rio de Janeiro, Brazil, 1 August 2000.

Lebedys, A. 2008. *Contribution of the forestry sector to national economies 1990–2006.* Forest Finance Working Paper: FSFM/ACC/08. Rome, Italy, FAO (also available at www.fao.org/docrep/011/k4588e/k4588e00.htm).

Livelihoods and Forestry Programme. 2009. *Community forestry for poverty alleviation: how UK aid has increased household incomes in Nepal's middle hills.* UK Department for International Development–Nepal. Kathmandu, Nepal: Livelihoods and Forestry Programme (LFP).

Locatelli, B., Kanninen, M., Brockhaus, M., Colfer, C.J.P., Murdiyarso, D. & Santoso, H. 2008. *Facing an uncertain future: how forests and people can adapt to climate change.* Forest Perspectives no. 5. Bogor, Indonesia, Center for International Forestry Research (also available at www.cifor.cgiar.org/publications/pdf_ files/media/CIFOR_adaptation.pdf).

Lohrberg, F. 2007. *Landscape laboratory and biomass production - a "Platform Urban Forestry Ruhrgebiet" demonstration project.* Presentation to the 10th European Forum on Urban Forestry "New Forests after Old Industries". Gelsenkirchen, Germany, 16–19 May 2007.

Lopez-Casero, F. 2008. *Public procurement policies for legal and sustainable timber: trends and essential elements.* Presentation to the forum on China and global forest products trade, Beijing, China, 18–19 June 2008.

MacQueen, D. 2008. *Supporting small forest enterprises – a cross-sectoral review of best practice.* London, UK, International Institute for Environment and Development (IIED).

MAF. 2009. *A forestry sector study*. Wellington, New Zealand, New Zealand Government, Ministry of Agriculture and Forestry (also available at www.maf.govt. nz/forestry/publications/forestry-sector-study-2009).

Maffi, L. 2005. Linguistic, cultural, and biological diversity. *Annual Review of Anthropology*, 34: 599–617.

Maffi, L. & Woodley, E. 2010. *Biocultural diversity conservation: a global sourcebook.* London, UK, Earthscan.

McNeil, J. 2009. *Oakville's urban forest: our solution to our pollution – next steps*. Voluntary paper presented to the World Forestry Congress, Buenos Aires, Argentina, 18–23 October 2009.

Milton, R.K. 1998. *Forest dependence and Participatory Forest Management: a qualitative analysis of resource use in Southern Ghana.* Norwich, UK, University of East Anglia. (PhD dissertation).

Mirjam A., Ros-Tonen, F. & Freerk Wiersum, K. 2005. *Forests, trees and livelihoods.* 15(x): 139.

Mochan, S., Moore J. & Connolly, T. 2009. *Using acoustic tools in forestry and the wood supply chain.* Technical Note FCTN018. Edinburgh, UK, Forestry Commission (also available at www.forestry.gov.uk/pdf/ FCTN018.pdf/$FILE/FCTN018.pdf).

Moloughney, S. 2009. What's next in herbs and botanicals? *Nutraceuticals World November 2009.*

Moore, G. 2007. *Future of smart paper.* Article on Pira's Profit through Innovation website (available at http://profitthroughinnovation.com/pulp-and-paper/future-of-smart-paper.html).

OECD. 2009. *What future for the agriculture and food sector in an increasingly globalised world?.* Workshop summary presented to the Organisation for Economic Co-operation and Development (OECD) Committee for Agriculture, Paris, France, 1 April 2009.

Ota, I. 2007. A forest owners' cooperative in Japan: obtaining benefits of certification for small-scale forests. *Unasylva,* 228(58): 64–66.

Padoch, C. & De Jong, W. 1992. Diversity, variation, and change in Ribereno agriculture. *In* K.H. Redford & C. Padoch, eds. *Conservation of neotropical forests: working from traditional resource use.* pp. 158–174. New York, USA, Columbia University Press.

Palmer, S. 2000. *Sustainable homes: timber frame housing.* Teddington, UK, Sustainable Homes (available at: www.sustainablehomes.co.uk/upload/publication/Timber%20Frame%20Housing.pdf).

Pescott, M. & Wilkinson, G. 2009. Codes of practice for forest harvesting – monitoring and evaluation. *Forest News,* 23(4): 6–7.

Peters, C.M. 2000. Precolumbian silviculture and indigenous management of neotropical forests. *In* D.L. Lentz, ed. *Imperfect Balance: Landscape Transformations in the Precolumbian Americas.* pp.203–223. New York, USA, Columbia University Press.

Petersen, F. & Kuhn, T. 2007. *Novartis and biodiversity: perspectives on access and benefit-sharing.* Business 2010. Montreal, Canada, Secretariat of the Convention on Biological Diversity (CBD).

Phelps, J., Webb, E.L. & Agrawal, A. 2010. Does REDD+ threaten to recentralize forest governance? *Science,* 328: 312–313.

Porter, M.E. 1990. *The competitive advantage of nations.* New York, USA, New York Basic Books.

Posey, D.A. & Balée, W. (eds). 1989. *Resource management in Amazonian indigenous folk strategies (advances in economic botany volume 7).* New York, USA, New York Botanical Garden Press.

Prasad, R. 1999. Joint forest management in India and the impact of state control over non-wood forest products. *International Journal of Forestry and Forest Industry,* 50 (198): 58–62.

Pretty, J., Adams, W., Berkes, F., Ferreira de Athayde, S., Dudley, N., Hunn, E., Maffi, L., Milton, K., Rapport, D., Robbins, P., Sterling, E., Stolton, S., Tsing, A., Vintinnerk, E. & Pilgrim, S. 2010. The intersections of biological diversity and cultural diversity: towards integration. *Conservation and Society,* 7(2): 100–112 (also available at www.conservationandsociety.org).

Renner, M. 1991. *Jobs in a sustainable economy.* Washington, DC, USA, Worldwatch Institute.

Roberts, G., Parrotta, J. & Wreford, A. 2009. Current adaptation measures and policies. *In* R. Seppälä, A. Buck and P. Katila, eds. *Adaptation of forests and people to climate change – a global assessment report.* IUFRO World Series Volume 22. pp. 123–134. Helsinki, Finland, International Union of Forest Research Organizations. 224 pp. (also available at www.iufro.org/download/file/4485/4496/Full_Report.pdf).

Romano, F. & Reeb, D. 2006. *Understanding forest tenure: what rights and for whom?* Rome, Italy, FAO (also available at ftp://ftp.fao.org/docrep/fao/009/ah250e/ah250e00.pdf).

Rosenbaum, L., Schoene, D. & Mekouar, A. 2004. *Climate change and the forest sector. Possible national and subnational legislation.* FAO Forestry Paper 144. Rome, Italy, FAO (also available at www.fao.org/docrep/007/y5647e/y5647e00.htm).

Scherr, S.J., White, A. & Kaimowitz, D. 2003. *A new agenda for forest conservation and poverty reduction: making markets work for low-income producers.* Washington, DC, USA, Forest Trends.

Schreckenberg, K., Degrande, A., Mbosso, C., Eoli Baboule, Z., Boyd, C., Enyong, L., Kanmegne, J. & Ngong, C. 2002. The social and economic importance of Dacryoides edulis in S. Cameroon. *Journal of Forests, Trees and Livelihoods,* 12(2):15–40.

Schumpeter, J. 1934. *The theory of economic development*. Boston, USA, Harvard University Press.

Schwab, J. (ed.) 2009. *Planning the urban forest, ecology, economy, and community development*. APA Planning Advisory Service, 2009. ISBN 978-1-932364-57-6.

Secretariat of the Convention on Biological Diversity. 2002. Bonn guidelines on access to genetic resources and fair and equitable sharing of the benefits arising out of their utilization. Montreal, Canada, Secretariat of the Convention on Biological Diversity.

Shackleton, S., Shanley, P. & Ndoye, O. 2007. Invisible but viable: recognising local markets for non timber forest products. *International Forestry Review*, 9 (3): 697–712.

Shepherd, G. 2010. *The ecosystem approach in Anjouan, Comoro Islands: managing the integration of diverse landscape choices*. Paper written for Darwin Initiative and Bristol Zoo Gardens.

Spathelf P & Nutto L. 2004. Urban forestry in Curitiba: a model for Latin-American cities? In: Konijnendijk, C.C., Schipperijn, J. & Hoyer, K.K., eds. *Forestry serving urbanised societies*. Selected papers from conference held in Copenhagen, Denmark, 27–30 August 2002. IUFRO World Series Volume 14. IUFRO, Vienna, pp. 357–365.

Stern, N. 2006. *The economics of climate change. The Stern review*. Cambridge, UK, Cambridge University Press.

Stoian, D. 2005 Making the best of two worlds: rural and peri-urban livelihoods options sustained by non timber forest products from the Bolivian Amazon. *World Development*, 33: 1473–1490.

Sunderlin, W.D., Hatcher. J. & Liddle. M. 2008. *From exclusion to Ownership? Challenges and opportunities in advancing forest tenure reform*. Washington DC, USA, Rights and Resources.

Sunderlin, W.D., Dewi, S., Puntodewo, A., Müller, D., Angelsen, A. & Epprecht, M. 2008. Why forests are important for global poverty alleviation: a spatial explanation. *Ecology and Society,* 13(2): 24 (also available at www.ecologyandsociety.org/vol13/iss2/art24/).

Sylva Foundation. 2010. myForest website (available at http://sylva.org.uk/myforest/index.php).

Takacs, D. 2009. *Forest carbon: law + property rights*. Arlington, USA, Conservation International (also available at www.conservation.org/Documents/CI_Climate_Forest-Carbon_Law-Property-Rights_Takacs_Nov09.pdf).

Tyrväinen, L., Pauleit, S., Seeland, K. & de Vries S. 2005. Benefits and uses of urban forests and trees. In: Konijnendijk, C.C., Nilsson, K., Randrup, T.B. & Schipperijn, J., eds. *Urban forests and trees.* pp. 81–114. Berlin, Germany, Springer.

UN. 2010. COMTRADE – the United Nations Commodity Trade Statistics Database (available at http://comtrade.un.org).

UN. forthcoming. *UNECE-FAO forest products annual market review 2009–2010*. United Nations Economic Commission for Europe: Timber Section, Geneva, Switzerland. Rome, Italy, FAO (also available at http://timber.unece.org/index.php?id=303).

UNECE/FAO. 2005. European forest sector outlook study 1960-2000-2020: main report. Rome, Italy, FAO (also available at www.fao.org/docrep/008/ae428e/ae428e00.htm).

UNECE/FAO. 2007. State of Europe's forests 2007: the MCPFE report on sustainable forest management in Europe. Jointly prepared by the MCPFE Liaison Unit. Warsaw: UNECE and FAO (also available at www.foresteurope.org/filestore/foresteurope/Publications/pdf/state_of_europes_forests_2007.pdf).

UNFCCC. 2010. *Text to facilitate negotiations among Parties*. Issued as an official document (FCCC/AWGLCA/2010/8) for consideration at the eleventh session of the AWG-LCA, 9 July 2010 (also available at http://unfccc.int/resource/docs/2010/awglca11/eng/08.pdf)

von Hippel, E. 1988. *The sources of innovation*. Oxford, UK, Oxford University Press.

Wagberg, P. 2007. *Innovation and research for success in the new media landscape*. Paper presented to the Forest-Based Sector Technology Platform conference, Hannover, Germany, 15–16 May 2007.

Wolf, K.L. 2004. *Human services provided by urban forests economic valuation opportunities*. Seattle, USA, Center for Urban Horticulture at the University of Washington.

World Bank. 2010. *Global economic prospects – summer 2010: fiscal headwinds and recovery*. Washington, DC, USA, World Bank.

World Health Organization. 2008. *Traditional medicine fact sheet 134*. World Health Organization. Geneva, Switzerland (also available at www.who.int/mediacentre/factsheets/fs134).

Wynberg, R.P. & Laird, S.A. 2007. Less is often more: governance of a non-timber forest product, maula (*Sclerocarya birrea* subsp. *caffra*) in Southern Africa. *International Forestry Review*, 9(1): 475–490.